Life in Tanganyika in The Fifties

Godfrey Mwakikagile

Copyright (c) 2010 Godfrey Mwakikagile
All rights reserved under international copyright conventions.

Life in Tanganyika in the Fifties

Third Edition

ISBN 978-9987-16-012-9

New Africa Press
Dar es Salaam
Tanzania

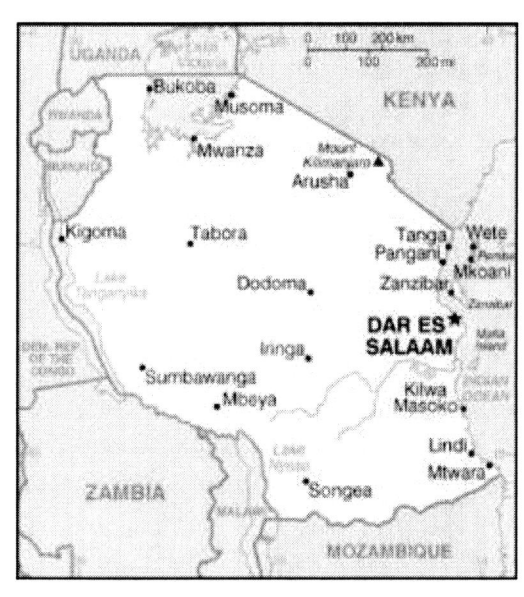

Contents

Acknowledgements

Introduction

Part I:

Chapter One:
Born in Tanganyika

Chapter Two:
My Early Years:
Growing up
in Colonial Tanganyika

Chapter Three:
Newspapers in Tanganyika in the Fifties: A History
Linked with My Destiny as a Reporter

Chapter Four:
Tanganyika Before Independence

Part II:

Narratives from the White Settler Community and Others in Colonial Tanganyika in the Fifties

Appendix I:
Sykes of Tanzania Remembers the Fifties

Appendix II:
Paramount Chief Thomas Marealle Reflects on the Fifties: An Interview

Appendix III:
The Fifties in Tanganyika: A Tanzanian Journalist Remembers

Appendix IV:
Remembering Tanganyika That Was: Recollections of a Greek Settler

Appendix V:
Other European Immigrants Remember Those Days in Tanganyika

Appendix VI:
Princess Margaret in Tanganyika

Acknowledgements

I WISH to express my profound gratitude to all the ex-Tanganyikans who have contributed to this project.

It would not have taken the shape and form it did without their participation and support. I am also indebted to others for their material which I have included in the book.

Also special thanks to Jackie and Karl Wigh of Australia for sending me a package of some material from Tanganyika in the fifties, including a special booklet on Princess Margaret's visit to Tanganyika in October 1956 and other items.

As an ex-Tanganyikan myself, although still a Tanzanian, I feel that there are some things which these ex-Tanganyikans and I have in common in spite of our different backgrounds.

We lived in Tanganyika during the same period; we are around the same age, at least most of us; we share perspectives on how life was in Tanganyika when we lived there around the same time; and many of us have not lived in what is now Tanzania for many years. In fact, I have lived in the United States longer than I did in Tanzania.

And I have never gone back in all those years. But I intend to, one day, and spend the rest of my life in my native land.

This book focuses on life in Tanganyika in the fifties, the decade before independence. It was a period of transition from colonial rule to sovereign status for Tanganyika and most of us witnessed this fundamental change and historic event even if it meant very little to many of us in terms of political significance because we were too young to understand what was going on during that time.

I remember the celebrations and fireworks on independence day in December 1961 in the town of Tukuyu in Rungwe District in the Southern Highlands Province. But to me it was no more than a festive occasion. I was only 12 years old and politics meant nothing or very little to me and other youngsters of all races.

Many of those youngsters are now parents and grandparents and some of them have contributed to this work which is one of the most important projects in my life.

I found them in different parts of the world: in Britain, South Africa, Australia and New Zealand; in the United States, Russia, Canada, Dubai, Tahiti, Italy, Turkey and other countries. And most of them were as enthusiastic as I was about the project. It brought back old memories, and even tears to at least one or two of them.

It may also have inspired and encouraged some of them to start writing their memoirs about those days. And they were good old days in many respects.

Not everything was good, but they were the good ol' days for many people. And they are still fresh in the memories of many ex-Tanganyikans living in different parts of the world including Africa itself.

In fact, some of them told me they had already started writing their memoirs and about the years they spent in Tanganyika long before I got in touch with them. One of them said she had already written a book and was just waiting for it to be published.

And quite a few of them know about Tanzania today more than I do because they have been there in recent times and through the years. Many of them visit Tanzania on regular basis for obvious reasons. I remember one in Britain who was on her way to Tanzania around the same time I got in touch with her.

Others told me they go to Tanzania quite often, some every year. They have solid ties to Tanzania; they were born and brought up there and they are involved in different projects including charitable work.

And they all remember those days with fondness, when life was simpler and safer, and the people friendlier.

One ex-Tanganyikan who spent more than 40 years in Tanganyika, later Tanzania, told me that he even remembers when he could sleep in the back of his truck, wide open, without fear of being attacked by anybody. And he did that many times when he was travelling as a missionary.

But not anymore! Those days are gone. And they are gone forever! However, the memories are still there to be savoured and cherished.

One ex-Tanganyikan remembered, with nostalgia, a song in Kiswahili and asked me if I also still remembered the song. I said I did.

She was talking about *Tanganyika, Tanganyika, nakupenda kwa moyo wote*, which means, "Tanganyika, Tanganyika, I love you with all my heart"!

Many ex-Tanganyikans who left Tanganyika, and Africa, left their hearts in Africa, and in Tanganyika in particular. Their great enthusiasm for this project is proof of that.

And to all of you, I say, *Asante sana* – Thank you very much.
Mungu ibariki Afrika - God bless Africa
Mungu ibariki Tanganyika - God bless Tanganyika
Mungu ibariki Tanzania - God bless Tanzania.

Introduction

DURING a period when many people in Kenya, Uganda and Tanzania – as well as in Rwanda and Burundi – are talking about forming an East African federation under one government, with Arusha in Tanzania as its capital, it may sound anachronistic when some of us in Tanzania are nostalgic about the good old days as life was in Tanganyika before the union with Zanzibar which led to the creation of the United Republic of Tanzania in 1964.

But that is indeed the case. And in many fundamental respects, they were the good ol' days! And we remember those days with nostalgia. And that is where we now turn to.

This work focuses on life in Tanganyika in the fifties. My focus was partly dictated by my interest in the autobiographical aspect of this enquiry because the fifties were some of the most important years of my life.

They were my formative years, as were the early sixties, and had a great impact on the development of my personality. What I am today has a lot to do with what happened, and what I learned, in those years.

The fifties were also a turning point in another respect. The years signalled the end of an era and the beginning of a new one.

It was the decade in which colonial rule was finally coming to an end. It was also the decade in which direct European influence reached it peak after decades of colonial rule since the 1890s when the Germans acquired the territory which came to be known as German East Africa or *Deutsch Ostafrika* as the Germans called it.

The years before the fifties also witnessed a transformation in the lives of Africans because of the political, social and economic impact colonial rule and European influence had on them.

Roughly speaking, it was a transition from the traditional to the modern way of life. The people basically lived the same way as they did before the coming of Europeans but there were some changes in their lives which had never been witnessed before.

Therefore the years before the fifties provide an important background which helps us better understand what happened during that very important decade which is remembered, probably more than anything else, as the last years of colonial rule in Tanganyika.

The social transformation of Tanganyika had been a gradual process through the years. Although it began in most parts of the country with the advent of colonial rule when the country was first colonized by Germany, there is no question that most of the changes which took place occurred during the British colonial period.

The British ruled Tanganyika longer than the Germans did, and they had an impact on the country which last longer. Even today British influence is clearly evident in what is now Tanzania.

Probably the only exception in terms of early penetration by foreigners was along the coast where Africans had been in contact with the Arabs and other foreigners mainly from Asia for centuries long before colonization by Europeans.

The Portuguese also had early contacts with the coastal people in the 1500s but their impact was minimal compared to that of the Arabs whose culture became dominant especially after the introduction of Islam.

But my focus is on the fifties not only because of the significance of the decade as an integral part of my life but also as a very important period in the history of Tanganyika which witnessed the beginning of the end of colonial rule in the largest country in East Africa.

It is a bygone era, yet relevant to my life today as it was back then.

The perspectives I have on things and how I look at the world and other people all have their beginning in the fifties more than in any other period in my life.

It is a crucible in which my personality began to develop and in which it was shaped; it is also a decade, especially the late fifties, which was the beginning of my political awakening even though I did not have any firm political beliefs because of my young age.

But I began to see things, although from the perspective of a child, in a way I did not before because I listened to the news on the radio and read some newspapers published in Kiswahili. The kind of awakening or awareness I had was mainly about important historical events and current affairs we were taught in primary school and which my father also taught me and told me about at home.

It was not the kind of awareness which entailed analysis of those events and the news. That is why, for example, when independence came on 9 December 1961, it was just another day of celebration for me, as much as it was for other children, since I did not understand and did not have the political maturity to comprehend the significance of this momentous event in the history of our country.

All I heard was that we were now free. We were going to rule ourselves. The British were no longer our colonial rulers. Fine words indeed! But what next? I had no answer to that; nor did many others including adults.

Apart from the autobiographical aspect, the fifties were also very important in another respect. It was a landmark on the road towards independence for most African countries. It was in the fifties that political agitation was most intense, and sustained, across the continent in the quest for freedom from colonial rule. And Tanganyika was no exception.

The fifties were also critical in yet another fundamental respect. As the struggle for independence gained momentum not only in Tanganyika but in other African countries as well, race relations came into sharp focus because it was a period of reflection and introspection. It was also a period of transition involving whites who monopolized power as the colonial masters and non-whites, especially black Africans, who were determined to end such monopoly.

Thus, the struggle for independence had unintended consequences and sometimes conveyed the wrong message as if it was a conflict between whites and blacks or between whites and non-whites; which was *not* the case. It was simply a struggle for equality transcending race.

Yet, important as this struggle was for all those involved regardless of race, I decided not to focus on that in this study but instead chose to highlight stories of human interest from the fifties if for no other reason than that as human beings we have a lot of things in common, far more than we want to admit, and which we sometimes ignore or overlook when we focus on our differences or when we have arguments.

We share the same emotions, we feel the same pain, we all cry and laugh and know how to love and hate. No race has a monopoly on that. It is a common denominator which unites and defines us as human beings and as mere mortals with frailties.

While politics and ideologies, religions and cultures can and do divide us, human emotions and common feelings unites us. And while man has an almost infinite capacity for evil, the opposite is equally true that he has an enormous capacity to do good. That is one of the most significant things about Tanganyika in the fifties.

Even if only in a limited way, there is no question that Tanganyika in the fifties demonstrated the brighter side of human nature, for, with all the differences we had as Tanganyikans during colonial rule in a society that was defined and structured on the basis of race by the colonial authorities, we were still able to find common ground on which we recognized each other as fellow human beings even if some people felt that they were better than others.

But the mere fact that the people usually – although not always – got along fine shows that there was a recognition on the part of all the races that there was something inherently good in every human being and it could bring us together provided there was a will to do so.

I remember Nelson Mandela saying that even some of the most racist whites in South Africa – or anywhere else for that matter – had some good in them; a point he underscores in his autobiographical work *Long Walk to Freedom*. I would also hate to believe that all the bigots we had in Tanganyika among all the races were pure evil like Hitler!

Although Tanganyika was a colonial society, it was definitely not apartheid South Africa. There were no laws prohibiting racial intermingling, although this was rare by choice and because the colonial authorities – which does not mean *all* whites – did not encourage it. Racial separation was also sanctioned by custom, not by legal strictures, and many people of all races in Tanganyika were more comfortable living with their own kind, although there is really only one kind, and that is mankind.

And because Tanganyika was a UN Trusteeship territory, the British colonial rulers knew that they were obligated to guide the country towards independence even if they dragged their feet for various reasons including the desire to maintain the privileged status of the white settlers as long as they could.

But even under the worst of circumstances in terms of race relations as was the case in apartheid South Africa before that abominable institution was abolished, there were people of all races who worked together to create a better world in which all human beings would be treated as equals.

It happened in South Africa; it happened in Kenya where in spite of Mau Mau there were whites and blacks who worked together; and it happened in my own home country, Tanganyika, where we did not even have racial tensions and animosities which could have driven the races even further apart and plunged the country into chaos.

Paradoxically, we were so close yet so far apart.

All that was needed was to break down racial barriers, accept each other as fellow human beings on equal basis, and end colonial rule which had instituted a hierarchical society based on race to the detriment of race relations; although, I must concede, there were people who were not interested in improving race relations even under the best of circumstances because they were bigots, and so blinded by prejudice that they couldn't even see that the different races united us, more than they divided us, as fellow human beings. Tanganyika in the fifties demonstrated this simple truth in both ways but, ultimately, justice prevailed.

The bigots even among whites were outnumbered by people of goodwill in the white settler community. Many of them saw the coming of independence not as a triumph of black supremacy over white supremacy – both of which are equally evil – but as a victory for equality and justice for all. In fact, the majority of whites stayed in Tanganyika after the country won independence.

Many of them left in the following years but usually for reasons other than race, although the policy of Africanization was interpreted, or misinterpreted, as a racial assault on whites. Still, among all the East African countries, Africanization was slowest in Tanganyika, and deliberately so, under the leadership of Julius Nyerere. And his definition of Africanization included people of all races who were citizens of Tanganyika, therefore African, just like the rest of us with a black skin.

The biggest disincentive to staying in Tanganyika among most whites and other people – including many black Tanganyikans – was economic when the country started implementing socialist policies and enforcing stringent measures to achieve nationalization.

But it is also true that there were bigots among Africans who made their position very clear during the struggle for independence, especially after they broke away from the Tanganyika African National Union (TANU) in 1958 to form the African National Congress (ANC) which, in spite of sharing the same name with the ANC of South Africa, was radically different from its counterpart.

The South African ANC embraced people of races like TANU did under Nyerere in Tanganyika; while the ANC in Tanganyika did not. And there was a battle between these two competing visions for the future of Tanganyika.

But the bigots who wanted Tanganyika to be the exclusive domain of blacks, like their counterparts among the white settlers who wanted to perpetuate white domination, also lost under sustained assault by true multi-racialist leaders such as Julius Nyerere and other stalwarts in TANU, the party which led the campaign for independence on the basis of racial equality and which was open to members of all races even in the leadership positions of the party at the national level.

All this happened in the late fifties, years which became a defining moment in the history of Tanganyika, charting out a new course and pointing where the country was headed in the future after winning independence.

It was also an important lesson in human relations, not just in race relations, since there were differences among whites themselves, bigots versus non-bigots, as much as there were among blacks who also had their own share of bigots. And from all this emerged a vision focusing on humanity transcending race.

And it is a vision that sustains us today wherever we are as human beings. For, whether we like it or not, we are all bound by our humanity regardless of the differences we may have in terms of background, outlook and beliefs which have caused so much misery and suffering throughout history when people choose to focus on their differences instead of focusing on what they have in common. As Dr. Martin Luther King said: "We must all learn to live together as brothers (and sisters) or we will all perish together as fools."

Part I:

Chapter One:

Born in Tanganyika

THE period during which I was born witnessed some of the most important events and changes in the history Tanganyika, the land of my birth, and indeed of the entire African continent. It was the dawn of a new era.

It was only a few years after the end of the Second World War in which many Africans, including two of my uncles, fought and in which many of them died; fortunately, both of my uncles survived and returned safely to Tanganyika.

It was also a period of political ferment in which the campaign for independence started in earnest in Tanganyika, the largest British possession in East Africa, and in other colonies on the continent.

I was born at 6 a.m. on Tuesday, 4 October 1949, in Kigoma, a port on Lake Tanganyika in what was then the Western Province in western Tanganyika. It was during British colonial rule and Tanganyika in those days had seven provinces: Western, Central, Lake, Northern, Coast, Southern and the Southern Highlands. The capital of the Western Province was Tabora.

My parents came from Rungwe District in the Southern Highlands. Rungwe District is in the Great Rift Valley and is ringed by misty blue mountains and is home to the Nyakyusa, my ethnic group, who today are one of the largest in Tanzania with more than one million people.

My father worked as a medical assistant during British colonial rule and that is how he and my mother ended up in Kigoma. Before I was born, my parents also lived in other parts of Tanganyika where my father worked. They lived in Handeni, Amani, Muheza, and Kilosa. They were also in Tanga for some time.

I am the first-born in my family. I was born in a hospital in Kigoma.

I don't know if my father worked at that hospital and I don't even remember whether or not my parents told me where he worked when I was born. But I do know that it was he who filled out my birth certificate. And it was he who always reminded me of my birthday every morning when I was growing up that October 4th was my birthday. My mother also reminded me of that, but not as much as my father did and was not as punctual. As soon as I woke up, my father would remind me if it was my birthday.

He was one of the few Africans in Tanganyika in those days who had secondary school education. He went to Malangali Secondary School in Iringa where he completed standard ten and excelled in school. And he would have gone to Tabora Secondary School where he would have completed standard 12 but couldn't go any further because of family obligations. Instead, he went to Muhimbili National Hospital in Dar es Salaam in the mid-1940s for medical training and qualified as a medical assistant.

The hospital was then known as Sewa Haji and was later renamed Princess Margaret Hospital. It has always been the country's only national hospital and was renamed Muhimbili National Hospital after independence.

My father's assignment to Kigoma after working elsewhere in Tanganyika turned out to be one of the most important events in my life because that is where I was born. And it will always remain an important part of my life as my birth place more than anything else.

Unfortunately, in all the years I lived in Tanganyika, later Tanzania, I never got the chance to visit Kigoma as a youngster or as an adult. And I still haven't unto this day.

My parents never went back to Kigoma and I did not get the

chance to go there even when I worked as a news reporter in Tanzania.

But I have two very important items with me which always remind me of Kigoma as my birth place.

One is my photograph taken when I was one year and three months old. It also has my father's handwriting on it in black ink, still legible 57 years later which was my age when I was working on the second edition of this book in 2007. He wrote in English: "Fifteen months old."

In this photograph, I'm standing looking at the camera, chubby and wide-eyed, and he's holding my right hand in front of the house in which we lived. It was a wooden house with a grass-thatched roof.

When I look at that picture, I can see how much I have changed through the years. I look chubby when I was a baby less than two years old, yet when I was growing up, I never gained much weight and was always slim. Many people said I was skinny. I thought my weight was in proportion to my frame. And I have always been that way, slim.

Another item I cherish so much is my birth certificate which my father gave me when I became a teenager and was attending Mpuguso Middle School in Rungwe District in the Southern Highlands from 1961 to 1964.

Also on my birth certificate are reminders of two other important historical events in my life: when I was baptized, by whom, and in what church.

I was baptized by Reverend Frank McGorlick on 25 December 1949, on Christmas day, two months and three weeks after my birthday. My birth certificate also bears his name in his own handwriting and it was issued by CMS, the Church Missionary Society, which did a lot of missionary work spreading Christianity in Tanganyika.

I remember when I was growing up that my parents used to tell me I was baptized as a CMS member. That was also the church my parents attended when they lived in Kigoma even before I was born until they returned to Rungwe District years later as members of the Moravian Church which was well-established in that district. They were members of the same church before they left Rungwe District.

The Moravian Church in Rungwe District was established in the 1890s by the Germans who were also the first colonial rulers of Tanganyika, while CMS missionaries first arrived in Tanganyika from Australia in 1927. The Church Missionary Society was established in Great Britain in 1799 and its founders included the renowned abolitionist, William Wilberforce. The missionary-doctor, Dr. David Livingstone, of the London Missionary Society, was also among its supporters.

Years later, when I became familiar with some Scottish names, I came to the conclusion that the minister who baptized me, Reverend McGorlick, was probably Scottish. And he left an indelible mark on me as the one who baptized me.

Reverend McGorlick came from Victoria, Australia. Decades later, I was able to get in touch with his wife Barbara in Australia who told me that they lived in Tanganyika, later Tanzania, until the early 1990s and that her husband died in 1993. I got in touch with her in 2005, as I did with their son Richard who also lived in Victoria, Australia. He grew up in Tanganyika, later Tanzania, as did the other children.

After I was born in Kigoma, my parents moved to Ujiji which is only a few miles away. It was there, in that very small yet famous place, where my sister Maria was born a year-and-half after I was. She was born in April 1951.

It was also in Ujiji where Henry Morton Stanley uttered those famous words on 10 November 1871 when he found the famous Scottish missionary doctor and explorer: "Dr. Livingstone, I presume?"

Dr. Livingstone had been missing for three years and the Royal Geographical Society sponsored an expedition to look for him in Africa.

Although I never got the chance to visit Kigoma and see the place of my birth, my sister Maria ended up living in Kigoma years later with her husband who was sent by his church to work there as a Seventh-Day Adventist pastor while she worked as a nurse. And I have always been interested in learning as much as I can about Kigoma - as well as other parts of the country - not only because it is my birth place but also because it is an integral part of my home country Tanzania. But because it is my birth place, there is no question that I have special interest in Kigoma in a way

I don't in other parts of the country.

And it has an interesting history. For example, not many people in Tanzania know that Kigoma was once a part of the Belgian colony of Ruanda-Urundi. Had it remained under Belgian control, my history would probably have been different. My father would never have been sent by the British colonial government to work in Kigoma, since it would not have been a part of their territory of Tanganyika. I would not have been born in Kigoma, or I may not even have been born at all!

But obviously, that was not my destiny. And Kigoma always brings back memories of my childhood in the fifties because that is where it all began, this short journey of mine into this world where we are mere mortals and which reminds me of one song by Jim Reeves, also sung by others, I used to listen to when I was a teenager in Tanzania in the sixties: "This world is not my home, I'm just passing through, my treasures are laid up, somewhere beyond the blue..."

But short as our presence is, in this world, we have to make the best of it. And in my case, my early life in Tanganyika played a critical role in determining what type of person I came to be years later. It is this land which I love from the very depth of my being, heart and soul. And it is this land that I will always love for the rest of my life.

It was in Tanganyika where I was born, and it was in Tanganyika where I was brought up. And it reminds me of another song we sang in Kiswahili in school and sometimes during national celebrations: *Tanganyika, Tanganyika, nakupenda kwa moyo wote*. In English it means: "Tanganyika, Tanganyika, I love you with all my heart."

It was also in Tanganyika where I spent one of the most important decades in my life and in the history of the country: the fifties. The fifties were my formative years. They were also the years when Tanganyika began its peaceful transition from colonial status to independence.

I witnessed some of those events during the transitional period especially in the late fifties. But I was still too young to understand exactly what they meant. I looked at things from a child's perspective, and simply having fun - chasing grasshoppers and butterflies - was more important to me than politics. And that is what I remember the most.

Even if they told me, I don't know if I would have been able to fully understand what was meant by *siasa*, which is a Swahili word meaning politics. And when I saw white people as child in the mid- and late-fifties, I saw them just as people. Yes, they looked different in terms of skin colour, but I still saw them as people nonetheless; and not as rulers or anything else.

Difference in skin colour meant absolutely nothing to me and other children in terms of an individual's worth as a human being, although even at that young age we noticed that white people had material things we didn't have. But we did not associate that with power or skin colour.

If someone tried to explain to me and other children the connection between skin colour and wealth or social status, we would have been confused. We just didn't understand why white people had things we didn't have, or why they lived in better houses than we did. Colonialism meant nothing to us at that age when we were under 10 years old.

And I had no reason to ask why white people were there, in Tanganyika, or where they came from, or why they had a different complexion. After all, there were Arabs and Indians in Tanganyika who also had a light complexion and even some Africans who had a light brown complexion.

Even my own mother had a light brown complexion. So did my brothers, some of my sisters, cousins, uncles and aunts; not white-looking or light-complexioned like the Indians and the Arabs we saw around when we were growing up but not dark-skinned either. Still, all that meant nothing to me.

I even remember my mother telling me when I was a young teenager in the early sixties that when we lived in Mbeya around 1953 and 1954, a British couple used to give me some cake and sweets and other things now and then whenever we passed by their house. And that only reinforced - even if not consciously - whatever notions I had, as a child, of a colour-blind society; which was, of course, not entirely the case as older people of all races knew very well. As a colony, Tanganyika was a colour-conscious society. Yet to a child, such colour-consciousness meant something different, if anything at all, even though it was a fact of life for all of us since our status was defined by racial identity.

Still, in spite of all that, there were people of all races who got along very well. They got along very well at work; many white families and their African servants were on very good terms and even their children played together, especially when house maids took their children with them to work or if they lived on the same premises although under separate roofs. A house maid is called *yaya* in Kiswahili.

Sometimes good relations between Africans and whites went beyond accepted norms. There were those who even ate and drank together, although usually in private, and whites who did that would normally avoid doing so in front of other whites. They did not want to be seen getting too friendly with Africans who were by colonial definition no more than servants of whites. And they did not want to be alienated from the white settler community of which they were an integral part simply because they wanted to be friends with Africans and people of other races.

Yet, there were those who defied convention. They were not the majority but they did exist, although no one cannot be sure how many in terms of numbers or percentage. For example, I remember my mother telling me in the late fifties and early sixties that there was a British couple who wanted to take me with them to Britain as a child to provide me with education and told my father that they would bring me back to Tanganyika every year on holidays but I would have the benefit of excellent education in the UK beginning at a very early age. She said my father seriously considered doing that, but she was strenuously opposed to the idea saying I was too young to go so far away.

They knew my father very well. They also knew my mother but they dealt with my father more than they did with my mother. Language was also a barrier on my mother's part. She did not know English like my father did. He spoke English fluently and even taught me the language at home when I first started learning English in 1961 at the age of 11. And that gave me an advantage over other pupils.

I don't remember exactly where or when this took place. But I know it was in the early fifties, either in Morogoro in the Coast Province or in Mbeya in the Southern Highlands when my parents and the British couple discussed the possibility of my going to school in Britain at a very early age under their guardianship.

And there was something about this British couple which stayed in my mind through the years, especially when I was growing up in Kyimbila in Rungwe District in the Southern Highlands about four miles from Tukuyu.

Their interest in my education showed that there were ordinary whites in Tanganyika, who were not colonial administrators but simply ordinary people who lived and worked there, who were concerned about the well-being of Africans yet couldn't do anything to improve the situation because they did not have the power or the means to do so. It was probably only a minority of them but there were such people.

In fact, some of them never left Africa. They stayed in Tanganyika even after independence because it was their home even if they were not born there, although some of them were, or they moved to other parts of Africa, mainly South Africa. Some also moved to what was then Southern Rhodesia and a few to Kenya. Their heart was, and still is, in Africa.

And when I was writing this book while living in the United States, I got in touch with some ex-Tanganyikan Britions and other whites living in different parts of the world including Britain, Australia and the United States who still had relatives or friends living in Tanzania and involved in various activities, including philanthropic work, together with black Africans. They told me that their relatives and friends never left Tanganyika after the country won independence.

Even some of those who left Tanganyika after independence *still* maintained strong ties with the country and were involved in various activities helping the people in different parts of what is now Tanzania today. As Marion Gough stated in her email to me from England on 17 January 2006:

> Tanganyika was my home and is still very much in my blood. I try to get back as much as I can and am in the process of fund raising to help the building of an Orphanage.
>
> I have sent two shipments of text books, papers and pens to two different schools, together with several computers (used). I had such a happy, if not, lonely, childhood that I feel I must return the privilege.

And as she stated in another email on 21 January 2006:

Jambo Godfrey,

I am raising funds for the building of an Orphanage in Mufindi and going to get all the info ready to contact big companies to see if they would be willing to help, after a little research of course. If you know of any that are sympathetic to Africa please give me a nod. The Charity in USA is called Mufindi Orphans.

It is going to be built by the Foxes. Geoff Fox (father) lives in Mufindi and has done so for 40 years. He has four sons and each helps run the company and safari camps in Ruaha, Mikumi and Katavi ,also a Highland lodge in Mufindi. They look after several villages by employing a lot of staff and they grow their own food for the camps, use local craftsmen and materials for the camps.

Bruce lives in Gloucester which is 1/2 hour away from me and we keep in close touch. Great family so enthusiastic for Africa. Bruce has stopped a lot of poaching and is also fighting to keep the Ruaha River flowing as a lot of water has been taken off for the rice fields! Therefore a lot of the wetlands has been destroyed which makes the land flood instead of sinking into the water table.

Sorry could go on for ever, will close here before I get carried away.

Hope the pics don't come out too big.

Take care,

Marion

I, of course, almost left Tanganyika myself even before independence when I was still a child.

Had I left with the British couple and gone to school in Britain at so early an age when I was under 10 years old, my life would probably have taken a different turn and I don't know where I would have ended up eventually. But it was not meant to be. Instead, I remained and grew up in Tanganyika although I did not stay there. As fate would have it, I ended up in the United States after spending my first 23 years of my life in Tanganyika, later Tanzania. But that is another story.

Yet when I look back at all those years since my childhood in Kigoma and Ujiji in western Tanganyika, I know - and I am glad - that I was exposed to other people and other cultures when I was growing up and in such a way that I ended up being what I am today as an open-minded person tolerant of other people's views and values as well as beliefs as long as they don't interfere with my well-being. As the saying goes, the right to swing your arm ends where my nose begins.

But it was with the innocence of a child that I looked at the world, and it was with this kind of innocence that I left Kigoma with my parents when my father was transferred to Morogoro in the Coast Province in the early fifties.

Although I hardly remember Kigoma to enable me to compare the life there with the life in Morogoro, I know that Morogoro was different. It was in the Coast Province with a strong influence of Islamic culture and only about 120 miles from Dar es Salaam, the capital, from where almost everything new started before spreading to other parts of the country.

By remarkable contrast, Kigoma was far in the hinterland - it's still there, of course, just as Morogoro is where it was back then - and being a port on Lake Tanganyika, it was linked to what was then the Belgian Congo just across the lake and played a major role as a hub of activity in the cross-cultural interaction between Congo and Tanganyika as much as it still does today.

It was also in Kigoma where Che Guevara had a supply base during his mission to the Congo in the mid-sixties and to where he sought sanctuary after his mission failed.

Although it was far from the coast, Kigoma was linked to Dar es Salaam by a railway which ran - and still runs - across the country from east to west forming the main artery of the railway network in what was then Tanganyika and which is now Tanzania. Although sparsely populated, Tanzania is a large country, bigger than Nigeria in terms of area, and Kigoma is more than 700 miles from Dar es Salaam.

While my memories of Kigoma are virtually none since I was only a baby under three years old when I was there, my recollections of some of the events in Morogoro are vivid mainly because of the "traumatic" experiences I had as a child in that "coastal" town.

It was also in Morogoro where my brother Lawrence was born in September 1952. He was the third-born but, tragically, he died in August 2005 in Mbeya. Coincidentally, it was also in Mbeya where my sister Gwangu was born in 1954 when we lived there after leaving Morogoro. She was the fourth-born. But her life also ended in tragedy. She died in Rungwe District in July 2004. And my mother died at home in our village of Mpumbuli, Kyimbila, in November 2006 about one month before her 77th birthday.

All these tragedies were compounded by the fact that they

occurred when I was far away in the United States.

And whenever I think about my siblings who passed away, I also remember them in terms of the fifties. We all had our beginning in the early fifties, although I was born two months before the beginning of the decade in which both of them were born.

But it was in the early fifties that I really became aware of my existence in this world and when my personality started to be formed.

And it was in Morogoro where my memories of the fifties started to crystallize and reflect some of the most vivid images of my life which I clearly remember even today.

Chapter Two:

My Early Years: Growing Up in Colonial Tanganyika

LIFE in Tanganyika in the fifties meant different things to different people - African, European, Arab, and Asian (mostly Indian and Pakistani), the four main racial categories in the country. But it had one thing in common. Life was simpler, and the people, friendlier. There was less crime in those days, far less than what you see today.

But it was also colonial life, although sometimes barely perceptible. To children like me under 10 years old, it meant very little in terms of racial domination. Life went on as usual as if all the people got along just fine. And they did on many occasions but not all.

Even for those who got along just fine, it was still colonial rule. We all lived in a tiered society, racially stratified, with whites on top, Asians and Arabs in the middle constituting some kind of buffer zone, and blacks at the bottom.

It was a heap of vast black masses at the bottom. And they are the ones who propped up this lopsided structure with their cheap labour made even more abundant because of their numerical preponderance in a country that was overwhelmingly black.

Yet, in spite of all the interdependence, with Europeans and Asians - and sometimes Arabs - providing goods and services needed by a significant number of Africans especially those living in towns, and the cheap labour and raw materials provided by Africans to sustain the colonial system, there was little interaction among or between the races. The most that you could see was between Africans and Asians. And that was only during business transactions when Africans went to Indian shops in towns to buy the items they needed.

In the case of Tanganyika, the distance between the races, especially between Africans and Europeans, seemed to be even greater than in neighbouring Kenya because of the smaller number of the white settlers in the country. The distance was magnified even in terms of perception.

Whites were not only fewer in Tanganyika than in Kenya but were also less visible because of their smaller number, yet no less dominant as colonial rulers. But, the fewer they were, the farther they also were from Africans in terms of interaction, although that was not true in all cases. Still, it was extremely rare for Europeans and Asians to socialize with Africans. The races were in most cases far apart and preferred things to be that way.

However, there was one fundamental difference. The difference in this relationship was between the Europeans on the one hand and the Africans as well as the Asians and the Arabs on the other. And it had to do with power.

It was the Europeans who instituted the social hierarchy based on race and who sanctioned the asymmetrical relationship between the races to their advantage as the rulers of Tanganyika in order justify colonial rule. In that sense, the Asians and the Arabs were equally victims of racial domination by whites even if some of them did not think that they were being victimized like blacks.

But although there is no question that the Europeans were the rulers of a country that was overwhelmingly black African (there are also white Africans and Africans of Asian and Arab origin as well as others on the African continent), for many blacks, life went on as it did before the coming of the white man.

That was especially the case in the rural areas, including villages near towns and not only those far away from the urban centres, where the most visible alien intrusion in traditional life since the advent of colonial rule was the tax collector and sometimes, although rarely, a black policeman in khaki uniform and black boots coming on foot to make an arrest.

However, there was fundamental change in institutions of authority in the sense that an alien power had been imposed on us. All of us including traditional rulers became colonial subjects. African chiefs and other traditional rulers lost their power. They no longer had the same power they had before as the ultimate authority in their traditional societies.

Therefore the biggest change which took place when colonial rule was introduced was political. Africans lost power and independence. Attitudes towards life in general, and even towards traditional authority, also changed, although gradually, because of the dominant role European rulers played in the political arena. So it was a dramatic change when power shifted from Africans to Europeans.

Less perceptible were the changes which took place in other areas of life. One was the cultural arena.

Most of the people in the rural areas did not see themselves as victims of cultural imperialism in the same way the few educated Africans did. Their traditional way of life and values remained virtually intact unlike that of their brethren who lived in towns or those who acquired some education especially at the secondary school level and beyond.

The more education one had, the more acutely aware one became, of the racial disparities and introduction and sometimes imposition of alien values by Europeans.

But in many cases it was also far less of an imposition than a willingness by many Africans who had some education to accept European ways of life as some kind of achievement in life. In fact, a significant number of them saw it as a badge of honour to be Europeanized, live and act like Europeans.

It showed that they were now "civilized," or more "civilized" than their brethren - those who continued to live the traditional way of life in the villages and even in towns and also those who had less education.

Yet nationalist sentiments were strong especially among some politically conscious members of the African elite, although even they were not dismissive of all aspects of alien cultures including British in spite of their uncompromising stand in defence of the African traditional way of life. As Julius Nyerere said:

A country which lacks its own culture is no more than a collection of people without the spirit which makes them a nation. Of all the crimes of colonialism there is none worse than the attempt to make us believe we had no indigenous culture of our own; or that what we did have was worthless...

A nation which refuses to learn from foreign cultures is nothing but a nation of idiots and lunatics... But to learn from other cultures does not mean we should abandon our own.

Nyerere was quoted by Dr. Graham L. Mytton, former head of the BBC's International Broadcasting Audience Research (IBAR), in his book *Mass Communications in Africa*, and by Don Moore in his article, "Reaching the Villages: Radio in Tanzania," published in *The Journal of the North American Shortwave Association*.

And as one British official in Tanganyika admitted in 1955: "We ignore their tribal dances and try to give them cricket. I'ts awful." He was quoted by American journalist John Gunther in his book *Inside Africa*.

Gunther visited Tanganyika in 1954. Among the places he visited was the newly established radio station in Dar es Salaam.

The station was founded in 1951 in response to a proposal by a BBC official who felt that there was a need for such a station which should produce programmes for a native audience in Kiswahili. It was named the Dar es Salaam Broadcasting Station (DBS) and was later renamed the Tanganyika Broadcasting Service (TBS) and then the Tanganyika Broadcasting Corporation (TBC).

And as Sala Elise Patterson stated in a dissertation for a master's degree submitted to the School for Oriental and African Studies at the University of London entitled, "State Control, Broadcasting and National Development," focusing on Tanzania as a case study :

Radio broadcasting began in Tanganyika in July 1951 in an unused attic of a house in Dar es Salaam. Aimed at city residents, the unit was called the Dar es Salaam Broadcasting Station (DBS).

One year later the colonial government invested 10,000 GBP to upgrade the radio service realizing the importance of broadcasting in the territory to further the colonial process. Another 55,000 GBP was invested from the colonial fund in 1954.

Then on May 8, 1956, the colonial authorities inaugurated the new and improved Tanganyika Broadcasting Service (TBS) with a 20-kilowatt transmitter that increased broadcasting capability to reach as far as Johannesburg.

In July of the same year, the government consolidated their national broadcasting and established the Tanganyika Broadcasting Corporation (TBC) officially as an independent broadcasting body that took over the functions of the TBS.

The colonial government closely monitored programming and the Governor had absolute power to prohibit the broadcast of any programme deemed inappropriate.

When Gunther visited the station in 1954, he was highly impressed by the staff's performance. It was a professional operation totally staffed by native Africans, in spite of the fact that the station had started, as Gunther wrote, "with little more equipment than a microphone and a blanket hung over a wall." It became so successful that it served as a model for broadcasting services in many other British colonies in Africa and elsewhere.

I remember listening to TBC when I was growing up in Rungwe District in the Southern Highlands in the 1950s and early sixties. And I still remember the names of some of the radio announcers, mainly David Wakati and Eli Mboto. Although the reception was poor most of the time, we still were able to listen to the news and to a variety of music, mostly Swahili and Congolese, broadcast from Dar es Salaam more than 300 miles away.

At first, there was not much interest in establishing a radio station because of the relatively small European population in Tanganyika, unlike in neighbouring Kenya where there was a significant number of white settlers. The British government did not encourage its citizens to emigrate and settle in Tanganyika mainly because the territory was not a typical British colony like Kenya but a UN trusteeship territory under British tutelage only for a limited, though not specified, period of time after which the country would become independent.

There were, however, some parts of Tanganyika which attracted a significant number of white settlers. For example, even before the British took over Tanganyika from the Germans after World War I, Lushoto in the Usambara mountains in the northeastern part of the country was a kind of "winter capital" for the Germans.

But, in spite of the relatively small number of whites in

Tanganyika, there was an obvious need for a radio station for the indigenous population, although the broadcasts had a short radius and were initially limited to Dar es Salaam, the capital, which itself had Africans in the majority.

Even in the capital Dar es Salaam, European influence on the lives of most Africans was limited when compared to what happened in Nairobi, Kenya's capital, and elsewhere in Kenya especially in the "White Highlands" in the Central Province which had the largest number of white settlers in the country including Boers from South Africa. In fact, it was Boers who founded one of Kenya's most well-known towns, Eldoret.

In the case of Tanganyika, British cultural influence was very limited in terms of everyday life and only had significant impact on the elite. The most visible change in the African way of life was in the towns which were the administrative centres for the colonial rulers. That is where the District Commissioner, whom we simply called DC, and his white staff worked and lived if the town was the district headquarters. If the town was the capital of a province, you had the provincial commissioner, known as PC, as the head.

That is where you would see the colonial rulers and other whites, working and living there, although in some parts of the rural areas, there were also whites who owned farms and hired black labourers to work on coffee and tea plantations and other large farms.

In Tanganyika, white settlers could be found in places such as Lushoto in the Usambara mountains in the northeastern part of the country where they owned coffee farms and also a school exclusively for white children known as Lushoto Prep School; in Arusha in northern Tanganyika where they also had large farms and a school for white children called Arusha School; in Moshi near the slopes of Mount Kilimanjaro of majestic splendour where they also had a primary school exclusively for white children; and in the Southern Highlands Province where they also built the most prestigious school for white students in the whole country called St. Michael's and St. George's School in Iringa District near the town of Iringa, and another one in the town of Mbeya known as Mbeya School in the same province.

Mbeya School, which is in my home region, was established in

1942 in buildings which were once a German School. It was closed in 1963 as an exclusively European school and became a secondary school for students of all races after Tanganyika won independence. But it became almost exclusively black after students of other races sought education elsewhere.

Besides the German School which became Mbeya School, another European school which was founded in Tanganyika to educate pupils of the same national origin was the Greek School in Moshi where there was a number of Greek farmers and other Greeks engaged in different pursuits.

The school also served Greek children from Arusha which also had a significant number of Greek settlers. As Gregory Emmanuel whose family settled in Tanganyika stated in his article "Grandfather Gregory Emmanuel 'Nisiotis' (1875 - 1977)":

> A large number of Greeks, many from Tenedos, came to Tanganyika, where Greeks became the second largest expatriate European community (Germans being the largest group).
> In both Moshi and Arusha there were thriving Greek communities and the need arose for a Greek school.
> As the house at Lambo was vacant, Grandfather leased it to the Greek community and it became the first Greek school in East Africa. It was a boarding school and was the first school attended by my father, Costas. (He told me that a student who sleepwalked was taken during the night by a leopard.)

Coincidentally, another school, Kongwa School, which was open to white children of all nationalities started as a primary school on 4 October 1948, exactly one year before I was born on 4 October 1949.

It evolved from the abortive groundnut scheme funded by the British Overseas Food Corporation at Kongwa.

After the groundnut scheme failed and was abandoned in 1954, its buildings were converted into a secondary school, upgraded from a primary school. Then in 1958, the students at Kongwa School were transferred to a new school in Iringa, St. Michael's and St. George's.

All the European schools in Tanganyika were co-educational, attended by white children and students of all ages depending on the kind of school they went to. For example, St. Michael's and St. George's was a secondary school. And it was highly competitive with a reputation for academic excellence.

Many of its former students became very successful in life in different parts of the world, including Tanganyika itself, which became Tanzania, and have been holding reunions now and then to renew ties and reminisce on life in Tanganyika in those days.

In many ways, they were the good old days. Life was also much safer and simpler, and the people a lot friendlier than they are nowadays when everybody is busy fending for himself, with a large number of individuals preying on others in different ways besides robbery.

Although I did not attend St. Michael's and St. George's School after independence, there are many things which the former students and I agree on in terms of how life was in school and in Tanganyika in general in those days.

And we have another thing in common. They went to school in the same province where I come from: the Southern Highlands.

Even after independence, St. Michael's and St. George's stood out among all the schools in Tanzania. It had students up to Form VI (standard 14) and was renamed Mkwawa High School and admitted students of all races, which was not the case before Tanganyika became independent in 1961.

It was in the area of education where the colonial authorities instituted some of the most rigid structures of racial separation in the country.

They sanctioned inequality in the allocation of funds and provision of facilities including teachers which ensured that the children of the white settlers would get the best education and enjoy a privileged life style at the expense of Africans and, to a smaller degree, Asians whose status was no better than that of the Africans as colonial subjects; although they were treated better than Africans in many cases.

Arabs had their own Koranic schools and were not really an integral part of the mainstream in terms of formal education in the Western intellectual tradition.

But the bottom line was that even if the Asians - as well as the Arabs - were treated better than the Africans, they were still colonial subjects, therefore not equal to whites. And provision of separate educational facilities and funds affected their lives as well; although even in this case they were favoured by the colonial government when compared with Africans. As David Nettelbeck states in "Educational Separatism and the 1950s" in his book, *A History of Arusha School*:

> Because of the Government's lack of resources and unwillingness to take a strong initiative in educational provision, and in pursuance of the G.I.A. policy, there grew up three racially distinct systems of African, Asian and European education with each of the three subdivided into state controlled, state aided, and wholly private schools.
>
> In the African sector for example in 1937, there were 9,500 pupils in Government schools, 19,500 in aided schools and 100,000 in private schools. These latter were often sub-standard bush schools, and catechetical centres or Koranic schools along the coast. It was not until 1955 that the Government required these kinds of schools to be registered.
>
> In the same year, there were 985 places in Government schools for Indian children and another 3,318 in grant aided schools. The Indian community were quick to take advantage of the G.I.A. system and fulfil the requirements thus only 320 of their children were that year in private schools.
>
> For the European community in the 1930s, the Government made direct provision in three ways. Arusha School, primarily for boarders, opened in 1934; a correspondence course was based in Dar es Salaam; and there was also a junior primary school in Dar es Salaam. The enrolment figures in 1937 show 59 children in the latter two, and 60 pupils at Arusha School.
>
> There were in addition 704 grant-aided places for European children, a significant proportion of these being in national community schools for the Dutch, German and Greek children. Another 15 places were in a private school. The above figures are taken from the enrolment statistics 1931 - 1948 in Appendix G.
>
> There is another way of looking at these statistics and that is to see the percentage of children being educated from each community. Listowell states that in 1933, 51% of the European children, 49% of the Asian and 2% of the African were at school.
>
> By 1945 7.5%, of the African children attended school though few got beyond the fourth primary grade and none could attempt the entrance exam for tertiary study at Makerere in Uganda. By 1959, 40% of African children attended at least the first four years of primary education, and in 1961, 55% of the age group entered the first primary grade.
>
> The present Government of Nyerere aims at universal primary education by 1980. (The comparative cost per head of population has been referred to above and is detailed in Appendix J.)
>
> In 1930 an Education Tax was introduced with the primary object of affording security to the Government for the repayment of loans made to non-African communities. In 1932 the Indian and European communities were taxed for their education on a poll Tax basis and, in addition, fees were charged at their schools. Nevertheless the Government was making a far more generous per capita provision for European and Indian children than it was for African

children.

The table in Appendix J shows the total expenditure for each community and the per capita cost from 1931 - 1937. Also the table in Appendix K shows that in 1955/56, 33.7% of the money spent by the Government on European education was collected in fees, 15.4% came from the European Education Tax and 49.1% from Central Revenue. In 1959 the central revenue provided for European Education an amount equivalent to 1% of the total territorial expenditure.

In 1956, £3,618,555 held by the Custodian of Enemy Property from funds collected from confiscated properties during the Second World War was distributed equally between the Tanganyika Higher Education Trust Fund for establishing tertiary education facilities, St Michael's and St George's School, a lavish secondary school for European children at Iringa, Indian education, and African education.

This 4 way split seem superficially fair but as President Nyerere has pointed out, the allocation on a per capita basis was equivalent to shs- 720/- to each European, shs. 200/- to each Asian and shs. 2/- to each African.

In 1948 and 1949, the three existing education systems described above were formalized by two ordinances, the Non-Native Education Ordinance and the Non-Native Education Tax Ordinance. This legislation brought into being an Indian Education Authority and a European Education Authority, each composed of representatives of the communities they were to serve.

They were responsible for the development and general over-sight of the systems, and for managing the education funds according to the budget approved by the Legislative Council.

There was also an Advisory Committee for Other (non-native) Education, which included Goan, Mauritian, Seychellois, Anglo-Indian, and Ceylonese children.

What began in 1948 as a very minor offshoot of basic Government responsibility for the development of the country with only 8,000 Asian and 300 European children, had become by 1961 a major concern catering for 28,000 Asian and 2,500 European children.

The three educational systems established along racial lines for Europeans, Indians and Africans - in descending order in terms of quality - were formalized in the 1940s and 1950s. And they mirrored the racial hierarchy in colonial Tanganyika instituted by the British colonial rulers. They were abolished in January 1962, soon after the country won independence on 9 December 1961, and all schools in Tanganyika were opened to students of all races.

Although the British constituted the largest group of whites during colonial rule, the white settler community in Tanganyika was a constellation of nationalities. It included many other whites such as Greeks, Germans, Italians, Afrikaners, Jews, Poles, Swedes, Danes, Russians, and Lithuanians. And that is not an exhaustive list. The white settler community was in some ways a microcosm of Europe.

There were even a few Americans in Tanganyika; for example, the first owner of the New Arusha Hotel, Kenyon Painter, a millionaire banker from Ohio. He went to Tanganyika for the first time in 1907 and started building the New Arusha Hotel in 1927. It was completed in the same year.

The hotel was formally opened in January 1928 and the opening ball - in December 1927 - was attended by the Prince of Wales, Edward VIII.

Painter continued to live in the United States but he made several hunting trips to Tanganyika, especially Arusha. He died in 1940.

Before he arrived, there was only one tiny hotel in Arusha owned by a Jewish couple, Jane and Goodall Bloom, and they named the hotel, Bloom's, and it was the first Arusha Hotel. That's why when Kenyon Painter built his hotel, he called it the New Arusha Hotel.

Kenyon Painter bought 11,000 acres of land near the town of Arusha and he played a major role in establishing coffee farms in the region. He also built the first post office in Arusha, a church, a hospital, and a coffee research centre at Tengeru, 16 miles from Arusha.

The New Arusha Hotel became a historic landmark and a centre of social activity for many people including Hollywood stars such as John Wayne whose famous movie, "Hatari," which means danger in Kiswahili, was filmed in Arusha in 1962. There was also a sign in front of the New Arusha Hotel which said:

THIS SPOT IS EXACTLY HALF WAY BETWEEN THE CAPE AND CAIRO AND THE EXACT CENTRE OF KENYA, UGANDA, AND TANGANYIKA.

Arusha also was, and still is, one of the famous towns on what is known as The Great North Road from C to C, that is, from Cape Town to Cairo. And as someone described the two main hotels in the town of Arusha and the town itself in 1957:

Also in the main street were Arusha's two famous hotels.

The New Arusha displayed a board announcing that it was exactly midway between Cape Town and Cairo, and the Safari Hotel boasted an unusual copper topped bar to which a baby elephant had been led in for a drink in a recent Hollywood film Hatari (Danger).

Mount Meru overlooked the pretty garden town beyond the golf course and the main road to Nairobi to the north.

The streets in the residential areas were lined with purple jacarandas and the well kept gardens displayed a profusion of tropical zinnias, petunias and marigolds mixed with the roses, hollyhocks, ferns and carnations of England.

At 5000 feet above sea level, the climate was perfect after the sultry heat of the coast and the early mornings were a delight with dew-dappled lawns, mists and a nip in the air, mingled with the fragrant scent of cedar hedges.

It was the kind of climate which attracted many whites to the region. Today Arusha is the headquarters of the East African Community (EAC) comprising Kenya, Uganda, Tanzania, Rwanda and Burundi and is virtually the capital of East Africa and of the proposed East African Federation to be formed by 2013, if at all.

Other whites who lived in Arusha included Germans, Greeks, South Africans, Italians, and the British. They had farms around Arusha and some of them had small businesses in town.

Some of the crops grown in this fertile region included cereals, cherries, apples, citrus, coffee, cocoa, vanilla, and rubber. They were grown mostly by the Germans but other Europeans participated as well.

At the beginning of World War II, there were about 3,000 Germans and Italians living in Tanganyika. That was out of a total population of about 8,000 whites in the country. During the war itself, there were about 3,000 Italians including those who were held as prisoners of war in camps in Tanganyika; 9,000 Poles, 500 Greeks, and 180 Cypriot Jews, among many others.

According to the British Foreign and Commonwealth Office, the total number of Italians who were interned in Tanganyika, mainly in Arusha and Tabora, and in Uganda and Southern Rhodesia during World War II was almost 15,000. The number given in May 1945 was 14,900.

Many whites came to live in Tanganyika after the Second World War. Also after Germany was defeated in World War I, she lost her colony of German East Africa which became Tanganyika, taken over by the British, and Ruanda-Urundi, by the Belgians. After the British took over the colony, they also used it for detaining prisoners of war (POWs) who included Germans and their allies.

Many of them ended up staying in Tanganyika. The Italians, for example, did not have any historical connection to Tanganyika like the Germans who were the first colonial rulers did, but they settled in the country in significant numbers. Most of them had been preceded earlier by a group of Italian missionaries as far back as the 1920s.

The Italians who were interned in Tanganyika during World War II were sent back to Italy after the war ended but many of them returned because they liked living there. They also felt that Tanganyika had better prospects for them than Italy did.

Many of them were craftsmen and worked in technical fields and in construction and knew that their skills were in great in demand in an underdeveloped colonial territory like Tanganyika. In fact, some of them had done the same kind of work when they in internment camps in Tanganyika.

The situation got even much better for them and the other prisoners of war or detainees in Tanganyika after 1947 when the property which had been confiscated from foreigners including some Italians by the "Custodian of the Enemy Properties," in essence the British colonial government itself, was returned to them.

Therefore the 1950s was a period when Tanganyika witnessed the arrival of a significant number of Italians who came to settle in the country in addition to the ones who were already there.

Some of them were employed on farms, for example on sisal plantations in Morogoro in the Coast Province, on tobacco farms in Iringa in the Southern Highlands, and in the cultivation of coffee and pyrethrum in Arusha and Moshi in the Nothern Province.

Other Italians went to work in the mines, mostly gold. They went to Geita in the Lake Province where they worked for the Gold Mining Company, in Musoma where they were employed by Tangold Company, and in the diamond mines of Mwadui in Shinyanga where they worked for the Williamson Diamonds Ltd.

of Mwadui. There were, of course, people of other nationalities as well working in these mines, including the British and Afrikaners.

It was also during the same period that another development took place which improved prospects for a number of Italians seeking employment in Tanganyika in the 1950s.

Two projects were launched under the direction of the M. Gonella Company based in Nairobi. These were the construction of some oil depots at Kurasini in Dar es Salaam and of the first sewerage system also in Dar es Salaam, the country's capital in the Coast Province.

An average of about 200 Italians came to Tanganyika every year in the fifties to live or seek employment. The number may have been small but when looked at in the larger context of all the immigrants who came to Tanganyika in those years, we see that the figure was not really that small and Italy was one of the main countries of origin of the immigrants who settled in Tanganyika in the 1950s.

In 1952, a census was done and it showed that there were 17,885 Europeans living in Tanganyika. A total of 12,395, or 69.3 percent of the white population in the country, were British. Greeks were the second largest group with 1,292 people, followed by the Italians with 1,071; the Dutch, with 515; the Germans, 499; the Swiss, 496; and the Americans, with 331.

Other sources arrive at pretty much the same figure showing that the population of white settlers in Tanganyika in the fifties was much closer to 20,000. That was about a third of those in Kenya.

Some cited a higher figure. For example, *Time* magazine, in one of its 1965 editions stated: "Tanzania, which as Tanganyika once had 22,700 whites, now has 17,000."

But all these settlers had one thing in common. They were white and therefore members of the white settler community. Although they settled in significant numbers in only a few parts of Tanganyika, the areas where they settled were mostly in the fertile and cooler regions at high altitudes with temperatures most whites were comfortable with. There were, however, also significant numbers of whites in Dar es Salaam in the Coast Province because it was the capital and commercial centre of colonial

Tanganyika.

Other whites were spread throughout the country living in different places such as Lindi, Nachingwea, Masasi and Mtwara in the Southern Province and other parts of the region; Kilosa in the Coast Province; Dodoma in the Central Province; Tabora in the Western Province; Mwanza and Bukoba in the Lake Province and other parts of Tanganyika.

Yet, even in areas with significant numbers of whites such as the Southern Highlands which were "extensively" occupied by the British, there was little interaction with Africans besides servants, farm labourers and house boys and maids, whose relationship with whites was defined by their subordinate status. There was also some interaction of the master-servant type in towns as well where whites lived and worked.

And the relationship couldn't be anything but that in a colony and racially stratified society dominated by Europeans even if most Africans in Tanganyika rarely saw a white person in their lives or at least during the period of colonial rule. Most of them lived in villages and spent their entire lives without going into towns where whites were.

And even when they went into towns to buy and sell things, they did not always see white people, although many of them did on a number of occasions now and then in their lives.

I remember when I was growing up in Rungwe District in Mpumbuli Village, Kyimbila, about four miles from the town of Tukuyu which was the district headquarters, I rarely saw whites when I went into town. That was in the late fifties when I was under 10 years old and quite often ventured into town, walking or sometimes catching the bus.

The only time we saw quite a few whites was when they played golf and tennis in the town of Tukuyu. I remember when we passed by as children, they now and then gave us tennis balls which we used to play with as soccer, popularly known as football. And it was the right size of "football", or "soccer ball," for us as little boys between 6 and 9 years old.

To us the whites, who were mostly British, were friendly and we saw them simply as white people who were in town playing golf and tennis. Politics was the last thing on our minds. We did not have the slightest idea of what was going on. We didn't even know why they came to Tanganyika all the way from Europe.

Even our knowledge of geography was very limited at that age. To us, our home district was the entire world. We couldn't envision anything beyond the misty blue mountains which form a ring around Rungwe District in the Great Rift Valley. Next to that, as our world, after we grew a little older and learnt more about geography, was our province, the Southern Highlands Province; and then Tanganyika, our country.

We hardly knew about the rest of East Africa when we were six and seven years old and did not even know much about the neighbouring countries of Nyasaland and Northern Rhodesia which border our region.

We did not learn that in standard one and standard two until later when we were in standard three and standard four. And why whites were in Tanganyika, and when they came to Tanganyika and to Africa in general, was in the realm of history and politics far beyond our knowledge at that age.

The whites who came to Tukuyu to play golf came from Mbeya, about 45 miles away. Some even came from Northern Rhodesia, which is Zambia today. And there were, of course, those who lived in Tukuyu, although not many. From what I remember, it was only a few of them who lived in the town of Tukuyu.

The town was first built by the Germans, the first colonial rulers, and was named Neu Langenburg. They are the ones who first made it the headquarters of Rungwe District. The town was destroyed twice by earthquakes, first in 1910, and again in 1919, but was rebuilt by the British after they took control of Tanganyika after the end of the First World War. And it is still the headquarters of Rungwe District today.

Among the whites whom I remember when I was growing up in Rungwe District in the late fifties were the District Commissioner (DC), the most powerful man in the town of Tukuyu and in the whole district of no fewer than 300,000 people during that period; the manager of Shell BP petrol station, a British like the DC, also in the town of Tukuyu where my father once worked under him as an assistant manager in the late fifties, and about whom I have more to say elsewhere in the book; and the manager of Kyimbila Tea Estate and his wife, both British, about a mile-and-a- half from our house whom I also address in another chapter in this book.

He and his wife lived on the premises at Kyimbila next to Kyimbila Moravian Church of which my family and I were members and whose pastor, Asegelile Mwankemwa, was my mother's uncle. He is also the one who helped raise my mother and her brothers after their parents died. My grandmother, my mother's mother, was his sister.

I don't remember any of the names of the whites I just mentioned except one, although when we were in primary school - I went to Kyimbila Primary School from 1956 to 1959 about two miles from Tukuyu and two miles from our home - we knew the name of the district commissioner (DC) of Rungwe District.

But I do remember the name of one provincial commissioner, Pearce. He was PC in the late 1950s and lived in Mbeya which was then the capital of the Southern Highlands Province. The former capital was Iringa but it was moved to Mbeya, although I don't remember exactly when; it was sometime in the late fifties, I believe.

The most visible symbol of colonial authority I remember when I was eight and nine years old in the late fifties was a wooden sign on the outskirts of the town of Tukuyu which said, "Native Authority." I remember it very well, almost 50 years later, and even exactly where it was. It was a white sign with black capital letters.

It was on the right-hand side of the road right at the foot of a small hill when on the way to Tukuyu, and on the left on my way home; on the same road that went all the way to Kyela, a town near the border with Nyasaland. It was very close to a junction where there was an Anglican Church. The other road led to a place called Makandana which was only about a mile from the town of Tukuyu.

I did not know what kind of sign it was - for direction, warning, or what - and it meant absolutely nothing to me. I had not even started learning English during that time, until later when I went to Mpuguso Middle School. It was a boarding school. I first went there in 1961, the same year I started learning English. I was 11 years and three months old when I started learning the language in January that year.

I was a day student from 1961 to 1962 before I was enrolled as a boarder in 1963. It was an all-boys school with a reputation for rigorous intellectual discipline and was one of the best middle schools in the Southern Highlands Province and in the whole country. It was also one of the oldest.

Among its alumni was Jeremiah Kasambala, son of a chief from the area who later became one of the first cabinet members under Nyerere when Tanganyika won independence. Others through the years included doctors, lawyers and academics; and a general in the Tanzania People's Defence Forces (TPDF) who also became head of a military college, my first cousin, Owen Mwambapa.

It wasn't until a few years later after I was at Mpuguso Middle School that I understood what that (Native Authority) sign meant after I learnt some English, and even much later before I understood its political significance as a demarcation line between the colonizer and colonized.

It symbolized colonial power enforced by indirect rule, a system of administration first introduced by Lord Lugard in Northern Nigeria under which the colonial government ruled vast expanses of territory through native rulers including chiefs in my home district of Rungwe.

The town of Tukuyu was under direct rule by the district commissioner (DC), and the rest of the district under indirect rule through native authority; hence the sign, "Native Authority," showing where direct rule ended and where indirect rule began. Africans and Indian shopkeepers who lived in the town of Tukuyu were under direct rule of the white colonial administrators who also lived there.

But if the colonial authorities felt that direct intervention was warranted, they did not hesitate to exercise their power.

I remember one tragic incident in the late fifties when two Nyakyusa chiefs and their people in Kyela were involved in a bloody conflict, the exact nature of which I never understood; some said the conflict was over land, which seemed to be a plausible explanation, given the scarcity of land in Rungwe District of which Kyela was then an integral part; today Kyela is a separate district and has been one for years.

When the conflict erupted, an urgent message was sent to

Mbeya, the provincial capital, and within the same day, the colonial authorities dispatched a contingent of Field Force Units (FFU) to stop the fighting. The FFUs, which still exist in Tanzania today, specialize in riot control and in stopping other violent conflicts and have a reputation for being tough and using weapons when necessary.

It was one of those instances during my life time when the British invoked *Pax Britannica* in the quest for peace under the Union Jack in their colony of Tanganyika. The FFU riot policemen were black but their officers white.

There were other whites I remember in Rungwe District including missionaries; for example, Catholic priests at Kisa Catholic Mission about five miles from our home. They used to walk most of the time all the way from Kisa to Tukuyu and back. I remember they were dressed in black robes.

There was also another white man whom I remember very well. He used to drive down the road near our house on his way to Ilima coal mine and back to Tukuyu and Mbeya. They said he was the owner of the coal mine which was about 15 miles from our home and the Nyakyusa called him Tojilwe, obviously a corruption of his name, whatever it was; today, it sounds like Trujillo or Torrijos to me.

He could have been Spanish, I don't know, if his name was indeed Trujillo or Torrijos, what my fellow Nyakyusas called Tojilwe.

The mine was almost mid-way between Tukuyu and Kyela, a town near the Tanzania-Malawi border, and the road goes all the way to Malawi, which was then Nyasaland in those days.

Although Tojiliwe was in charge of the coal mine at Ilima – now officially known as Kiwira Coal Mines - which was about 15 miles from our home in Mpumbuli village in the area of Kyimbila, and the people who did all the hard work were Africans, to him they were just that, coal miners.

His relationship with the coal miners was basically no different from the relationship other whites had with Africans in general. Few whites interacted with Africans on personal basis. Africans were no more than colonial subjects under the imperial flag fluttering under the tropical sun.

The interaction was minimal for racial and cultural reasons, as well as for reasons of personal taste probably on both sides. Africans who may have wanted to associate with whites - usually for social status more than anything else as members of "civilized" society which by colonial definition meant white - were inhibited in their desire by their well-founded fear and suspicion that they would not be accepted, let alone as equals, by a people who were their masters as colonial rulers and many of whom probably considered them to be inferior; while some whites, on the other hand, did not want to mingle with blacks because they did not consider them to be their equal in any conceivable way including mental capacity.

Africans dealt mostly with Indians who owned shops where African customers bought a variety of items such as clothes, soap, cooking oil, salt and sugar. And they communicated very well. I remember many Indians in Tukuyu who spoke Kinyakyusa, our "tribal" language, with their customers. And some of them knew the language very well.

Although many Africans probably did not notice or feel the colonial presence and white domination did not have a direct impact on their lives everyday, there were those who were acutely aware of the disparities in life among the races purely along racial lines. They knew the disparities or inequities were not merely accidental but a product of deliberate decisions by the colonial rulers who instituted a system of racial hierarchy to maintain colonial rule.

What set them apart from the other Africans besides their political consciousness was education. They were mostly educated, with secondary school education or higher and sometimes even less, and they worked directly under the supervision of whites especially in towns. And they are the ones who led the struggle for independence, not only in Tanganyika but in other African countries as well.

There was another politically conscious class of Africans who constituted a critical mass during the struggle for independence. These were the workers in towns. They formed trade unions demanding better wages and conditions at work which eventually led to demands for political equality and representation at the local and national levels.

Most of them were not educated in the traditional sense. They never got the chance to go to school, although a significant number of them did and had at least primary school education enabling them to read and write as well as count. But because they worked directly under whites, they became very much aware of the difference in living conditions among the races and they were among some of the most politically conscious people in Tanganyika and in all the other colonies across the continent.

Their consciousness was best demonstrated on a number of occasions when they went on strike to force the colonial authorities to meet their demands, a strategy which helped galvanize the independence movement.

In fact, the labour union leaders became some of the most prominent leaders in the independence struggle. For example, Rashid Mfaume Kawawa, a prominent labour union leader in Tanganyika, became prime minister and later vice president of Tanganyika and later of Tanzania. And in Kenya, Tom Mboya, another highly influential labour union leader, became the most prominent national leader after President Jomo Kenyatta and his heir apparent. He also held senior cabinet posts including the ministry of economic planning and development until his assassination in July 1969 at the age of 39.

I remember there were even songs by Kenyan musicians played on the radio, the Tanganyika Broadcasting Corporation, which in those days we simply called TBC, in the late fifties about Tom Mboya when he was one of the brightest stars on the Kenyan political scene even before independence.

In the case of Tanganyika, the late fifties were a turning point in the independence struggle, as much as they were for neighbouring Kenya, and witnessed among other things the departure of one of the last two governors of this vast country, the largest among the East African British colonies.

I witnessed some of those events, although I was only 8 and 9 years old.

I remember when Sir Edward Francis Twining, one of the last two governors of Tanganyika, came to Tukuyu in 1958. It was a farewell visit.

He was the governor from 18 June 1949 (about four months before I was born) to June 1958. He was succeeded by Sir Richard Gordon Turnbull who was the last governor of Tanganyika from

15 July 1958 until independence day on 9 December 1961. Twining died in June 1967, and Turnbull in December 1998.

I remember the day Governor Twining came to Tukuyu in 1958 to say good-bye. I was about eight-and-a-half years old. It was a bright, sunny day, in the afternoon.

I was then a pupil in standard three at Kyimbila Primary School about two miles from Tukuyu and our head teacher made arrangements for us to go and see the governor.

So, we were in school only half of the day and we walked the two miles to the town of Tukuyu to see the governor for the last time; it was also the first time most of us saw him on that day.

Paul Bomani, left, with Julius Nyerere, right, in the Lake Province in the 1950s. Bomani was a major leader of the Sukuma, Tanganyika's largest ethnic group, and campaigned for independence with Nyerere. He was president of the Sukuma Union and later president of the Tanganyika African National Union (TANU) in the Lake Province.

I even remember his attire. He was dressed in white. He also had on a white hat and white gloves. And Nyakyusa dancers performed the traditional dance called *mang'oma* in farewell to him.

There were also many whites on the scene. Some had accompanied him from Dar es Salaam and Mbeya and others simply came to see him.

Also on the scene was the Provincial Commissioner (PC) of the Southern Highlands Province from Mbeya, the provincial capital, and the District Commissioner (DC) of Rungwe District who lived right there in Tukuyu, the district headquarters.

I remember it was a festive occasion. People were in jovial mood. Politics seemed to be the last thing on their minds, as the dancers swayed and swivelled to the rhythm and drum-beat of *mang'oma*, the most popular Nyakyusa traditional dance.

And the others who were there joyously clapped their hands for the governor when he climbed up the steps of the Barclays Bank building from where he waved to the crowd, smiling.

I remember the area well. The Clock Tower and the golf course were only a few yards away on the right hand-side when you faced the Barclays Bank Building.

Although I was too young to know what was going on in the country in terms of politics and the campaign for independence under the leadership of the Tanganyika African National Union (TANU) whose charismatic leader, Julius Nyerere, electrified his audiences by his mere presence even before he spoke whenever he campaigned in different parts of Tanganyika, I was still able to tell that there was no hostility of any kind towards the governor and other whites on the part of the Africans who were there on that day.

And that seemed to be the case even during the campaign for independence itself.

There were no attacks on the British and other whites, and the people of all races seemed to get along just fine even if they did not mingle.

The campaign for independence was peaceful and was waged along constitutional lines.

Oscar Kambona, one of the founders and first secretary-general of TANU. He became minister of home affairs and later of foreign affairs after independence and was close to President Nyerere until July 1967 when he went into exile in Britain. He returned to Tanzania in 1992 to form an opposition political party and died in London in July 1997after suffering several strokes.

When reflecting on the transition from colonial rule to independence, Nyerere himself said that Tanganyika won independence by peaceful means, and there was no hostility towards whites even after the country won independence. As he stated in parliament during a debate on the citizenship bill when a few members wanted only black Africans to be citizens after Tanganyika became independent, as reported in the *Tanganyika National Assembly Debates* (Hansard), in October 1961 less than two months before the country won independence from Britain:

> If we in Tanganyika are going to divorce citizenship from loyalty and marry it to colour, it won't stop there...until you break up the country....They are preaching discrimination as a religion to us. And they stand like Hitlers and begin to glorify race. We glorify human beings, not colour.

Nyerere was furious when he heard a few members of the National Assembly speaking against citizenship for whites, Indians, Arabs and others. He was known to be very calm, tolerant and kind but he lost his temper during the course of the debate and accused them of racism and talking rubbish and behaving like Nazis.

Julius Nyerere in the early 1960s.
Photo sent by Andrew Nyerere, his eldest son.

Earlier as a little boy, before Nyerere gave that speech in the National Assembly in October 1961, I witnessed an event which embodied his vision of a multiracial society.

The reception the governor, Sir Edward Twining, was given by Africans and other people on that day in Tukuyu in 1958 during his last visit there was in many ways highly indicative of how things were going to be after Tanganyika won independence: people of different races and ethnic groups living and working together in harmony without hate and fear of each other or one another in the best interest of the country and for the sake of peace and stability enjoyed by all.

Governor Edward Twining's farewell visit marked the beginning of the end of British colonial rule in Tanganyika.

But, at that tender age, little did I or any of the other children - including many adults - know that independence was only three-and-a-half years away after 42 years of British colonial rule.

Julius Nyerere in the early days of independence in the sixties.
Photo sent by Andrew Nyerere.

Chapter Three:

Newspapers in Tanganyika in the Fifties: A History Linked with My Destiny as a Reporter

NEWSPAPERS in Tanganyika have a long history. I was a witness to some of that history because I read some of the newspapers which were published in the 1950s. And I still have vivid memories of some of the pictures I saw in the newspapers during that period.

I remember seeing pictures of the Mau Mau fighters in Kenya in some of the newspapers published in Kiswahili in the late 1950s. One of the most memorable aspects of those pictures was the hairstyle of some of the Mau Mau fighters. They had dreadlocks, a hairstyle that was new to me and to many other people during that period not only in Tanganyika but in Kenya itself where the war was going on.

Some of the Mau Mau fighters were sent to Tanganyika where they were detained in what was then the Central Province and in other parts of the country including the Coast Province. And the Mau Mau uprising was one of the most important stories in the Swahili newspapers I read during those days.

I remember reading those newspapers especially in 1958 and 1959. They included *Mambo Leo*, *Mwafrika*, *Baragumu*, *Mwangaza*, and *Kiongozi*.

There was also one newspaper which was published in Kinyakyusa, my tribal language. It was called *Lembuka* which means "Wake Up" in the Nyakyusa language. It was first published in 1953 by the Rungwe African District Council and lasted until 1957. The paper was also published in Swahili.

Some of the newspapers were published by missionaries. They included *Lumuli* which was published by the Roman Catholic Church in Mwanza from 1936 until 1964. It was published in the Sukuma language. Coincidentally, the meaning of *Lumuli* in Sukuma is almost the same as in my tribal language Nyakyusa. In Sukuma, *Lumuli* means "torch," and in Nyakyusa it means "light."

Another newspaper published in my home district of Rungwe was *Ushindi* which means "victory" in Swahili. It was published in the town of Tukuyu by the Moravian Church which I belonged to as did the rest of my family. In fact, my great uncle – my mother's uncle and brother of my grandmother on my mother's side – was the pastor of the Moravian Church at Kyimbila which we attended. His name was Asegelile Mwankemwa.

The newspapers which I remember the most – or the most memorable ones – in terms of news were *Mambo Leo* and *Mwafrika*. And among all the newspapers, *Mwafrika* was the most well-known and most popular among Africans.

It was first published in 1957 and the editor of the paper, Joel Mgogo, came from my home district. He became the editor of *Mwafrika* in 1958. Years later, his younger brother, a graduate of the University of Dar es Salaam, was my history teacher at Tambaza High School in Dar es Salaam from 1969 to 1970.

The newspapers were read not only in Tanganyika but in Kenya as well. The common denominator was Kiswahli, a language spoken in both Kenya and Tanganyika, which enabled the people in both countries to read the newspapers.

But while I witnessed some of the most important events in the history of our country during the last decade of colonial rule in the fifties and read the Swahili newspapers published during that period, I was not fortunate enough to have been a witness to what had taken place long before then. I was not there because I was not born then. Therefore I have relied on the historical record to write what I have written here about the newspapers published long before I was born.

One of the most important sources of information about newspapers published in Tanganyika during that period is Martin Sturmer whose work proved indispensable in writing this chapter. His work also helped illuminate some of the themes I have addressed about Tanganyika in the fifties which is the focus of my book.

Also, his information about the newspapers published in Tanganyika in the fifties has served to complement what I already know about the events and the newspapers during that period. As a primary source of information myself about those newspapers and some of the events which took place in the fifties since I was there during that period and read some of the newspapers, I may have a different perspective from what he has on some of the issues he and I have addressed in our works. But his work nonetheless serves as a vital source of information. I have found it to be very useful in writing this chapter and in complementing my observations and analysis.

And it's a long history. As Martin Sturmer states in his book *The Media History of Tanzania*:

"The first newspaper in Tanzania, *Msimulizi* (Storyteller), was published by the Anglican Universities' Mission to Central Africa (UMCA) on Zanzibar in 1888....

Kwetu (Home) became Tanganyika's first African-owned newspaper....The first issue of *Kwetu* appeared on November 18th 1937 in a run of 1,000 copies. All the material was in Swahili, except the leading article which was translated into English....

In its contents, *Kwetu* focused on topics which were popular among the indigenous community, such as racial discrimination, economic exploitation, and European control of the political system." – (Martin Sturmer, *The Media History of Tanzania*, Ndanda Mission Press, Ndanda, Mtwara, Tanzania, 1998, pp. 29, and 55 – 56).

Although I have focused on the fifties, I have also incorporated into my work some details from Sturmer about the newspapers which were published before then, and thereafter, in order to present a more comprehensive picture because the years before the fifties provide a very important background to what took place during the last decade of colonial rule in Tanganyika. And newspapers played a very important role in shaping those events not only by reporting what took place but also by shaping public opinion in varying degrees.

Most of the coverage was not in the best interest of Africans even in some of the highly influential newspapers published in Swahili because of the nature of colonial rule. The interests of the white settlers and rulers were paramount. Even at a young age in the late fifties, I noticed the difference in living standards between Africans and Europeans when I was growing up in Rungwe District in the Southern Highlands of Tanganyika; a subject I have also addressed in one of my books, *My Life as an African: Autobiographical Writings*.

All that was part of our colonial heritage and history going all the way back to the time when the Germans became the first Europeans to rule our country. It was also during the German colonial period that some of the most important newspapers in the history of colonial Tanganyika were first published.

I also have some memories about the occupation of our country by the Germans. There even used to be a German colonial settlement in my home area at a place called Kyimbila only about a mile from our house. And a large cemetery of Germans buried there since the 1890s during their years as the rulers of Tanganyika still exists today. Some of the people buried there may even have been eulogised in some of the German newspapers published in Tanganyika during those years.

The first newspapers to be published in Tanganyika were published about 100 years ago.

The newspapers were first published when the country was a German colony known as *Deutsch Ostafrika*, meaning German East Africa which included what is now Rwanda and Burundi. They were published in German.

After the Germans lost the colony during World War I, the British took over as the new rulers and published their first newspaper in 1916. It was published by the East African Expeditionary Forces of the allies who defeated the Germans. The newspaper was called *The Morogoro News*.

The first edition was published on 16 September 1916, and it was the first English newspaper to be published in Tanganyika.

It was a four-page bi-monthly dealing mainly with the military situation in Tanganyika during and immediately after the war and its main article was on the "liberation" of Morogoro from the Germans.

Another English newspaper launched during that time was the *Tanga Post and East Coast Advertiser*, although it did not last long. Its first edition was published on 6 September 1919 just two months-and-a-half after a government paper, the *Tanganyika Territory Gazette*, first appeared on 24 June 1919.

The last issue of the *Tanga Post* appeared on 25 June 1921 but other papers followed through the years and immediately after the war, including the *Dar es Salaam Times*, a weekly, which was first published on 19 November 1919.

It was subtitled *The Voice of Tanganyika* and was the first paper in the country devoted almost exclusively to the well-being of the white settlers and also published many articles about the white settler community in neighbouring Kenya.

The *Dar es Salaam Times* lasted until 26 December 1925 when the last issue was published. By that time, the paper was 12 pages, twice its original size. It did not die but simply changed its name to *Tanganyika Times* to reflect its wider audience which included white settlers who lived in other parts of Tanganyika besides Dar es Salaam.

The first issue of the *Tanganyika Times* was published on 2 January 1926. And it was still a weekly paper like the original *Dar es Salaam Times*, but also had a sister paper which was a four-page daily launched only two days later on January 4$_{th}$. Both the daily and weekly editions of the the *Tanganyika Times* lasted until June 1930, overwhelmed by another paper, the *Tanganyika Standard*, which was launched in the same year.

Although all these English papers may give the impression that Tanganyika was now solidly under British control, which it was, it is also important to remember that the advent of British colonial rule in Tanganyika cannot be attributed to total defeat of the Germans in Tanganyika in World War I.

The Germans in Tanganyika led by General von Lettow-Vorbeck were actually never defeated in World War I. They waged a brilliant guerrilla campaign together with their African soldiers against vastly superiors forces in terms of weaponry and manpower which drew worldwide attention, admiration and respect even from their enemies.

They surrendered only after the armistice was signed in November 1918 and would have continued to fight had Germany itself not agreed to the terms to end the war, up to that time the bloodiest in world history.

Although the Germans in Tanganyika surrendered to the Allied forces led by the British, including soldiers from South Africa under General Smuts, they were not humiliated in the coverage of their defeat in the pages of *The Morogoro News*. However, the newspaper did not last long and after five editions, it ceased publication.

There followed a number of newspapers through the years published in English, and eventually in Kiswahili as well, which were aimed at specific audiences and along racial lines.

Some of the most important newspapers in Tanganyika, in both English and Kiswahili, were founded by Tanganyikans of Indian origin and others by Indians in Kenya. Newspapers for people of Indian and Pakistani origin were also published in Gujerati.

The most influential English newspaper in Tanganyika was founded in 1930. It was named the *Standard*, a sister paper of the *East African Standard* based in Nairobi, Kenya, and the first edition was published on January 1st.

It still exists today and was renamed *Daily News* in 1970 after it was nationalized about a year after I first joined its editorial staff as a news reporter in June 1969 when I was still a high school student in Form V at Tambaza, formerly H.H. The Aga Khan High School, in Dar es Salaam.

And the first newspaper to be published in Kiswahili was *Mambo Leo*, meaning Today's Affairs or Affairs of Today. It was a monthly newspaper published by the Department of Education and first came out in January 1923. Although it was aimed at the indigenous population, it was not African in orientation and was primarily a colonial organ intended to portray a good image of the colonial government among Africans.

Africans wanted to start their own newspaper but economic problems and stringent rules by the government discouraging such a venture made it virtually impossible for them to do so.

In spite of that, an attempt was made by some Africans to launch an African newspaper to suit their taste. And that happened in March 1932 when *Anga la Tanganyika*, meaning The Sky of Tanganyika, was first published.

The first edition appeared on March 4th. The paper was founded by Shaaban Said Mnubi who was also its editor. It had a print run of 200 copies. But only a fifth of those were sold and Mnubi was forced to stop publication.

After the paper died, another effort was made to launch an African publication in Tanganyika. This led to the founding of *Kwetu*, meaning Our Home (from the Swahili expression *nyumbani kwetu* which literally means our home).

The First edition of *Kwetu* appeared on 18 November 1937 and had a print run of 1,000 published every 18 days. It was founded by Erica Fiah, a Ugandan from Kampala, who lived in Dar es Salaam and was active in African economic and political associations in that town.

He was also the editor of the paper and is credited with starting what is considered to be the first African-owned newspaper in Tanganyika. As he stated in his letter of application to start the newspaper he sent to the Colonial Chief Secretary of the Government of Tanganyika on 4 May 1936 and which is kept in the Tanzania National Archives: "The aim of our paper will be to promote social and economic and political interests of the sons of the soil."

It became a popular newspaper among Africans because it addressed their concerns. Issues covered included racial discrimination, economic exploitation and control of the government by Europeans to the exclusion of Africans who constituted the majority of the population.

Kwetu also had an English supplement to reach a wider audience including the white settler community as well as the colonial authorities most of whose members did not know Kiswahili or well enough to understand the Swahili edition.

Another Swahili paper founded during that period was *Dunia*, meaning The World, in 1939 by M.D. Patel, editor of the *Tanganyika Opinion* which was aimed at the Asian community.

Dunia was basically a counterpart of the English edition,

Tanganyika Opinion.

Most of its articles were translations of the articles published in the *Tanganyika Opinion*, although it also had letters written by Africans in Kiswahili. Patel, the editor, also wrote editorials now and then articulating grievances aired by Africans and *Dunia* has the distinction of being the first daily newspaper published in an African language in Tanganyika.

But it did not last long and ceased publication in 1946 soon after World War II.

In September 1947, attempts were made to launch a Swahili and English paper named *The African Voice*. But those attempts failed.

And in May 1948, another independent newspaper, the *Tanganyika Herald* founded in the late 1930s by V.R. Boal for the Asian community in Tanganyika, also ceased publication. It reappeared in 1959 and lasted until 1963.

Two other Swahili newspapers were launched during that period and became influential in their own way themselves, although not as much as *Kwetu* was in terms of expressing indigenous discontent against the colonial administration and some elements of the white settler community and as outlet for black nationalist sentiments which were sometimes expressed in pretty strong language.

One of those papers was *Baraza*, meaning The Council, a weekly. But it was not a Tanganyikan newspaper. It was Kenyan. It was started in 1939 by the East African Standard Ltd. in Nairobi.

But although it was not a Tanganyikan paper, it had a bigger audience and circulation in Tanganyika than it did in Kenya. It was very popular among Africans in Tanganyika during that time but did not articulate nationalist sentiments the way *Kwetu* did, although it had the potential to be a potent force in political agitation had it chosen and been allowed to do so.

The other Swahili newspaper, besides *Kwetu*, was *Zuhra*, The Wanderer. It was launched in 1940 and was a daily newspaper. It was also very popular among Africans, although not as much as *Kwetu* and *Baraza* were, probably because of its limited circulation. The paper was available only in Dar es Salaam and its outskirts.

It was started by a Tanganyikan of Asian descent, M. Machado Plantan, and was edited by Mathias E. Mnyampala, a poet who was active in African politics. He later became a judge.

Although the paper was not against the colonial government in its editorial policy, it did now and then publish comments critical of some of the colonial practices. Mnyampala walked a fine line and avoided antagonizing the colonial authorities while at the same time paying attention to his African audience by trying to please both sides.

He used to publish articles which were sympathetic towards the colonial government, yet at the same time wrote comments critical of the views expressed in some of those articles, thus making it clear that he was not sympathetic towards the colonial rulers and against his own people who, as colonial subjects like himself, did not have the same rights the white settlers had. But he also knew that not all whites were against Africans.

The paper did well through the years and existed until the early the fifties, thanking the colonial government for allowing it to continue to exist and for doing some good things for Africans, yet at the same time making it clear that there are things the colonial rulers could do to serve the interests of Africans and make their lives better.

But it should also be remembered that all these papers were launched just before or during the Second World War, and economic conditions made it very difficult for them to continue to exist. Therefore it was during this period that the number of independent newspapers began to go down.

The decline was compounded by the fact that the colonial government was really not interested in seeing these newspapers flourish since they did not serve its interests and those of the white settlers and would therefore have not kept them afloat even if the owners sought financial assistance from the colonial rulers.

World War II also had a profound impact on *Kwetu*, the Kiswahili newspaper which was highly influential especially among politically conscious Africans but which was not a daily; *Kwetu* was published once every two-and-a-half weeks.

It continued to be published even during those difficult times but financial problems during the war made it impossible for the newspaper to continue and in May 1945 ceased publication. But

Erica Fiah did not give up and in January 1946 resumed publication.

This time the paper was published as a monthly. However, continuing financial problems made it extremely difficult for the paper to be published on regular basis and from July 1946, it appeared only rarely.

To save the paper, Fiah sought assistance from the Indian community in Tanganyika, mainly in Dar es Salaam, in February 1947 and succeeded in getting the help he needed to relaunch the paper.

From 1948 he started publishing *Kwetu* again and turned it into a weekly. He even wanted to start a daily newspaper but failed to do so for financial reasons. However, the weekly edition became successful and continued to speak for Africans and defend their interests.

But the colonial government did not agree with what Fiah was doing. The two were at opposite ends on fundamental issues in spite of the fact that the paper had been allowed to exist and circulate among Africans and articulate their views. Tanganyika was still a colony and not ready for the kind of sentiments expressed by *Kwetu* in pursuit of nationalist aspirations of the indigenous population. And so in March 1951, *Kwetu* ceased publication and Africans were left without a newspaper that could speak for them.

Ironically, *Kwetu* was forced to close down during the same period when political agitation among Africans was getting stronger. It was also during the same decade that the struggle for independence gained momentum.

Only three years after *Kwetu* was virtually banned, although not in a strictly legal sense, the Tanganyika African National Union (TANU) was founded in July 1954 to lead the struggle for independence and became one of the most successful nationalist movements in colonial history in the entire world.

It was also during the fifties that Swahili newspapers made a dramatic entry on the scene and had a profound impact on the course of events and the country's history during the struggle for independence. They also had mass appeal since they were published in a language the vast majority of the people knew and understood.

And it was these people who provided the strongest support for the independence struggle led by Julius Nyerere who himself had an uncanny ability to connect with the masses in spite of his reputation as an intellectual, hence a member of the elite.

On the other side of the racial divide were two influential papers, the *Tanganyika Standard* serving mostly the white settler community, and the *Tanganyika Opinion* aimed at the Asian community. Because of the continuing success of these papers, the colonial government felt that there was a need for an African paper to serve Africans.

Its first Swahili newspaper, *Habari za Vita* (War News), a weekly which focused on World War II to project a good image of the government among Africans, was renamed *Habari za Leo*, meaning Today's News or News of Today, in 1945. It was free of charge like its predecessor *Habari za Vita* and, because of that, was snatched up as soon as it rolled off the press.

But *Habari za Leo* pursued the same editorial policy another major Swahili newspaper, *Mambo Leo*, did and which had an even bigger print run of 50,000 copies. Both papers had many articles about the British royal family but little coverage of the nationalist aspirations of Africans and other political subjects.

Another government monthly published in Kiswahili was *Sauti ya Kweli* (Genuine Voice), founded in 1959, but it was not published on regular basis. And it was no match for *Mambo Leo* and *Habari za Leo* in terms of circulation and appeal. It also came too late on the scene as a government paper to stem the nationalist tide since it was launched at a time when the country was on the verge of independence.

The government was aware of that and knew Africans did not have a newspaper covering current affairs to their satisfaction, although it had no interest in helping advance the nationalist cause espoused by African leaders.

So in 1951, it launched *Mwangaza*, The Light, which during that time was the only Swahili daily newspaper in Tanganyika. And it was significantly different from the other Swahili papers in its editorial policy, besides the staunchly pro-African *Kwetu*, in the sense that it was more liberal and sympathetic to the nationalist cause and other African concerns than the other papers were, although *Zuhra* under Mathia Mnyampala as editor tried to address some of those issues even if not in-depth the way *Kwetu* did.

When *Mwangaza* was launched in 1951, it was printed in Dar es Salaam and Tanga and consequently had its largest circulation and readership among Africans in those towns which were also the largest in Tanganyika, with Tanga being the second-largest for decades until it was surpassed by Mwanza in the 1970s. The paper grew steadily through the years and was later printed in Lindi as well, and reached a print run of 9,000 copies in 1956.

But Africans were not wholly satisfied with *Mwangaza* anymore than they were with *Mambo Leo* and *Habari za Leo*, all of which had been started by the colonial government and were therefore colonial organs intended to soothe Africans, although there was no alternative press to which they could turn among themselves to meet all their needs. They did, nevertheless, make attempts to do just that when some of them started their own newspapers in the fifties.

This trend was pioneered by C.H.B. Hakili in 1951 when he launched *Wangaluka*, meaning Good Morning in the Nyamwezi language, which was published in Kiswahili and Kinyamwezi. It was a monthly and was the first paper in Tanganyika during British colonial rule which did not appear in Dar es Salaam. It was, instead, based in Nzega, a town and district north of Tabora, the capital of the Western Province which was also the largest in colonial Tanganyika.

Then other papers followed, published in vernacular languages and in the lingua franca of Kiswahili.

In 1952 two African papers were started. One was *Bukya na Gandi*, which means Fresh News in Haya language, and was launched by Ewald R. Munseri in Bukoba District in what was then the Lake Province.

It was a weekly paper, published in Kihaya, English, and Kiswahili and chose the line of least resistance to the colonial authorities. It had a subtitle, "Truth, Tact and Tolerance" but did not publish anything critical of the government and was not required to post bond as most or all the others papers were required to, as long as they were not supported or published by the colonial government itself.

The editor of *Bukya na Gandi*, Ewald Munseri, was considered by some people to be the most experienced and best educated African journalist in Tanganyika during that time. He worked for several years in the Information Office of the colonial government in Kampala, Uganda, and after he returned to Tanganyika, served as assistant editor of *Habari za Leo* and *Mambo Leo* in Dar es Salaam before he left to start his own newspaper in his home district of Bukoba.

He said one of the reasons he started this independent newspaper was to fight tribalism among his people, the Haya, one of the largest ethnic groups in the country.

Although he did not openly articulate nationalist sentiments, his efforts to combat tribalism among the Haya definitely helped to advance the nationalist agenda of the African leaders who wanted all the different ethnic groups in Tanganyika to unite and work together in the quest for independence and future well-being of the country after the end of colonial rule.

His paper became popular and its print run rose from 1,000 in 1952 to 3,000 in 1955. Encouraged by the high circulation and popularity of *Bukya na Gandi*, Munseri started another paper in 1955, a monthly published in Kihaya and entitled *Bahaha Twemanye*, Bahaya, Let Us Know Each Other.

And in 1956, he founded a weekly paper published in Kiswahili, *Tanganyika Mpya*, meaning New Tanganyika. Like the other two papers he started and which were also published in his vernacular language, Kihaya, *Tanganyika Mpya* was published and edited in Bukoba.

And its title alone, *Tanganyika Mpya*, was indicative of the times and the paper was buoyed by the nationalist tide sweeping across the country.

However, *Bahaya Twemanye* was not very successful and ceased publication before independence. But the other two papers he started, *Bukya na Gandi* and *Tanganyika Mpya*, continued to exist until 1962 when he is said to have come under political pressure, forcing him to stop publishing the papers. And that was before nationalization of assets by the government started.

But whatever the reasons were, which forced him to give up publishing the two papers, may be including tribal loyalty since one of his papers, *Bukya na Gandi*, was also published in his native language of Kihaya, Munseri's future as a journalist was not jeopardized or compromised in any way.

After he stopped publishing the papers, President Nyerere appointed him to a high government post in the Ministry of Information; an appointment which may also be attributed to the fact that one of the papers he founded, *Tanganyika Mpya*, was unquestionably nationalist in orientation and did not survive or thrive on ethno-regional loyalties and sentiments.

A few years later, I also joined the Ministry of Information and Broadcasting in 1971 as an information officer, although when I worked at the ministry headquarters in Dar es Salaam, Munseri was not in the Information Services Department which was then known as Maelezo in Kiswahili. I'm not even sure he was anywhere else in the Ministry in Dar es Salaam or in some other part of the country. I was there for only a few months before going back to the *Daily News*.

The other independent African newspaper, besides *Bukya na Gandi*, which was founded in 1952 was *Wela*, which means Grain in the Gogo language. It was launched in Dodoma which was also the capital of the Central Province in those days, and now the official capital of Tanzania, and was published in English and Kigogo.

It was edited by Geoffrey P. Masekas who worked for the colonial government in the Dodoma Local Treasury and dealt mostly with local news. The paper also included articles or items on practical advice covering a wide range of topics including farming and how to get some of the things people needed in life.

And an older paper, *Zuhra*, which was first published in 1940 as a daily and disappeared from the scene in 1950, resurfaced in 1952 but as a weekly, not as a daily as it once was. However, the paper faced a lot of problems and was not published on regular basis during the next 10 years until it ceased publication in 1962 after the country won independence the previous year on 9 December 1961.

As independent African newspapers continued to grow in number and circulation in the fifties, the colonial government became apprehensive of the situation, fearing that it was losing whatever influence it had on the indigenous population.

To reverse the trend, it launched *Siku Hizi*, meaning These Days, as a counterweight in 1952, the same year in which three

African papers - *Bukya na Gandi*, *Wela*, and *Zuhra* - were started, with *Zuhra* being re-launched that year after an absence of about two years.

Although the government publication was also a picture magazine designed to attract a larger and wider audience among Africans, its English edition had a limited number of readers. Therefore it had a print run of no more than 1,000 copies while its Swahili counterpart, *Siku Hizi*, had 9,000.

One of the other government papers, *Mambo Leo*, also played a significant role in trying to neutralize nationalist sentiments among Africans and the influence of nationalist leaders among their people.

Just a few years earlier in 1948, the United Nations issued a report stating that the policy of indirect rule being pursued by the colonial government was detrimental to the well-being of Africans as a collective entity because it reinforced ethno-regional loyalties, mostly on tribal basis. The colonial government knew that was true and had no intention of abandoning this policy because it helped the colonial rulers to stem the nationalist tide across the country.

To help achieve this goal, Sir Edward Twining, the governor of Tanganyika during that period, gave the chiefs even more powers and freedom under the Native Authorities in 1951, virtually turning these administrative units into semi-autonomous entities under the "control" of the chiefs who were beholden to the colonial government.

And as a government publication, *Mambo Leo*, did a lot to try and project a positive image of the government among its readers. It published many pictures of African chiefs who had been offered free trips to England to meet, and wine and dine, with British leaders and even showed some of them being entertained at the royal court.

They were also awarded medals, badges and high-sounding titles as true servants in Her Majesty's Service upholding the ideals of the British Empire. For example, I came across some pictures of bronze medals awarded in 1953 to Regent Ramadhani Nasibu of Bunyongo in Kibondo, northwestern Tanganyika, and another one in the same year to Chief Ali Kipanya of Nguruka in Shinyanga.

They were bronze medals with the Queen's image on one side and these words around it: Queen Elizabeth the Second. On the other side was an image of the giraffe, with the name Tanganyika Territory across it.

The chiefs and their underlings were highly valued by the colonial rulers who used them as a shield against the nationalist forces campaigning for independence.

The government went even further to undermine the nationalist cause by launching 23 monthly provincial publications in 1952 and 1953 intended to project a good image of the government among the indigenous people.

The publications came in varying degrees. Some of them were simple typescripts circulated as duplicated copies and having only a small audience, while others were newspapers with a print run up to 3,000 copies. They had a total print run of 26,000 and most of them were published in Kiswahili in order to reach the largest and widest audience possible among Africans.

There were, however, a few which were published in native languages. For example, there was a paper published in Tukuyu called *Lembuka*, which in my native language, Kinyakyusa, means Awaken.

It was also published in English and targeted one of the largest ethnic groups in Tanganyika to win support for the government in its competition with African nationalists for influence among the people during the very same period when political awakening among Africans was very high in the decade preceding independence. In Mwanza was *Majyambele* which was also published in Kiswahili. And there were others.

The papers were edited by Africans with the help of the Native Authorities and district commissioners (D.Cs). And the government tried to encourage the growth of these papers as independent organs but still as instruments of government policy by encouraging them to portray the colonial rulers in a positive way, contrary to claims by African nationalists that the colonial rulers were not fair to Africans and the colonial system unjust.

However achievement of this goal was hampered by the fact that there were no trained African journalists to do the job. And most of what was published was confined to local news. There was also little criticism of government policies when the papers were first launched, although this changed later in a number of cases.

Parallel to this development on the African side was the launching of the *Sunday News* on 7 November 1954 to serve the interests of the white settler community and of the government on the other side.

The paper was a sister publication of the *Tanganyika Standard* and was launched exactly four months after the nationalist party of TANU was founded on July 7th in the same year. And Sir Edward Twining, the governor, had this to say in his congratulatory message published in the first edition of the *Sunday News*:

> I WELCOME the advent of a Sunday paper as an associate of the *Tanganyika Standard* which for a quarter of a century has kept the people of Tanganyika so well informed on world and local events of importance and interest.
>
> I feel confident that the views expressed in the new paper, the *Sunday News*, will be such as to enhance the harmonious relations we enjoy and that its standard of journalism will be on the very high level which we in this territory have come to expect from your organisation.

By the end of 1954, about 50 newspapers and magazines were being published in Tanganyika. But almost all of them were either government-owned and -controlled or not critical of the government.

There were no papers advancing the nationalist cause and TANU, as a political party espousing this cause, was new on the scene and did not have a paper or magazine of its own to propagate its message and advance the nationalist agenda.

But things were bound to change sooner rather than later during this period which witnessed the beginning of the end of British colonial rule in Tanganyika.

The second half of the 1950s can aptly be described not only as the beginning of the end of colonial rule but also as a period that was characterized by the emergence of the nationalist press as a twin to the nationalist campaign for independence.

There had always been a need for African newspapers run by Africans themselves. But the political climate during colonial rule was not conducive to the establishment of such papers. However, the situation changed in the late fifties and the desire among

Africans to have their own newspapers was given impetus by the independence movement which gained momentum during that period; and by an acknowledgement by the United Nations that the country was headed towards independence, although the timetable proposed by the world body did not conform to the nationalist aspirations of the African leaders such as Julius Nyerere, president of TANU, and Oscar Kambona, the secretary-general, and what they had in mind.

In January 1955, the UN said Tanganyika should be independent within the next 20 to 25 years. African leaders said sooner than that. As Nyerere himself said, the colonial government was going in the same direction as the nationalist movement but at a different pace.

There were other factors which led to the establishment of independent African newspapers. One was that TANU leaders wanted to have their own means to propagate their message. Another important factor was the monopoly the colonial government had over the dissemination of news which was often slanted; it was biased towards the government for obvious reasons. The major Swahili papers were owned by the government, and funded by the government.

In response to that, TANU leaders decided to start their own newspaper. And they did so in 1957 when they launched *Sauti ya TANU*, meaning The Voice of TANU, in Dar es Salaam.

The paper was edited by Nyerere himself. And it was the first African publication in Tanganyika which took an uncompromising stand against colonial rule and without fear of being intimidated by the authorities.

Had the leadership wavered on this important issue, TANU would not have been given the kind of support it got from the people across the country. And it was massive support within a relatively short period of time.

Just the year before, in February 1956, some white settlers opposed to independence - not all of them were - founded the United Tanganyika Party (UTP) with the governor's encouragement as a counterweight to TANU and to try to sway public opinion among Africans in favour of the new party as a truly multiracial "movement" and whose leaders felt that the people of Tanganyika were not ready for independence. The colonial government itself supported UTP.

In March 1956, the government's Public Relations Department which was responsible for the publication of all government newspapers replaced *Habari za Leo* with a new paper, *Baragumu*, meaning The Bugle, which supported UTP policies. Being a Swahili newspaper, its audience was overwhelmingly African. It was a weekly tabloid and, in spite of its support for UTP, had a promising start selling about 20,000 copies every time it was published.

But nothing could dissuade TANU leaders and their supporters from their commitment to independence and true racial equality after the end of colonial rule. And in pursuit of this goal, the leaders of TANU went on the offensive on all fronts to spread their message.

That was one of the reasons why their newspaper, *Sauti ya TANU*, was also published in English. As Nyerere explained, he and his colleagues wanted the government to know exactly what they were doing and that they were ready to pay any price to end colonial rule.

But in spite of their uncompromising stand, the leaders of TANU were not militant in their rhetoric and their publication *Sauti ya TANU* was equally moderate in tone most of the time. Nyerere also used the publication to help calm down some of his supporters who were espousing militant views.

However, *Sauti ya TANU* had limited circulation and therefore it could not reach a much wider audience. It was read almost exclusively by TANU members and did not circulate elsewhere.

But this loss was offset by Nyerere's enormous popularity across the country even among non-TANU members. And the chiefs, who were on the government payroll and were known to be subservient to the colonial authorities, were aware of that. They knew that Nyerere and his party TANU did not need them. They could be bypassed, as they indeed were, to reach the masses.

Afraid that they would be left behind and out of the picture, most of the chiefs concluded that it would be prudent not to ignore TANU, let alone antagonize its leadership, at this late hour.

The chiefs and other local authorities who were against Nyerere and his policies found out that they were losing support and popularity among the masses. And they adjusted accordingly.

Realizing that Nyerere could not be stopped, and also being fully aware that he did not need them, most of the chiefs decided to join TANU. And by the end of 1957, most of them had already become members.

And with this change also came a change in the way the local papers and other publications addressed issues including the struggle for independence. The papers in the provinces also had to adjust accordingly and, gradually, started to criticize some of the government policies.

Although it was a gradual transformation, there is no question that it had a lasting impact on the course of events leading towards the end of the fifties, the last decade of colonial rule in Tanganyika.

The same papers which not too long ago had supported the government were now supporting the independence movement and provided an important platform for the articulation of views expressed by the people across the spectrum and most of whom supported the nationalist aspirations of TANU.

And in a move which demonstrated Nyerere's far-reaching influence across the country and the depth of his commitment to independence, he appealed to the people to stop reading and supporting government newspapers and other publications. They heeded his call and, as a result, all the main government Swahili newspapers - *Mambo Leo*, *Mwangaza*, and *Baragumu* - lost readership and suffered enormously.

The government tried to save the papers by placing them under the control of an independent corporation, the Tanganyika National Newspaper Ltd. But it was too late by then. And the corporation itself was not quite independent since it was financed by the government.

The papers continued to suffer and, on 31 December 1958, *Mwangaza* ceased publication. It was a blow from which the government never recovered.

As TANU's popularity continued to grow, so did support from African papers. The most popular African newspaper which was also TANU's most important mouthpiece was *Mwafrika*, which means The African. According to its editorial policy, the paper was supposed to be impartial but there is no question that it was strongly pro-TANU.

The paper was launched in September 1957 by Kheri Rashidi Baghdelleh and Robert Moses Makange. It was published every two weeks.

It published articles and commentaries which were highly critical of the government; a move which increased the paper's popularity among Africans. The sales of this fortnightly went up from 4,000 to 20,000 copies within the first three issues; a spectacular achievement.

The publishers obviously knew that it was almost too late for the authorities to derail let alone stop the independence movement and went on to openly criticize the government without any fear of sanctions even by the governor himself. But they may have underestimated the authorities.

In 1958, Baghdelleh and Makange were arrested. However, their paper was not banned, obviously out of fear by the authorities that they would only make things worse by doing so.

A new editor, Joel Mgogo, took over, and *Mwafrika* underwent a transformation under his leadership. While the paper continued to be published as a fortnightly, a sister paper, also named *Mwafrika*, was launched as a daily in 1959 with an initial print run of 8,000 copies.

Although independence was only about two years away, TANU - with all its popularity across the country - decided to maintain some distance from *Mwafrika* despite the fact that it clearly agreed with the paper on fundamental issues including uncompromising opposition to colonial rule. But TANU leaders feared that the paper's ultra-militancy would alienate some people and tarnish the image of TANU as a moderate party embracing people of all races and backgrounds.

So they found an alternative, *Ngurumo*, another Swahili paper whose name means The Roar or Thunder, and they started supporting it financially as their new mouthpiece.

First published on 15 April 1959, *Ngurumo* was a daily newspaper. It became one of the most popular, and most influential, Swahili papers in the history of the country especially among ordinary workers.

When the founder of *Ngurumo*, Randhir Thaker, died, Surendra Thaker took over as editor of the paper. And there is no question that TANU's objectives neatly coincided with those of the founders of *Ngurumo*. As Surendra Thaker - in explaining why *Ngurumo* was started - said in an interview with Hadji Konde (who was assistant managing editor of the *Daily News* when I worked there as a reporter in the early 1970s) published in Konde's 1984 book *Press Freedom in Tanzania*:

> Our purpose was not economic. Our aim was to inform, to reach and mobilise the masses and explain to them about TANU's fight for them. At that time the big newspapers and the radio were in the hands of colonialists. So there was need for a Swahili daily.

The Thakers also felt that there was a need to help teach and spread Kiswahili as much as possible among all the people of Tanganyika. So, at the end of each month, they included a supplement entitled *Kaka*, which means Brother, to help achieve this objective. Although Kiswahili was widely spoken in Tanganyika, not everybody - including those who spoke it everyday - had thorough command of the language.

The year 1959 also witnessed the establishment of a publishing house by TANU. It was named the National Times Press. Nyerere wanted the papers in Tanganyika to reflect the broadest spectrum of society representing everybody regardless of social status. And they were to be published in Kiswahili and English, the country's official and major languages.

But financial problems and lack of equipment made this impossible. However, TANU managed to publish an English paper, *The National Times*, although for only a very short period.

Still, Nyerere's idea was not abandoned and the chief editor of The National Times Ltd., Haroon Ahmed, started three papers later in the same year 1959. And they were all weeklies: *Mwananchi*, meaning Citizen, with a print run of 10,000 copies; *National Weekly* with 5,000; and *Nootan Africa* with a print run of 2,000 copies.

Many of the papers published in Tanganyika in the 1950s were widely read. But there was a conflict of interest as well as of perceptions between the Africans who read those papers and some of the publishers.

Africans wanted the papers to support the struggle for independence and criticize the colonial government. But if the publishers did so, they would not get advertisers whose advertising money helped sustain those papers.

Most of the advertisers were Asian and European who did not want to offend the government by advertising in papers which criticized the colonial authorities. If they did that, they risked losing business licences and face other sanctions which would have made their lives difficult and would even have driven them out of business.

Europeans and Asians controlled trade in Tanganyika and anything that affected them negatively had an adverse impact on the rest of the country including publication of independent African newspapers.

Yet in spite of all that, the movement towards independence continued to gain momentum and, in the elections of 1958 -1959, TANU won a landslide victory.

Following this victory, and in what amounted to a concession by the colonial authorities and supporters of the United Tanganyika Party (UTP) which was opposed to independence, *Baragumu* - UTP's mouthpiece among the Africans and the only Swahili paper which openly supported the white settlers who were opposed to independence - was sold to the Kenyan East African Newspaper Ltd.

It was a new media group established in Nairobi in 1959 by Michael Curtis and Charles Hayes and was commonly known as the Nation Group. And it went on to launch some of the most successful newspapers in East Africa and on the entire continent, the *Daily Nation* and the *Sunday Nation* with the financial support of H.H. The Aga Khan.

The disappearance of *Baragumu* from Tanganyika also marked the end of an era. It was the end of colonial rule.

After *Baragumu* was bought by the Nation Group in Nairobi, it was merged with *Taifa*, which means Nation, which was owned by the same media empire. The merger led to the establishment of *Taifa na Baragumu*, The Nation and The Bugle, whose first edition was published on 23 July 1960. *Baragumu* had undergone a transformation.

The paper which had supported the colonial government and the white settlers who were opposed to independence in Tanganyika now supported TANU and its policies. Although published in Kenya, it was also - under the new name *Taifa na*

Baragumu - available in Tanganyika. When its first issue came out on 23 July 1960, Tanganyika was only about one-year-and-a-half away from independence. It was the first country in East Africa to win independence.

The end of colonial rule was the dawn of a new era, but one fraught with danger. After independence, the new nation had to face harsh realities of nationhood which have also been recorded by newspapers through the years.

The history of newspapers in Tanganyika is highly significant in many respects.

Most people, including reporters, don't even know that many different newspapers were published through the decades since the end of the First World War, and even before then during German colonial rule.

And even after the Germans lost what came to be known as Tanganyika, they still published some papers in German; for example, there was a German paper published in Lushoto in Usambara mountains in the 1930s where there was a significant German community. And there were others, in Arusha, Moshi, Mbeya, and elsewhere.

The newspapers served as a repository of knowledge. They recorded history in the making, and they helped interpret events.

It is not only a record of events but an integral part of the history of the country itself. It is also a study in human relations, and race relations, showing different perspectives on issues through the decades and how different people in different periods of history see each other across the spectrum.

It also shows that in spite of being an underdeveloped country, and in the "Dark Continent," or "In the Heart of Darkness" to use Conrad's title, Tanganyika was not isolated from the rest of the world as many people believe. The newspapers published in Tanganyika even during the first years of colonial rule show that this kind of isolation was more apparent than real.

During the struggle for independence, newspapers helped to spread the message, educate the people, and raise the level of political awareness among them, facilitating the campaign against colonial rule. On the other side, they helped the opponents of independence in their futile attempt to stem the nationalist tide.

Not every white person supported these opponents but they

used newspapers to propagate their message and even sometimes succeeded in creating the false impression that almost all whites were opposed to independence; which was not the case. And there were those who didn't care either way even if their views were not recorded in print. But a lot was recorded by the newspapers in Tanganyika during the colonial period.

The newspapers also mirrored and reflected two competing visions for Tanganyika.

One was pro-empire. It justified and defended colonial rule as was the case even during my time when I was growing up in the fifties when the United Tanganyika Party (UTP) founded by some white settlers tried to block independence and genuine racial equality. Not all whites supported the party or shared its vision but it had the potential to be a potent force in the country had it won more support not only from whites but from other people as well, including some Africans, who did not believe Tanganyika was ready for independence.

The other vision articulated by African nationalists including some whites and Asians - such as Derek Bryceson, Dr. Leader Sterling and Amir H. Jamal - who supported the independence struggle, disputed that, and undermined the rationale for imperial rule; with the leaders contending that Africans (who included Tanganyikans of all races since Africanisation according to Nyerere simply meant Tanganyikanisation regardless of race) had the right to rule themselves and were entitled to freedom like everybody else. They had the right to be free because freedom is a natural right. We are born free to live free. As Dr. Willie Abraham, a Ghanaian philosopher, says, independence is a state of nature.

There are, of course, those who dispute that, contending that not all those who yearn to be free are capable of being free. The chaos in many African countries since independence, some of which dissolved in anarchy - pulverized from within - is cited as proof of this. The pro-empire proponents say they have been vindicated by history. To their opponents, this is a discredited theory that has no basis in history and science, espousing the doctrine of racial supremacy.

Yet when Sierra Leone was destroyed during the civil war in the 1990s, it was the former colonial power, Britain, which effectively ended the war and restored law and order after Sierra Leonean leaders begged for help from their former colonial rulers. And the people of Sierra Leone were glad the British were "back."

In fact many of them, including a prime minister during that period, pleaded with Britain to restore former ties when Sierra Leone was an integral part of the British Empire; a polite way of saying they begged the British to come back and rule them again. As Max Hastings stated in his article, "The Return of the Dark Continent," in *The Daily Mail*, Johannesburg, South Africa, 13 August 2002:

> There was a vivid moment a couple of years ago during the first stage of the British intervention to support the struggling government of Sierra Leone. Its prime minister asked a visiting British politician, in the presence of journalists, if it might be possible for his country to become part of the British Empire again. Most of those present believed the Sierra Leonese leader was serious. The problems of African societies are so huge, so deep-rooted, that the few honest and decent politicians despair. They grasp at any straw to rescue their countries.

Even in my own country, Tanganyika, it was British troops which ended the army mutiny in January 1964 after President Nyerere reluctantly sought emergency assistance from the former colonial power. British forces in Kenya could not land in Dar es Salaam because the airport was in rebel hands. Therefore other forces had to be used.

A total 600 British special forces led by Brigadier Patrick Sholto Douglas, the same army officer who was the last commander of the King's African Rifles (KAR) when the country won independence, sailed from Aden to Dar es Salaam and disarmed the mutineers within a short period.

The mutiny started when soldiers of the First Battalion of the Tanganyika Rifles (simply known as the King's African Rifles before independence) seized key points in Dar es Salaam on 19 January 1964, releasing their British officers to Kenya. They were joined by the Second Battalion the next day with none left that was loyal to the government of Tanganyika; the country then had only two battalions and now its entire armed forces were in rebellion.

The mutiny was started by Sergeant Francis Hingo Ilogi and 19 other soldiers against the British officers who were still in charge of the army three years after independence. They wanted them replaced by African army officers, although there may have been another motive for the mutiny involving other people - especially labour leaders Victor Mkello and Christopher Kasanga Tumbo - who were not even in the army but who probably wanted to overthrow the government.

The British troops who ended the mutiny arrived in Dar es Salaam on January 24th and captured the mutineers. Some fled but were captured weeks later.

But the British did not stay long in Tanganyika. Soon after their arrival, Nyerere called an emergency session of the Organization of African Unity (OAU) in Addis Ababa and appealed for help from other African countries. Nigeria agreed to help and sent troops to Tanganyika to provide defence while the country reorganized its army and trained new soldiers to replace the mutineers.

One of the Nigerian army officers sent to Tanganyika during that time was Colonel Odumegwu Ojukwu who three years later led the secession of the Eastern Region of Nigeria which declared independence as the Republic of Biafra.

The British left in April 1964 and handed over security to a Nigerian battalion, coincidentally, in the same month Tanganyika united with Zanzibar to form Tanzania. Nigerian forces left in October the same year.

Some of the Nigerian soldiers stayed at the secondary school I attended in southern Tanzania. That was Songea Secondary School. They left three months before I went to that boarding school.

Yet in both cases, of Sierra Leone and Tanganyika (coincidentally, both countries won independence in the same year and from the same colonial power and were the only ones on the entire continent to win independence in 1961) the successful intervention of British troops - and even administrators in the 1990s and beyond in the case of Sierra Leone - was a vindication of *Pax Britannica* typical of what went on during the days of imperial rule when the British imposed peace and maintained law and order in their colonies; a glaring contrast to what happened in some of the African countries during the post-colonial period.

African nationalists may have been offended and humiliated

by that, as they indeed were and still are, but it is also true that their opponents cite that as evidence showing that some people are not capable of ruling themselves.

And there is incontrovertible evidence to show that Africa has had a number of failed states since the end of colonial rule. Although colonial rule was a system of racial inequality, it transformed Africa, for better or for worse, into a continent which has never been the same as it was in the pre-colonial era, and isolated.

People are divided on this subject. For example, Dr. Walter Rodney who taught at the University of Dar es Salaam where he wrote his best-seller, *How Europe Underdeveloped Africa*, contends in that book that the only positive development from colonial rule was when it ended. Others contend otherwise.

And there is no question that the colonial rulers laid the foundation for the modernization that has taken place in African countries through the years since the advent of colonial rule, much as some people may hate to admit this, including many whites, especially liberals, who are always sympathetic towards us even when we don't deserve such sympathy because of our own faults and failures, causing self-inflicted pain.

We just have to face the fact that it was the colonial rulers, not us, who introduced modern education and built the infrastructure in African countries which enabled African countries to modernize and develop even if in a limited way. None of this infrastructure - towns, roads and railways, telecommunications facilities, schools and hospitals, to name only a few - existed before the coming of Europeans. And we inherited all that at independence.

But much of what we inherited at independence when the colonial rulers left has been destroyed through the years under inept leadership.

The educational system has virtually collapsed or has been severely compromised in many African countries; the infrastructure, built by the colonial rulers, has crumbled; health facilities are in a shambles; corruption has been institutionalized; law and order is unheard of in many parts of Africa, and much more.

That was not the case during the colonial period. Schools and hospitals, even if they were few, worked. Roads and communications facilities were well-maintained. And there was law and order without which life is living hell.

In many fundamental respects, African countries are worse off today than they were at independence and under colonial rule.

There is external involvement in our plight but a lot of the problems millions of Africans face everyday have nothing to do with that. All those problems cannot be attributed to external forces. It is a sentiment shared across the continent and by many other people outside Africa.

One of the influential Africans who articulates this position is Moeletsi Mbeki, the younger brother of South African President Thabo Mbeki and head of the South African Institute of International Affairs. According to a report by BBC Africa, "Africa 'Better in Colonial Times'" published on 22 September 2004:

> The average African is worse off now than during the colonial era, the brother of South Africa's President Thabo Mbeki has said.
>
> Moeletsi Mbeki accused African elites of stealing money and keeping it abroad, while colonial rulers planted crops and built roads and cities. "This is one of the depressing features of Africa," he said.
>
> Moeletsi Mbeki also said that South Africa should support democracy in Zimbabwe, and not tolerate violence. President Thabo Mbeki has been accused of being too soft on his Zimbabwean counterpart Robert Mugabe.
>
> South Africa should "not tolerate use of violence, torture and rigging of elections and, if necessary, we should support the opposition," Moeletsi Mbeki said.
>
> **Downward spiral**
>
> He said that while China had lifted some 400,000 people out of poverty in the past 20 years, Nigeria had pushed 71 million people below the poverty line.
>
> "The average African is poorer than during the age of colonialism. In the 1960s African elites/rulers, instead of focusing on development, took surplus for their own enormous entourages of civil servants without ploughing anything back into the country," he said.
>
> In July, a United Nations report said that Africa was the only continent where poverty had increased in the past 20 years.
>
> Moeletsi Mbeki was addressing a meeting of the South African Institute of International Affairs, which he heads.

It is our responsibility to solve our problems. And if we

continue to blame other people and other forces - American imperialism, British imperialism and whatnot - for our condition, for the problems we have created ourselves, then we are not being responsible.

We fought for independence in order to be free but freedom itself entails - and demands - responsibility. Freedom without responsibility leads to anarchy, the kind that has destroyed a number of African countries including Sierra Leone, Liberia and Somalia. And many others have been torn by civil strife for the same reason, pushed to the brink of catastrophe.

It is also a subject I have addressed in one of my books, *Africa is in A Mess*: *What Went Wrong and What Should Be Done*. In fact, the title of my book comes from one of the statements Nyerere made not long before he died. He said, "Africa is in a mess."

We did not fight for independence so that we should have the opportunity to destroy ourselves.

It is, of course, true that we were free and ruled ourselves before the advent of colonial rule. Therefore the struggle for independence was no more than a struggle to regain our freedom and independence.

But it is equally true that, although we ruled ourselves before colonization, we did *not* have the countries we have in Africa today. Almost all of them with the exception of Ethiopia and the kingdoms of Ruanda and Urundi (as they were known back then before colonial rule) in sub-Saharan Africa were created by our European rulers; and Liberia by the Americans.

It is as if we needed Europeans to unite us because we did not have enough sense to know how important unity was, or we simply did not see the need to unite among ourselves.

In fact, many of us as members of ethnic groups or entities didn't even know about each other even in our respective regions, let alone across the continent, until Europeans came.

Europeans may have divided us - in fact only about 171 ethnic groups out more than 1,000 across Africa were split by colonial boundaries - but they also united us. As Nyerere conceded, colonialism created a sense of oneness among Africans.

But it is a oneness that has come under severe strain during the post-colonial era as has been clearly demonstrated by ethnic conflicts in many African countries simply because many people don't accept each other and would rather favour members of their own tribes than treat everybody as an equal.

That was not the case during colonial rule. Tribal or ethnic conflicts as open warfare were rare. It is as if we needed colonial rulers to maintain peace and hold us together.

Once they left, we turned against each on ethnic or tribal basis in an orgy of violence in many cases never witnessed before even in the past. And large chunks of Africa are still blood-soaked on an unprecedented scale.

Tanzania has been spared this scourge in its most virulent form. But tribalism is a potent force anywhere on the continent especially in sub-Saharan Africa and it is a potential danger that cannot be ignored even in Tanzania. We ignore it only at our peril.

In fact, since the introduction of multi-party democracy in Tanzania in the early nineties, unscrupulous elements have tried to exploit ethno-regional rivalries and loyalties in pursuit of partisan interests to the detriment of national unity.

They include leaders of the Civic United Front (CUF) in Zanzibar, especially on Pemba island; and Reverend Christopher Mtikila, the leader of the Democratic Party on Tanzania mainland who wants the union dissolved and is openly hostile towards Tanzanians of Asian origin, Arabs and other non-blacks and wants them expelled from the country. And there are others of his ilk, with the same warped mind.

Mtikila espouses doctrines reminiscent of the African National Congress (ANC) in Tanganyika in the late fifties and early sixties when the party was led by Zuberi Mtemvu and was virulently anti-white, anti-Asian and against other non-blacks even if they were citizens of Tanganyika. The party's doctrine of Tanganyika for Tanganyikans echoed the sentiments of other racial purists whose invocation of the slogan "Africa for Africans" meant only one thing: Africa for black Africans.

It was divisive then, and it is divisive today. And so is tribalism which has torn the social fabric of many African countries and continues to do so. It is a continental phenomenon and a perennial problem.

Although Tanzania may have been spared the agony, it is not immune from this deadly disease, this malignant cancer of tribalism and racism, and may one day suffer the same way other African countries have. As Professor Haroub Othman, a Tanzanian originally from Zanzibar who taught at the University of Dar es Salaam, stated in his lecture, "Mwalimu Julius Nyerere: An Intellectual in Power," delivered at the University of Cape Town on 14 October 2005:

> Julius Nyerere was always non-racial in his perspective, and this at times got him into conflict with his colleagues both in the ruling Party and Government.
> During the days of the struggle for Tanganyika's independence, he rejected the position of the "Africanists" within TANU who put forward the slogan "Africa for Africans", meaning black Africans.
> In 1958 at the TANU National Conference in Tabora when some leaders strongly opposed TANU's participation in the colonially-proposed tripartite elections, where the voter had to vote for three candidates from the lists of Africans, Asians and Europeans, Julius Nyerere stood firm in recommending acceptance of the proposals. This led to the "Africanists" marching out of TANU and forming the African National Congress.
> It is extremely worrying that this racist monster is reappearing now in Tanzania. Some politicians in their quest for power are using the racist card, as manifested both at last May's Chimwaga Congress of the ruling party, CCM, and in the on-going election campaigns.
> It is very unfortunate that no stern measures are being taken against this trend, thus giving the impression that the country's leadership is condoning it.

Tanzania remains an island of stability in a turbulent region. But if racism and tribalism go unchecked, it could end up being one of the deadliest theatres of conflict because of a combination of highly combustible elements in the country including a large number tribes or ethnic groups (126); significant numbers of racial minorities, and disruptive religious forces especially of the fundamentalist kind among both Christians (exemplified by Reverend Christopher Mtikila) and Muslims especially in Zanzibar who want turn the isles and coastal regions of Tanzania into a hotbed of radical Islam or Islamic fundamentalism intolerant of others.

One of the best examples of the malignancy of racism in Tanzania was the virulent campaign against Dr. Salim Ahmed Salim, an Arab, whose presidential ambitions in 2005 were thwarted by black nationalist elements within the ruling party itself (CCM) who questioned his credentials as a national leader simply because he is an Arab; although he is also of Nyamwezi and Manyema descent on his mother's side, an ancestry rooted in two ethnic groups native to western Tanzania and eastern Congo, respectively, with the Manyema also being resident mainly in what is now Kigoma Region. His mother has roots in Tabora, western Tanzania, but she also Arab.

His most vociferous opponents were fellow Zanzibaris, black delegates from the ruling party, Chama cha Mapinduzi (CCM) - which means the Party of the Revolution or the Revolutionary Party - at the party's convention at Chamwino near Dodoma in central Tanzania where the ruling party's leaders chose their presidential candidate in April 2005.

His enemies also claimed that he was not a Tanzanian because his father was born in Oman. Yet, as Dr. Salim explained, and as many people who know about his family equally stated, both of his parents were born in Zanzibar; so were his grandparents.

It's also interesting that his political enemies never questioned the credentials of Amani Karume, the president of Zanzibar and son of the first president of Zanzibar Abeid Karume, although his mother is an Arab if being Arab or partly Arab - or being white or of Asian origin - is indeed a disqualification in the quest for leadership in Tanzania. Yet Amani Karume's partial Arab identity or ancestry was never a major factor, if it was one at all, in his quest for high office.

Salim Ahmed Salim also was one of the youngest and strongest supporters of the Zanzibar revolution when it was taking place.

Still, his detractors raised questions about his credentials as a national leader and as a true patriot, and in spite of the fact that President Nyerere trusted him and even wanted him to be the next president of Tanzania after Nyerere stepped down from the presidency in 1985.

During the 2005 presidential campaign, Salim himself publicly stated at a press conference in Dar es Salaam that Mwalimu Nyerere asked him to run for president in 1985 in order to succeed him, and again in 1995, but declined to do so for a number of reasons.

One of those reasons, although he did not publicly say so, was that he faced stiff opposition from some black nationalist leaders in Zanzibar who were resolutely opposed to his candidacy in 1985 and in 1995. And they were just as resolute and uncompromising in their opposition to his candidacy in 2005 as were a number of others on the mainland as well.

Dr. Salim also pointed out that there were many Tanzanians who were of mixed ancestry like him, and many others who were just Arab, Asian or of European stock and were entitled to equal treatment just like any other citizens of Tanzania.

He also reminded his detractors that if such discrimination continued, it would destroy Tanzania as Nyerere himself warned not long before Tanganyika won independence and again through the years when he was president.

Nyerere himself appointed Salim Ahmed Salim ambassador to the UN, minister of defence, minister of foreign affairs, and prime minister at different times through the years; something he never would have done if he did not trust him as a capable and credible national leader; if he thought he was an Arab supremacist as some of Salim's enemies claimed, and if he thought he was – together with Abdulrahman Mohammed Babu and other suspects – one of those who masterminded the assassination of Tanzania's first vice president and president of Zanzibar, Abeid Karume, as his detractors also claimed.

In fact, Dr. Salim held the largest number of the highest posts in the government, at different times, more than any other leader in the history of Tanganyika and Tanzania besides Nyerere himself who also once served as prime minister and had the defence and foreign affairs portfolios at other times directly under his control in the president's office.

No other Tanzanian leader had, at different times, served as minister of defence, minister of foreign affairs, deputy prime minister, and prime minister besides Dr. Salim. And he was, besides Foreign Affairs Minister Jakaya Kikwete, the strongest presidential candidate in 2005 (and was said to have the support of the political heavyweights in the ruling party including President Benjamin Mkapa himself) until some people fabricated a story linking him to an Arab supremacist group, accusing him of being a racist. As Ernest Mpingajira stated in his article "In Bed with the State" published in *Intelligence* in 2005:

In April this year, two very experienced editors, Said Nguba and Mhingo Rweyemamu, committed what amounted to professional impropriety.

They manipulated a picture of former OAU secretary-general, Dr Salim Ahmed Salim, and cast him as a member of an Islamic terrorist group Hizbu.

At the time this happened, Dr Salim was running neck and neck for the Chama Cha Mapinduzi presidential nomination against the eventual victor, Jakaya Kikwete. Dr Salim looked set to win the nomination to vie for the presidency in the October 30 General Election.

Within the CCM ranks, Dr Salim's encroachment on Kikwete's turf was a major threat and his wings had to be clipped at whatever cost.

The offensive picture was fished out of the archives, manipulated and published on page one of *Mwananchi* Kiswahili daily. It portrayed Dr Salim as a racist and an Arab supremacist who masterminded the assassination of Zanzibar's first president, Abeid Amani Karume.

Foremost diplomat

Naturally, Dr Salim protested, but the damage had been done. For the time being, Tanzania's foremost diplomat will never shake off this tag for the rest of his political life.

The two *Mwananchi* editors, Nguba and Rweyemamu, were given their marching orders by their employer but for Dr Salim, the die had been cast; he lost to Kikwete, who is likely to become Tanzania's president in the October polls.

Race seems to have gained prominence in Tanzanian politics, although not in national life, in a way it never did before, especially under Nyerere who did not condone such bigotry. And it is a threat to national unity.

It is a tragedy that while others, including the developed countries of Europe, talk about the imperative need for unity, we seem to glorify disunity on the basis of race, ethnicity, national origin and other irrelevant criteria.

Race is definitely a factor and a potent force. But tribal loyalty is paramount in African countries most of which are predominantly black. And as African countries are fractured along ethno-regional lines, we remain weak in a world where the weak are an expendable commodity especially in this era of globalization while at the same time we complain that we are being dominated by outsiders.

It is true that we should not be ruled by others. But it is also true that those who are opposed to African independence feel vindicated in their belief and argument that we cannot manage our own affairs, citing a number of cases of such incompetence. And this has profound implications for the future of Africa as much as it did during the struggle for independence when many people, including some black Africans themselves to be brutally frank, argued that we were not ready to rule ourselves.

It is a view that had many proponents during the colonial period across Africa.

In my country Tanganyika, it was the United Tanganyika Party (UTP) - supported by some white settlers and even by some educated black Africans - which, more than anybody else in the political arena, espoused this view which came into conflict with the nationalist aspirations of the majority of Tanganyikans.

Newspapers in Tanganyika played a major role recording and facilitating debate between these two competing visions although it did not become as intense as it did in some circles in apartheid South Africa and even in what was then known as Southern Rhodesia in the fifties.

Tanganyika did not have such a serious racial problem. And that explains why the country went through a peaceful transition from colonial rule to independence. Many whites who were not even citizens of Tanganyika did not want to leave the country after colonial rule ended. They felt at home, and safe, in Tanganyika under black majority rule.

The newspapers also recorded some of the most important events in the history of Tanganyika - hence of Africa and the rest of the Third World - because most of these papers were launched during the period of decolonization especially after World War II. Decolonization was a phenomenal event and one of the most important in the history of the world in the post-war era.

I have not gone beyond 1960 because the focus of this book is on Tanganyika in the fifties. I even tried to avoid 1960 but couldn't because of the fate of *Baragumu* and what happened to this Swahili newspaper in 1959; a succession of events which had the two years inextricably linked in this particular case as one period covering 1959 and 1960.

And from a personal perspective, the history of newspapers in Tanganyika is highly relevant to me.

I worked for a newspaper in Tanzania. It was the oldest and most influential English newspaper in the country. Founded in

1930 when the country was still a British colony known as Tanganyika, it was supported by the colonial government. It also supported the colonial government.

After independence, it eventually became a government newspaper when I worked there as a news reporter. And it is the same newspaper which helped me to go to school in the United States when Benjamin Mkapa was its editor.

I'm talking about the *Tanganyika Standard* which later became the *Daily News* with President Nyerere as the editor-in-chief, although his role at the paper was more symbolic than functional. The paper was run by the managing editor.

And it will always be an important part of my life. Always. I probably wouldn't be what I am today without it.

Chapter Four:

Tanganyika before Independence

WHAT IS TANZANIA TODAY did not come into existence until Tanganyika united with Zanzibar in 1964 to form one country.

I was born and brought up in Tanganyika. And it is Tanganyika that I focus on as the land of my birth where my personality and identity was shaped during British colonial rule in the fifties and in the first decade of independence in the sixties.

Tanganyika itself did not exist as a territorial entity until 1885 when it was annexed by Germany. It was created as a colony by the Germans whose claim to the territory was given formal recognition at the Berlin conference during the partition of Africa.

The German Colonization Society led by Dr. Karl Peters claimed the territory in 1884. He was supported by his home government under Bismarck and went on to establish the German East Africa Company to rule the territory.

In 1886 and 1890, the British and the Germans signed agreements which defined their spheres of influence in the interior of East Africa and along the coast previously claimed by the sultan of Oman who had moved his capital from Muscat, Oman, to Zanzibar.

In 1891, the German government took over direct administration of the territory from the German East Africa Company and appointed a governor with headquarters in Dar es Salaam, a port city founded by the Arabs and whose name means Haven of Peace in Arabic.

European powers drew territorial boundaries to define their

spheres of influence, creating the countries we have in Africa today.

In East Africa, the British had Kenya, Uganda, and Zanzibar; and the Germans, Tanganyika, and Ruanda-Urundi - what is now Rwanda and Burundi - which together formed one colony called German East Africa which existed from 1885 to 1919.

After that, the British took over what became Tanganyika following Germany's defeat in World War I. The Belgians acquired Ruanda-Urundi which became two separate colonies but administered together with Belgian Congo.

British formal presence on Tanganyikan soil began in 1914 at the beginning of World War I when the Royal Navy occupied Mafia island in the Indian ocean a few miles southeast of Dar es Salaam, the capital.

During World War I, German East Africa was occupied by the Allied forces including troops from South Africa led by General Smuts. It was - minus Ruanda-Urundi - renamed Tanganyika Territory in 1920 (named after Lake Tanganyika) and placed under the League of Nations mandate administered by Britain after American President Woodrow Wilson refused to assume responsibility for the former German colony as proposed by British Prime Minister Lloyd George of the Liberal Party.

In 1921, the Belgians transferred Kigoma district in western Tanganyika to British administration, making it part of Tanganyika. They had administered the district - together with Ruanda-Urundi - since the Allied occupation of the former German colony in 1916.

And in 1924, Britain and Belgium signed an agreement defining the border between Tanganyika and Ruanda-Urundi.

Until 1925, Tanganyika was administered in an improvised way and followed German administrative practices, after which the system of Indirect Rule was introduced.

Indirect Rule was first practised by Lord Lugard in northern Nigeria where he used traditional rulers including emirs to administer a vast expanse of territory.

In 1946, Tanganyika became a UN trusteeship territory; coincidentally in the same year the Nigerian federation was formed out of three massive regions created by the British: Northern Nigeria dominated by the Hausa-Fulani, Eastern

Nigeria by the Igbo, and Western Nigeria by the Yoruba. Nigeria itself was created in 1914 with the amalgamation of the North and the South which had been administered separately as if they were two distinct colonies but under the same colonial power.

When Europeans came to Africa and established colonies, they thought they could transform at least some of those colonies into a permanent home for white settlers as the British did in Australia and New Zealand, as well as in South Africa, Southern Rhodesia - what is Zimbabwe today - and Kenya. In fact, Kenya was declared a "White Man's Country" from the beginning of formal British occupation of the territory under Lord Delamere.

Neighbouring Tanganyika would have met the same fate had the British colonialists succeeded in establishing a giant federation stretching from Kenya all the way down to South Africa.

In fact, the governors of all the colonies in the region - Kenya, Uganda, Tanganyika, Nyasaland (now Malawi), Northern Rhodesia (Zambia today), and Southern Rhodesia met in Tukuyu, southern Tanganyika, in 1925 to work on a plan to form such a federation.

But, years later as political awakening among Africans began to take place, the proposed federation was strongly opposed by African nationalists who feared that the establishment of such a giant political entity would consolidate and perpetuate white domination over Africans who constituted the vast majority of the population throughout the region as much as they did in the rest of the continent.

Yet, in spite of such opposition, it is interesting to note that years later Ugandan leader Milton Obote took a firm stand against the dissolution of one federation, the Central African Federation (of Northern Rhodesia, Southern Rhodesia and Nyasaland), an imperial creation, arguing that it would not be in the best interests of Africa if the federation was dissolved.

He argued that it would be beneficial to Africa if the federation remained intact and became a supra-nation upon attainment of independence.

He was virtually alone among African leaders in his support of the continued existence of the Central African Federation - also known as the Federation of Rhodesia and Nyasaland - which was created in 1953. It was dissolved 10 years later in 1963.

And there were always whites in all these territories who supported Africans in their quest for justice and racial equality across the spectrum, including the former governor of Northern Rhodesia, Sir Roy Welensky, who also once served as federal prime minister of the Federation of Rhodesia and Nyasaland, although his espousal of the doctrine of racial equality did not go far enough.

But he at least acknowledged the genuine aspirations of Africans even if he may not have believed that black Africans really deserved the same rights as whites.

Another example, of genuine commitment to racial equality, was Derek Bryceson, a British, who emigrated from Kenya to Tanganyika in 1952 and who became a cabinet member soon after the country won independence.

Then there was Dr. Leader Sterling, also British, who first came to Tanganyika in the 1930s. He also became a nominated member of parliament and a cabinet member appointed by President Julius Nyerere.

Bryceson was also an elected member of parliament representing a predominantly black district, Kilosa, and never lost an election against black political candidates contesting for the same seat; nor did Amir Jamal, of Indian origin, representing Morogoro, who was also, like Bryceson, a cabinet member under Nyerere for more than two decades since independence.

And there were other whites - not only in Tanganyika but in other colonies as well, across the continent - who felt the same way, including those who privately expressed their interest in building multiracial societies on the basis of equality but did not express their feelings publicly for fear of offending and alienating other whites who were not as liberal or open-minded as they were. As Harry Hodson states in his autobiography:

> A new constitution for Southern Rhodesia, which would have kept the white majority in parliament but extended the black franchise, and which had the nucleus of a common electoral roll, had been proposed from London and was being hotly debated. (It was to avert this far from radical constitution that Mr Ian Smith declared UDI two years later.)
>
> Over his customary tankard of beer Sir Edgar Whitehead, the colony's Prime Minister, a taciturn, introspective character, gave me his opinion that if all went according to plan the reforms would give rise to a genuine multiracial government with a multiracial parliament.

Sir Roy Welensky, Prime Minister of the moribund Central African Federation, amid a great deal of bluster, agreed with Whitehead at least on the point that time and opportunity had to be used to break down race barriers.

Sir Robert Tredgold, who later became fainéant head of state under UDI, deplored the lack of communication between Africans and the great majority of Europeans: "the trouble with most of our people here is that they live in a deaf world."

Lord Malvern, who as Sir Godfrey Huggins had been Prime Minister of Southern Rhodesia for 10 years, and at 77 was as amusing, vigorous and earthy as ever, gave a luncheon party for me.

I reminded him that several years earlier, dining with the Round Table Moot, he had likened the mass of Africans in Rhodesia to the London East-Enders among whom he had worked as a young doctor -poor and ignorant, and like children, but as capable as they of education and advance. Did he hold to that? "Yes - and they will grow up just as quickly."

Yet these white Rhodesian leaders were not the most liberal kind. They were racist. For example, Godfrey Huggins, who was acclaimed as a great British liberal, said at a press conference in London in 1952:

There will be no Africans in a federal government (of Rhodesia - Northern and Southern - and Nyasaland formed in 1953).

They are quite incapable of playing a full part....They may have a university degree, but their background is all wrong.

It is time for the people in England to realize that the white man in Africa is not prepared, and never will be prepared, to accept the African as an equal either socially or politically.

His racist remarks were published in British papers and elsewhere. He was also quoted by Colin M. Turnbull in his book *The Loney African*, p. 90. I have also quoted him in my book, Godfrey Mwakikagile, *Africa and the West*, p. xiv.

But the mere fact that even such racist liberals at one time or another acknowledged the imperative need for change and knew that such change was inevitable; and the more enlightened amongst them articulated genuinely liberal sentiments - that Africans were entitled to racial equality - shows that there were whites who were interested in achieving racial harmony and equality; and a number of them were far more committed to achieving this goal than most of their leaders were.

They could be found in all African countries, including apartheid South Africa. And Tanganyika was no exception.

Therefore the struggle in all these African countries was essentially democratic and not racial - black versus white - best exemplified by the new dispensation in post-apartheid South Africa where common aspirations shared by blacks, whites, Indians, Coloureds and others led to the adoption of one of the most liberal constitutions in the world guaranteeing equality for all South Africans. As one black South African cabinet member said in his emphatic declaration that non-blacks in South Africa were also Africans just like black Africans: "Indians are in India, and Europeans in Europe."

And it's very interesting to know how the European settlers felt about their new life in the colonies they had established under the tropical sun far away from Europe.

In spite of the difficulties they faced living in underdeveloped regions of the world, they were still very much satisfied with their new life. That is why they did not want to leave or return to Europe except in some cases after independence when conditions became intolerable even for many black Africans who were born in those countries.

Political repression and worsening economic conditions became a way of life in many African countries after the end of colonial rule. And through the years, tens of thousands of Africans have left the continent in search of greener pastures especially in the West.

By the end of 2005, there were more than 5 million Africans living outside Africa, tens of thousands of them highly educated and trained professionals. And tens of thousands of African students who go to school in Europe, North America and other parts of the world every year don't return to their home countries or to any other part of Africa after they finish their studies.

At this writing, there were more than 30,000 Nigerian doctors living and working in the United States alone. In New York City, there were more than 600 Ghanaian doctors. In Chicago, there were more doctors from Sierra Leone than there are in Sierra Leone.

And that's just the tip of the iceberg.

About 50,000 Kenyan professionals live and work in the United States as I write now. That's without even counting those in the United Kingdom where, for historical reasons because of former colonial ties, they have gone to in the past in larger numbers than they have anywhere else.

Add Nigerians, Ghanaians, Tanzanians, Zimbabweans, Zambians, Sierra Leoneans and others who live in Britain, North America and other parts of the world including Australia. Also think about how many Africans from Senegal, the Ivory Coast, Guinea, Mali and other former French African colonies live and work in France alone. And why.

Then you can see why our continent is in such a mess. It is a continental crisis, a massive brain drain, and it is killing Africa because of rotten leadership - more than anything else - in most parts of the continent since the end of colonial rule.

And we have to be brutally frank about it. Glossing over the problem is not going to solve it.

Those are grim statistics. They tell a sad story about the conditions in our countries which force tens of thousands of highly educated people including professionals such as doctors, engineers, scientists and many others in different critical fields to flee the continent every year in search of better life in Western countries and elsewhere in the industrialized world. They constitute the critical mass without which Africa cannot develop. They keep on fleeing the continent. And it has been that way since independence.

In fact many Africans, especially the older ones, remember with nostalgia how life was in "the good ol' days" before independence when there was law and order and no shortages of essential items.

They also remember that they could get jobs, even if the jobs weren't paying much; and that in spite of difficulties, roads and railways were well-maintained, and the people could travel to different parts of the country without fear of being robbed or killed.

And they did not have to pay bribes in those days to get a job, buy a bus ticket or even a simple bar of soap or some toothpaste as happened in many countries across the continent after independence.

Those are some of the reasons why many people remember the fifties with nostalgia; a nostalgic feeling which may seem to justify or defend colonial rule although that is not the case.

It is simply a desire by many people to live better, even if simpler, lives.

And the deplorable condition in which tens of millions of Africans live more than 40 years after independence is a searing indictment against Africa's post-colonial leadership.

It is no wonder that millions of Africans who are old enough to have lived under colonial rule remember those days with nostalgia.

For whites, life was even better for them when compared with the way Africans lived. In fact, life couldn't have been better for some of them since many colonial administrators would not have been able to get in their own countries - in Britain and elsewhere in Europe - the kind of jobs they had in colonial Africa.

Since I focus on Tanganyika in this chapter, the examples I cite come from East Africa to illustrate my point. As Erika Johnson, writing about the 1950s in colonial Tanganyika, stated in *The Other Side of Kilimanjaro*:

> Robin [Robin Johnson was a District Commissioner, simply known as D.C. throughout British colonial Africa] maintains that there was no better life for a man in those days than that of a District Commissioner. It was a marvellous combination of an active open air life, coupled with a wide, varied and interesting amount of office work.
>
> You did long walking safaris through your area and slept under canvas, and in this way you got to know your parishioners and their problems.
>
> Responsible for a vast area, you were father, mentor and disciplinarian to everyone, sorting out family and tribal disputes. You had to do anything and everything: build roads, dams and bridges, dig wells and be a magistrate and administrator of law and order.
>
> Your problems could vary from shooting a rogue elephant despoiling villagers' crops to trying a stock thief in court.
>
> In later years, [Julius] Nyerere once said to a silent Robin that the D.C's had made little contribution other than collecting taxes!

From left to right: Kenneth Kaunda, Julius Nyerere, Jomo Kenyatta, Milton Obote

Many of those projects provided employment for a number of Africans. And they played a major role in building roads, dams and bridges, making bricks, digging wells and doing many other things, providing cheap labour.

In fact, I personally remember seeing African men doing hard work, building roads, in the town and on the outskirts of Mbeya and also working on the road from Mbeya to Chunya, a district north of Mbeya; and in Rungwe district working on the road from Tukuyu to Kyela, 30 miles south of Tukuyu close to the Tanganyika-Nyasaland (now Malawi) border, when I was a little boy under 10 in the 1950s.

They worked for the colonial Public Works Department, what was simply known as PWD, and rode in the back of Bedford lorries; they were British lorries imported from Britain. The lorries also were simply called PWD. I even remember their colour. They were painted green on the sides and white on top.

The African labourers worked hard, all day long, often in scorching sun.

The buses which used those roads, besides other vehicles, were the East African Railways & Harbours Corporation (EAR&H) buses. I remember they were Leyland buses.

The wages for Africans working on those roads and elsewhere were low but better than nothing if you needed some money to buy a few things now and then.

Many other Africans earned some money by selling agricultural products, and sometimes handicrafts, at open markets in villages and sometimes in town. In our case it was in the town of Tukuyu, built on small hills with a majestic view below and all the way down to Lake Nyasa clearly visible about 34 miles away on the Malawi-Tanzania border.

Some of the people at the market whom I remember vividly were Kikuyu women. They were originally from Kenya and had, like many other Kenyans, come to Tanganyika to take advantage of the opportunities available to make money in a country where the indigenous people, including my fellow Nyakyusa in Rungwe District, were supposedly not as aggressive as the Kenyans were.

The Kenyans were seen as "more enterprising," "more adventurous," and "more of risk-takers" than Tanganyikans; although all those are relative terms.

Even today, many Tanzanians are apprehensive about their future in the proposed East African Federation which is supposed to be consummated by 2013 or even later, if at all. They say the federation will be dominated by Kenyans and Ugandans who are more "aggressive" and better educated.

They also say problems of tribalism and racism, so common in Kenya, Uganda and in Rwanda and Burundi unlike in Tanzania, will spread to Tanzania and the country will lose the peace and stability it has enjoyed since independence.

When I recall the fifties and early sixties, I can understand why many of my fellow countrymen feel the way they do in terms of competition between Tanzanians and Kenyans as well as Ugandans in the economic arena, besides their fear of tribalism and racism becoming major problems in Tanzania - which will be no more - if the countries do indeed unite to form a supra-nation.

I remember what my mother said more than once in the late fifties and early sixties after she saw Kikuyu women at the market in Tukuyu when she now and then went into town to but a variety of items. She described them as very aggressive and determined to make money. They were the first to arrive at the market early in the morning before dawn to make sure that they had the best spots where they could attract the largest number of customers.

I went to the market myself a few times and I remember seeing them selling beans, rice and other items.

And what was so good about all this is that there was no hostility towards the Kikuyu on the part of the Nyakyusa. I don't remember hearing anyone saying these Kikuyus have come all the way from Kenya to Rungwe District, down here, near the border with Nyasaland and Northern Rhodesia to take over our market and steal our customers! It was business as usual, although many Nyakyusas were outmaneuvred on their own turf, at their own market, in their own town and home district, by these "strangers" from Kenya.

But some of them may have learnt a thing or two from these Kikuyu women who had mastered the art of salesmanship and tricks of the trade. However, most of the Nyakyusa women at the market were equally competent and were a perfect match for the Kikuyu and may even have welcomed the challenge from them to demonstrate their own marketing skills. The challenge itself was a source of inspiration to others to excel and was therefore a positive thing.

Besides the women and some men selling food and other items at the market in Tukuyu, there were other Africans - although not many - who worked in that town. My father was one of them. He was assistant manager at a Shell BP petrol station under a British manager. I remember the manager had a son who was around my age. Whenever I went to see my father now and then when I was in town for a walk or to buy a few things, I would see the boy there with his father.

It has been more than 40 years since I last bought some items from the Indian shops in the town of Tukuyu - they were the only ones, except one Somali shop owned by Rajab who knew my father well - but I still remember some of the owners and the names of those shops, Hirji, Merali, and Makanji which were also said to be the biggest in town. There were no African shops in Tukuyu in those days.

I remember that some Indian shop owners even spoke

Kinyakyusa, the native language of the Nyakyusa in Rungwe District, and they had good relations with their customers. I also remember seeing and listening to many Nyakyusa women negotiating with the shop owners over price when they were buying clothes, sugar, cooking oil, kerosene for their lamps in the villages and other items.

One of the popular items bought by some women was a cotton cloth called *mwasungo* in Kinyakyusa. It was black and cheap and the people who bought that were usually very poor. If you bought *mwasungo*, people would assume you had nothin'. Some people even made fun of the material. It's sad but it happened.

Hardly any African women worked in the town of Tukuyu except may be a *yaya* (house maid) here and there.

There were, however, a few men who worked as watchmen staying awake all night long outside Indian shops with their *pangas*, in spite of the fact that we never heard of anybody trying to break into the shops - which were also Indian family residences - even when there were no night watchmen at all at some of the shops.

My father was one of the few men who had a regular job in Tukuyu when he worked as an assistant manager at the Shell BP petrol station.

I also remember one very small African restaurant near the football field in the town of Tukuyu. The soccer field was also used by politicians to address mass rallies.

I remember my father took me to that restaurant quite often when we were in town and he knew the owners well.

But it was Africans working on road projects, building or repairing roads, who were probably the most visible people in the labour market of the formal sector besides teachers and other employees.

I saw them working on roads many times in the fifties. And I remember many of them liked to sing or shout a lot when they worked, repairing or building roads. They worked hard until late in the evening, sometimes until dusk.

I also once got into trouble with some of them when we lived in Mbeya. That was between 1954 and 1955 when I was around four and five years old.

I was not yet in school then, although that was not an excuse for what I did. And I remember I used to play a lot near the road going from Mbeya to Chunya. Our house was very close to the road just on the outskirts of Mbeya. The town was within walking distance from our house.

Almost everyday I would collect small stones, big enough for my size, and pile them up under a shrub near the road as I waited for the Bedford PWD lorries to come by. Because I was small, it was easy for me to hide. The lorries always carried African workers on their way to and from work. As soon as the lorries were getting ready to pass by, I would throw stones at them, targeting the labourers riding in the back of those lorries. And quite often I scored direct hits.

As soon as I did that, I would duck under the bush. They sometimes saw me but I would dash back home and the driver never stopped. But one day he did! I remember that very well. The PWD lorry was headed towards Chunya, without necessarily going that far. It was simply the direction the lorry went.

About two or three of the labourers jumped out of the lorry and came after me. I couldn't outrun them and they caught me. One of them grabbed my hand. I was so terrified that I thought they were going to do something bad to me. But my age and size saved me.

I was crying when they grabbed me and they ordered me to take them to my parents. I did, crying all the way. My mother was there and she gave me a severe tongue lashing in front of them and they let me go.

I expected the worst and would probably have been rewarded with that had my father been there during that time. He was a strict disciplinarian who regularly administered corporal punishment when we were growing up, especially in my case and my younger brother Lawrence. But he was at work in town and didn't come back home until in the evening everyday. I remember he worked for Brooke Bond in those days.

And that was the end of my adventure. I never tossed stones at PWD lorries again for a long time, although the thrill was not gone.

I think I did it again a couple of times or so much later after that incident. But basically, I stopped doing it.

That is one of my most memorable experiences when we lived in Mbeya in the fifties besides the circus I attended in Mbeya town and which I have described elsewhere in the book.

It was also when we lived in Mbeya that I saw a tortoise for the first time. There was a chap who used to go around showing the tortoise to earn some money. He would somehow coax the tortoise to stick his head out of his shell and the people would give him a few coins for performing the "trick". He actually did nothing; the tortoise did, and I believe only when it was ready to do so.

One day he came to our house. It was in the afternoon, on a sunny day, and I was playing outside. He showed the tortoise to my mother and to my sister Maria and we all, together with my brother Lawrence, looked at it.

I remember thinking how slow it moved when he put it on the ground. And to me, it looked sad because of the way it moved. I was simply too young to know that was simply its nature and that's the way it looked.

It was quite an experience and I learnt something from that, especially since that was the first time that I saw that kind of animal. I had never seen anything like it before. And I remember the day well, in fact very well.

But my favourite pastime even after I started school in Rungwe District was catching grasshoppers and butterflies. That was after my parents returned to their home district - hence ours as well - and I went there with them for the first time together with my brother and my two sisters.

None of us was born in Rungwe District, and none of us had been there before. But the rest of my sisters and my only other brother David were all born in Rungwe District after my parents returned there in the mid-fifties.

I used to play outside a lot and loved catching and feeding grasshoppers, giving them blades of grass. I treated them as if they were my "cows," and in fact I called them that.

After living in urban areas during the first five years of my life, it was quite a dramatic change when we finally went to live in the rural areas. And twice, I came perilously close to getting killed because of my adventures.

Before we settled in Kyimbila which is in the highlands of Rungwe District, we lived in Kyela in the southern part of the district. That was in 1955. Kyela is now a separate district but it was then a part of Rungwe District. It is mostly lowland, hot and humid and borders Malawi, what was then Nyasaland.

I had not started school when we lived in Kyela and did not enroll in primary school, Kyimbila Primary School, until we moved to the highlands in the northern part of Rungwe District, what the Nyakyusa in Kyela call Mwamba; the Nyakyusa in the highlands are also sometimes called *Bamwamba* by those in Kyela.

Bamwamba in Nyakyusa means those of the highlands or highlanders. And Nyakyusa highlanders call the Kyela area Ntebela, or lowland, and the people who live down there *Bantebela*, meaning, of the lowlands or lowlanders.

And it was when we lived in Kyela that I almost got killed when I was playing outside. We lived in a rural area, a few miles north of the town of Kyela.

I remember there was a mango tree on our land only a few yards from our house. I used to go to that tree almost everyday to play. And that is where I came face to face with two cobras. I think they were king cobras.

I was 5 years old and did not really know what they were. But I do know and remember very well that I did not take them seriously.

I also remember that I saw the snakes more than once around that tree, on the ground, and whenever I saw one or both, I used to throw stones and sticks at them, playing, and they would slither away fast.

One day, I remember one of the snakes stuck its head out of the grass facing me after I threw stones and sticks at it. That's when I ran back to the house and told my mother what happened; my father was not there during that time.

And that is when I realized how I came perilously close to getting killed by one of those snakes.

My mother told me I was playing with snakes, extremely dangerous snakes, and would have been killed had I confronted the one which stuck its head out, no longer afraid of me, if it ever was. It had its head puffed out while facing me, yet I did not have the slightest idea of what that meant because whenever I threw stones and sticks at the snakes around that mango tree, they ran away.

From then on, I was forbidden from going to that tree, although I think I went there again just out of curiosity. But I was more "cautious" than before. Obviously the word caution meant something different to me at that age.

But, thank God, I managed to get out of there alive and my parents and I, together with my brother Lawrence and my two sisters Maria and Gwangu, moved to Kyimbila in the northern part of Rungwe District in the highlands where my parents originally came from.

We settled in Mpumbuli village surrounded by relatives including my grandmother on my father's side, my aunts, uncles and cousins and felt really at home. All these relatives lived in the area of Kyimbila not far from our house.

Some of them lived right there in Mpumbuli. And it was when we lived there that I started going to school. I was six years old when I enrolled in standard one at Kyimbila Primary School in 1956, not long after we moved from Kyela the previous year.

It was also when we lived in Mpumbuli village that I once again came close to losing my life. Our house was only a few yards - not more than 20 or 30 yards - away from a small river called Lubalisi.

The river goes around our property of a few acres of land, probably not more than five acres since land is so scarce in densely populated Rungwe District, and serves as a demarcation line separating our land from the property of others.

I used to go to the river everyday, bathing and playing with crabs. It was also an area which was known to have pythons and other snakes. I never saw a python but I saw many small green snakes on tree branches and guava trees which grow in abundance in our area.

The guava trees were just wild plants and people in the area cut them down if they had to clear the land for farming. We ate guavas now and then but we never valued them as food or as a staple item of our diet. They were simply wild fruits and we plucked them from trees now and then just for fun.

Birds and monkeys valued them more than we did since we had plenty of food including bananas, maize, sweet potatoes, beans, cabbage and other vegetables in this highly fertile district where we also grow coffee and tea. I helped harvest coffee on our farm when I was growing up and I remember seeing small green snakes on coffee tree branches as well. But they were harmless and not aggressive.

I did, however, have a close encounter with one river snake when I was washing my legs in River Lubalisi one evening. I was standing on a big stone where I stood all the time whenever I went to the river, and was washing my legs when something just told me instinctively to look in the water behind the stone. And sure enough, there was something there, a snake, its head straight up moving slowly towards my heel trying to sneak up on me.

As soon as the snake saw me looking at it, it ducked back into the water and disappeared under the stone. I did not even finish washing my legs and ran back to the house where I did the rest. We had plenty of water stored in buckets for bathing, after heating it up, using firewood, but it was still a thrill for us, especially boys, to go to the river and bathe even if we could avoid that and bathe at home.

I don't know what would have happened had I been bitten by that snake. I don't know what kind of snake it was and whether or not it was poisonous. I just remember that it was a small black snake. If it was highly poisonous, I would have been in trouble.

Tukuyu Government Hospital was about four miles away. And we had no car. It was not until about five years later that my father bought a used Land Rover from an African businessman known as Mr. Katule. And even if we had a car back then, there is no guarantee that the hospital would have been able to save my life had I been bitten by a highly poisonous snake. I'm not sure – in fact I don't believe – it was equipped for that with the necessary staff and medicine.

But the worst never happened and so I lived to tell the story. Yet that was not the end of it.

I had another encounter, right on our property, and close to the same river, when I was severely tested and forced to "mature overnight." I was still under 10 years old.

There was a small shrub on our land right on the bank of the river – only about 20 yards from our house – we passed by whenever we went to draw some water for various activities around the house. We never drank the water from River Lubalisi and never used it for cooking. It was not clean. And since we were downstream, the people upstream polluted it even more for us everyday.

Fortunately, we had fresh, spring water coming straight out of a small high bank of a small stream – which was itself spring water – only about 50 yards away from our house and next to River Lubalisi on the other side of the river bank. Also our grandmother on my father's side did not live far from there; may be about 150 yards or so.

My sister Maria (second-born), my brother Lawrence and my sister Gwangu (third- and fourth-born, respectively, now both dead), and I used to go there almost every day to get some drinking water in different containers.

Although the water was supposed to be clean, our father did not want to take chances and bought a water filter to make sure that we all drank clean water in the house.

We even went there at night, sometimes, taking chances with creatures of the night we could run into anytime. But nothing ever happened to us.

But something happened to me at that shrub on the river bank close to our house.

One day when I was playing there, I noticed that there was a big hole under the shrub and was fully convinced right away that there was a big snake in there; my belief reinforced by what we had heard before that there were pythons in the area. Or it could have been some other creature. I was not sure but was still convinced that if anything lived in there, it had to be a snake.

It was during daytime under the tropical sun. And I had plenty of time to investigate or do whatever I wanted to do. I came up with an idea that if there was indeed a big snake or some other creature in there, I would be able to flush it out and see what it was, and fire would do the trick.

So, I collected some dry grass and banana leaves, and a few dry sticks, and piled them up on the hole. I struck a match and up went the flames. But within seconds, whatever was in that hole put out the fire. I heard some noise, like loud hissing or a small wind, and saw the ashes and sparks blown away and scattered around the shrub as the fire went out.

Until recently, I didn't know what it was or how the fire was put out so quickly within seconds right in front of me. I assumed it was a python in that hole and it put out the fire with a jet of saliva. But I could have been wrong. It could have been a different creature, although I doubted that seriously.

For decades, I left that to experts to determine or conclude whether or not the fire was, most likely, extinguished by saliva from a python or some other kind of large snake.

It was not until decades later that I came to know the truth. One of my nephews, Humphrey Mwaipopo, wrote me in October 2009 saying that there was a python in that hole. That's about 50 years later. Some pythons have been known to live that long, and may be even longer.

He wrote me from Tanzania in response to a letter I had written him when I was still living in the United States. I had written him to ask him if he knew anything about pythons near the river which is only a few yards from our house. I told him about the hole and what happened decades ago when I started a fire over that hole. He knew the hole very well since he spent a lot of time on that piece of land. He was partly brought up there by my mother, his grandmother, and he said my family members saw the python now and then and it was now very old.

He also told me that my uncle Johanne Mwambapa, now deceased like my mother, who was popularly known as Chonde and who was my mother's elder brother, wanted to shoot the python in that hole but older people in the village stopped him. They said the python belonged to the land and if he killed it, he would drop dead instantly!

So, now I know it was a python in that hole.

And that was not the end of my close encounter with nature in Mpumbuli village in the fifties when I was growing up.

On another day, my father and I were going back home from my grandmother's – his mother's – house on the other side of River Lubalisi about 150 yards away from our house. It was night time and as we got to the bank of the river getting ready to cross, I saw an animal sitting on the left hand side very close to where we used to get our spring water.

My father also glanced at the animal but didn't say anything. I didn't either. After we crossed the river and had climbed up a small hill leading to our house and were only only a few yards away, may be 50 yards or so before we reached home, my father said the animal we just saw was a leopard!

And he made the right decision not to tell me that when we were crossing the river. I probably would have panicked. I don't know if the leopard would have attacked us or not had I screamed or made some other kind of noise. But it's possible any commotion could have been misinterpreted by the leopard as an attack on it, triggering an attack on us.

It was also at the same crossing on another night when I was going back home that I heard some noise in the bushes on the opposite bank. It was loud as if something big was slithering towards the river. And it was indeed. I was sure it was a python! Nothing slithers like that unless it is a snake. And if it's snake, it's a big one. And if it's a big one, it's a python, especially in that area. The conclusion was obvious to me, since there were pythons in the area.

As I was getting to cross the river, I heard some loud splashing and as if something big was wiggling in the water like as huge snake. And I was right. After it crossed the river, I heard it slithering and going into the bushes on the same side of the bank where I was when I was getting ready to cross. And I still remember the noise. The creature slithered like a huge snake. It could not have been but that. And I believe it was a python.

Miraculously, in all the years I lived in Mpumbuli village, eight years altogether before I went to boarding school at the age of 13, I never heard of anyone or any animal being eaten by a python. We had two cows and I took them grazing a few times but nothing happened.

And my uncle Johanne Chonde Mwambapa, who was about 13 years older than my mother and who even helped to raise her (she was the last-born in the family), once gave me a small pig as gift when I was about seven or eight years old.

It was in the evening when he gave me the pig at his house and I had to take it home with me about a mile-and-a-half away, going down a hill, crossing a stream, climbing up another hill, crossing the Tukuyu-Kyela road, then going down another hill and finally crossing River Lubalisi and climbing yet another hill to get to our house.

I also had to go through some bushes on the way home from my uncle's house. Yet nothing happened, although the pig made a lot of noise almost all the way.

That's in an area with pythons. None of them may have been hungry. But if there were any in that area during that time, they would have heard the pig squealing. And pythons are known to have a keen sense of hearing. Some experts say they can detect the slightest movement a hundred yards away.

The worst incident I knew of involved our dog, Jack, a German shepherd, who was almost killed near the bank of the same river at the south-end of our property.

Our father went looking for the dog along the river bank on our land and when he found him he noticed that the dog couldn't walk well.

We never found out what happened to Jack but our father suspected that a python might have tried to kill the dog. But that was only speculation and it probably wasn't the case since it takes only a few seconds for a python to wrap around its prey and squeeze it to death once it gets hold of it.

It was also in the same area where my father found our dog that two of my cousins and I had a close encounter with another python.

My cousin Bello Mwambapa, now deceased, who was the son of another elder brother of my mother, and Newton Mwankusye, the son of my mother's elder sister, came to visit us one day.

We were walking around and I told them I wanted to take them to the area where my father found our dog near the same river Lubalisi.

We were eating some bananas on our way there, an area that was also only a few yards from our house. After we got to the place, we stopped and kept on talking. Then I threw a banana peel on some tall grass and shrubs very close to where we were standing, telling my cousins that was the area where my father found our dog Jack. As soon as the peel landed on the grass, we heard some noise, and something big and heavy slithering away going downhill towards the river.

I'm sure it was a python. We had been standing there, talking, for about five minutes. We didn't have the slight idea that we were standing in front of a python only a few feet away. Obviously, the python knew all the time that we were there and was just listening to us. It could very easily have attacked one of us but it probably wasn't hungry and didn't feel threatened.

Those are some of the most memorable events in my life when I was growing up in Mpumbuli village in Kyimbila and which were in sharp contrast with what I experienced during the first five years of my life in Kigoma, Ujiji, Morogoro, and Mbeya where we lived in urban areas.

I had other experiences, of course, in the mid- and late fifties; for example, when our headmaster at Kyimbila Primary School who was also married to my mother's first cousin sent all the boys in the school down the valley near our school to hunt.

The Nyakyusa don't do that to boys - working hard on the farm is manly enough - but in his own peculiar way, what he did to us was probably a form of initiation into manhood he felt, rightly or wrongly, that we needed!

But he opened another window for us into the world since he was the one who taught us geography at Kyimbila Primary School.

I remember well that it was when I was in standard four at Kyimbila Primary School in 1959 that our headmaster taught us about African countries, including the names of some leaders such as Kwame Nkrumah, Nnamdi Azikiwe and Jomo Kenyatta besides Julius Nyerere. And I still remember the map he used in class, although I don't have vivid memory of everything he taught us in geography.

But I remember that the map he used, and obviously the one that was most current in those days, had a only few huge patches, some red, some green and I think others beige, orange or yellow.

I remember two distinctly. One was green and covered most of West Africa and was labelled French West Africa. The other one was red and was labelled British, although I'm not sure it said British East Africa.

But I remember that all the colonial territories had names - Kenya Colony, Uganda Protectorate, Tanganyika Trust or Trusteeship Territory or simply Tanganyika Territory, Zanzibar Protectorate in our East African region - and some of them were identified by their colonial rulers; for example, British and French Somaliland, Portuguese Guinea, and so forth.

So, while I lived in a village, my school attendance at Kyimbila Primary School and later at Mpuguso Middle School which was a boarding school about three miles south from our house - and which was almost perfect attendance - opened my eyes to the rest of the world I had never known before. But it was formal education complemented by my firsthand knowledge of rural life in Rungwe District after we left Mbeya in 1955. It was a dramatic change in my life starting with a transition from urban to rural life in those days in the fifties and it left an indelible mark on my mind.

All this dramatic transformation in my life took place in what was then the Southern Highlands Province when I finally went to live a typical African way of life in a village where I also learnt Kinyakyusa, my "tribal" language, for the first time. I had learnt some earlier, listening to my parents and other relatives we had in Mbeya including my aunt, my mother's eldest sister (she died in 1993 at the age of 102), and her children but not enough.

Up until then, I spoke Kiswahili. And my playmates in Morogoro, who were not Nyakyusa, also spoke Kiswahili. But all that changed when we moved from Morogoro to Mbeya in the Southern Hilghlands Province. And it is a province that I will always remember, and always cherish, the way it was back then.

The province was under a British provincial commissioner, called PC. The town of Mbeya was the provincial capital, where my parents and I together with my siblings lived on the outskirts in the early and mid-fifties before we moved to Rungwe district, about four miles south of the town of Tukuyu, which is 45 miles south of Mbeya.

During those days of colonial rule, Tanganyika was divided into seven provinces: The Southern Highlands Province, the Southern Province, the Central Province, the Western Province, the Lake Province, the Coast Province, and the Northern Province. After independence, the Southern Highlands was divided into Mbeya Region and Iringa Region; so were the rest, also broken down into smaller regional administrative units called Regions.

I also remember that the fifties were a period when many people from Tanganyika went to work in the mines in South Africa. Some of them came from my area of Kyimbila which has several villages including Mpumbuli, my home village, about four miles from the town of Tukuyu. One of the people who went to work in the mines in South Africa was my cousin Daudi who lived in a different part of Rungwe District several miles away from Kyimbila.

Coincidentally, Daudi's father William, my father's elder brother, migrated to South Africa in the mid- or late forties never to be heard from again, except once or twice when he wrote my father back then not long after he settled in South Africa. Until this day, we don't know what happened to him or if he got married again and had another family in South Africa. If he did, we will probably never know about that.

Although I was under 10 years old in the fifties, I remember that the people who went to work in the mines were flown from Mbeya to South Africa. I remember talking to some of those who came back, including my cousin Daudi, and asking them about South Africa.

They had plenty of stories to tell about the City of Gold and how big it was. They also told us stories about the fights they had in the mines with people of other ethnic groups. The Nyakyusa, the people of my ethnic group, had a reputation on the mine compounds as fierce fighters. I heard the same story about twenty years later in the seventies when I came to the United States.

One of the people who stayed with me and other African students in Detroit, Michigan, in the United States in the seventies was Ndiko, a South African; I don't know if he spelt his name as Ndiko or Ndhiko.

He was with us for only a few weeks and I remember that when I told him that I was a Nyakyusa, he got excited and started telling me how tough the Nyakyusa were as fighters in South Africa; a spirit which, I believe, can partly be attributed to ethnocentric tendencies common among many groups whose members think, wrongly, that they are better than others as fighters and probably in many other ways, although not everybody believes that. I am one of those who don't.

Anyway, Ndiko (or Ndhiko), also had a relative, Lindiwe Mabuza, who taught at Ohio University in Athens, Ohio, and when he and I went to visit her in 1974, she said the same thing about the reputation of the Nyakyusa as fierce fighters on the mine compounds in South Africa. I also remember she tried to help me get a scholarship from Ohio University but I returned to Detroit where I graduated from Wayne State University.

She eventually returned to South Africa after the end of apartheid and served as a member of parliament. She was later appointed by President Nelson Mandela as South Africa's ambassador to Germany in 1995. When I was writing this in November 2009, she was South Africa's high commissioner (ambassador) to the United Kingdom.

When I first visited her at Ohio University in 1974, I was relatively new in the United States. I moved from New York to Detroit towards the end of December 1972 after staying in New York for about two months with a relative-in-law, Weidi Mwasakafyuka, who worked as a diplomat at the Tanzania Mission to the UN. He later served as Tanzania's ambassador to France in the 1980s.

He was the only person I knew when I first landed on American soil. I left Dar es Salaam on November 3rd and arrived in New York the next day. I went straight to Greensboro, North Carolina, before going back to New York. I stayed in Greensboro for only a few days.

Coincidentally, Weidi also came from Mpumbuli village, my home village in Kyimbila in Rungwe District, and was the second person from our village to go to school in the United States. He graduated from the University of California-Los Angeles (UCLA) and from Carleton University in Canada in the sixties. He did his postgraduate studies at Carleton.

E. Weidi Mwasakafyuka (United Republic of Tanzania) making a statement at a meeting of the UN Special Committee of 24 on Decolonization, Conakry, Guinea, 12 April 1972.

I was the third from our village to go to school in the United States. The first one was Henry Mwakyoma, a cousin on my mother's side, who graduated from the University of Virginia where he first went in the late fifties.

I remember when he came back to Tanganyika, he used to come to our house and tell us stories about life in the United States. He was one of the first people who inspired me to go to school in America. And he remains one of the people whom I remember the most from the fifties.

Unfortunately, Henry died many years ago in the 1970s, a victim of a brutal attack by thugs in Mbeya who literally beat him to death, according to reports I got from relatives when I was in the United States. He happened to be in the wrong place at the wrong time in that town. Times had really changed through the years. Those kind of attacks and crimes were unheard of in Tanganyika in the fifties.

The fifties were without question some of the most important years of my life. They were my formative years as much as the sixties were. And I remember listening to many inspiring stories which helped to enlarge my mental horizon at such an early age. And they have remained a source of inspiration throughout my life. My father was one of the people who liked to tell stories about hard work and success in life and played a critical role in shaping my personality when I was growing up.

I also remember hearing stories of valour about the Nyakyusa during my time and in the past including their successful campaigns against the Ngoni in the 1830s, '40s and '50s when the Ngoni tried to invade and penetrate Nyakyusaland. The Nyakyusa also successfully repelled the Sangu who invaded our district in the 1870s and 1880s from neighbouring Usangu in Mbeya District. Like the Nyakyusa, the Sangu had a quite a reputation as fierce fighters. But they were no match for the Nyakyusa who stopped their incursions into Nyakyusaland.

The few white missionaries who settled in Rungwe District also tried to intervene and act as mediators in the conflicts not only between the Nyakyusa and the Sangu but also between the Nyakyusa and the Safwa, then the largest ethnic group in Mbeya District until they were later outnumbered by the Nyakyusa. They also played a mediating role in other conflicts including intra-tribal (or intra-ethnic) disputes but not always successfully.

But, besides the Nyakyusa, it was the Ngoni whom I remember the most for their reputation as fighters mainly because I interacted with them in the sixties. Their legendary reputation as fighters sent a chill down the spine and many of their neighbours were afraid of them, except a few like the Nyakyusa, and the Hehe who, under their leader Chief Mkwawa, once defeated the Germans.

Originally from Natal Province in South Africa, the Ngoni settled in Songea District in southern Tanganyika, as well as in Sumbawanga in the western part of the country where they came to be known as the Fipa, which is their ethnic name and identity even today. They had a reputation as fierce fighters even in South Africa itself before they left during the *imfecane* in the 1820s and '30s headed north, finally settling in what is now Malawi, Mozambique and Tanzania. Some of them even went to Congo after going through Tanganyika.

I went to Songea Secondary School which was a boarding school in Songea District, the home district of the Ngoni, in southern Tanzania and talked to many Ngonis including some who were old enough to be my parents when I was in my teens back then in the sixties. Almost without exception, they all recalled the stories they were told by their elders when they were growing up on how the Nyakyusa and the Ngoni fought when the Ngoni tried to invade and conquer Nyakyusaland, to no avail.

They told me that the Nyakyusa *ni watani wetu*, a Swahili expression meaning they are our friends and we tell jokes about each other. Many of those "jokes" have to do with how hard the Nyakyusa fought to repel the Ngoni invaders after the Ngoni failed to steal Nyakyusa cows and women!

Some of the Ngoni also went to work in the mines in South Africa - where they originally came from - but not in significant numbers as the Nyakyusa and other people from the Southern Highlands did, especially from Rungwe and Mbeya Districts in a region bordering what was then Northern Rhodesia, now Zambia.

Northern Rhodesia itself attracted many mine workers from my region and many of them settled in that country. Even today, you will find many Nyakyusas who settled in Kitwe and other parts of the Copperbelt many years ago after they went to work there in the mines. For example, in 1954 the Nyakyusa in Kitwe formed an organisation to preserve, protect and promote their interests as a collective entity.

The Lozi, members of another ethnic group from Baraotseland or Barotse Province and one of the largest in Zambia, also formed their own organisation around the same time, as did others and some even before then including the Ngoni. And they were all cited as examples of ethnic solidarity among the mine workers in Kitwe and other parts of the Copperbelt in Northern Rhodesia. The Nyakyusa presence in what is now Zambia is still strong even today.

In fact, one of my mother's first cousins who was older than my mother emigrated from Tanganyika to Northern Rhodesia as a young man in the early 1940s. He was the son of my mother's uncle Asegelile Mwankemwa who was the pastor of our church, Kyimbila Moravian Church at Kyimbila in Rungwe District. He also lived in South Africa for a number of years before returning to Northern Rhodesia where he eventually became a high government official after the country won independence as Zambia.

He returned to Tanzania in the 1990s to spend his last days in the land of his birth. Tragically, he had forgotten Kinyakyusa and did not know Kiswahili after so many years of absence from Tanganyika, later Tanzania, and could communicate only in English and Bemba, one of the major languages in Zambia. All his children were also born and brought up in Northern Rhodesia.

And he was just one of the many people from my district who migrated to Northern Rhodesia and even some of them to South Africa. Jobs in the mines in both countries was the biggest attraction, encouraging many Tanganyikans to go there in those days.

The town of Mbeya was their main departure point heading south and was the largest town in the region. It was also the capital of the Southern Highlands Province when I was growing up.

The people who had been recruited to work in the mines in South Africa boarded planes called WENELA. I remember that name very well because I heard it all the time when I was growing up in the fifties. The people would say so-and-so has gone to Wenela, meaning to work in the mines in South Africa. The term became an integral part of our vocabulary in the 1950s, probably as much as it was even before then among the Nyakyusa and others.

The name WENELA was an acronym for the Witwatersrand Native Labour Association which was responsible for the recruitment of cheap labour among Africans in neighbouring countries including Tanganyika to work in the mines in South Africa. They were sometimes recruited to work in other sectors of the economy but primarily in the mines.

Many of the people who were recruited in Tanganyika were flown down there unlike, for example, those from Basutoland (now Lesotho) or Bechuanaland (now Botswana) who, because of their proximity to South Africa, were transported by buses.

But many people from Tanganyika were also transported by road from Mbeya in the Southern Highlands to Broken Hill in Northern Rhodesia. And from there they were taken to Mungu in Barotseland, the western province of Northern Rhodesia, and then flown to Francistown in Bechuanaland; and finally transported by railway to Johannesburg.

Working in the mines was hard labour, with little pay. But it was still something for people who virtually had nothing in terms of money. That's why they were drawn down there.

I remember my cousin Daudi worked for three years in the mines in Johannesburg. But when he came back to Tanganyika, he hardly had anything besides a wooden box he used as a "suitcase" - and which was the only popular and common "suitcase" among many Africans in those days - and may be a couple of shirts, two pairs of trousers, and a simple pair of shoes he wore when he returned home. In fact, he came straight to our village, from Johannesburg, to live with us.

My father was also his father, and the only one had, since his own biological father migrated to South Africa. His father left behind two children, Daudi himself, and his only sister, Esther, who was also younger than Daudi. Tragically, she died only a few years after Daudi returned from South Africa.

He went to South Africa to earn some money, yet returned hardly with any. It was hard life not only for him but for most

Africans who went to work in the mines and even for those who remained in the villages.

He was brutally murdered in Tanzania in the late 1970s when he was working at a sugarcane plantation in Kilombero, Morogoro Region, in the eastern part of the country.

In general the people were not starving in Tanganyika in the fifties. There was plenty of food especially in fertile regions such as the Southern Highlands where I come from. And my home district of Rungwe is one of the most fertile in the entire East Africa and on the whole continent. Almost anything, any kind of food, grows there: from bananas to sweet potatoes, groundnuts to beans, and all kinds of fruits and vegetables, besides cash crops such as coffee and tea, and much more.

But the people were poor in terms of financial resources. They had very little money. And that is why some of them went all the way to South Africa and to neighbouring Northern Rhodesia to work in the mines.

Some of them also ended up in Katanga Province, in the Congo, which is about 300 miles west from my home region of Mbeya. With all its minerals as the treasure trove of Congo, Katanga Province was another prime destination for job seekers from neighbouring countries who were looking for jobs in the mines.

The Nyakyusa from my home district were some of the people who ended up there. For example, I vividly remember a photograph of a Nyakyusa family published in the *Daily News*, Dar es Salaam, when I worked there as a news reporter in the early seventies.

They had lived in Congo for about 40 years but were expelled from the country and forced to return to Tanzania in what seemed to be a xenophobic campaign fuelled by anti-foreign sentiments in spite of the fact that members of this family, as well as many others, had lived in Congo for decades and their children were born and brought up there.

Therefore there was quite a contrast in terms of living standards between Africans and Europeans as well as between Africans and Asians; also between Africans and Arabs. Africans were the poorest. But there was no hostility, at least not overt, on the part of Africans towards whites and others in spite of such disparity in living standards; not to the extent that the social order was threatened in a way that could have led to chaos in the country.

For me as a child growing up, life was good as much as it was for many other youngsters. Our parents took care of us. I was never hungry. I always had clothes, although not shoes all the time. My father even gave me pocket money to buy sweets, soft drinks such as Fanta, Sprite and Coca Cola; cake and other delicacies as well as other things I wanted to buy including marbles we boys used to play a game called *goroli* in Kiswahili. It was one of my favourite games.

And for the colonial rulers as well as other whites, life was much better than ours in many respects. They usually had a lot more money than we did; and they had many things we didn't have.

There are also some things I remember about the kind of relationship some of us had with them as children.

There is one thing in particular which always comes to mind when I recall those days as a young boy in Rungwe District in the 1950s and how I saw whites.

I remember British men and women playing golf and tennis in Tukuyu, the administrative capital of Rungwe district, four miles from our home village and about 30 miles from the Tanzania-Malawi border. Many of them were friendly and they used to give us tennis balls now and then when we passed through the golf course. Quite a few of them came from as far away as Mbeya, the provincial capital, 45 miles north of Tukuyu, and some even from neighboring Northern Rhodesia, now Zambia.

I was, of course, too young then to know what was going on in terms of colonial domination, or what it meant to be ruled by the British or Europeans in general. But I do remember that whenever we saw them, they seemed to be very happy and satisfied with their lives, which were made much easier by African servants in almost every European household. It was unthinkable not to have one, since they all could afford it. African servants provided cheap labour.

But Africans also needed the money and they were glad to have jobs as house maids and as house boys or as farm workers working for Europeans. They also, the men especially, had to have a way to earn some money in order to pay taxes. Otherwise they would be in serious trouble with the colonial authorities. And like in every other country, there were those who simply did not want to pay taxes even if you told them, and could prove to them, that the money would be used to help them as well.

Europeans were in full control and the colonial authorities had no interest in sharing power with Africans, Asians or Arabs on equal basis as equal citizens of the same country. Yet there were whites who worked with Africans and other non-whites for the benefit of all. Therefore it would be a mistake to say that there were no whites in Tanganyika or in other parts of Africa who were interested in the well-being of Africans.

In fact, many of them were Africans themselves as citizens of African countries. Or they considered themselves to be Africans because they were born and brought up in Africa even if they retained British citizenship or that of any other European country. And when some of them had to leave for different reasons, they were sad they had to go, leaving a country or countries they knew as their home.

In spite of all that, there are still millions of white Africans in Africa, mostly in South Africa, about five million of them. And there are tens of thousands of others elsewhere in different countries on the continent. Their identity as Africans and allegiance to Africa inspired coinage of the term "white tribes" of Africa.

But there were some who were die-hard colonialists and had no intention of sharing power or identifying with non-whites - black Africans, Asians and Arabs - as fellow Africans. They were the ones who were opposed to independence in spite of the fact that there were whites who supported the nationalist aspirations of the Africans in their quest for independence or simply acknowledged the fact that independence would come some day whether they liked it or not.

As we saw earlier, in Tanganyika, some British settlers formed the United Tanganyika Party, known as UTP, to stem the nationalist tide that started to sweep across the country. But in spite of the differences they had with those who felt that Tanganyika should be a truly multiracial society ruled on democratic basis, there was no bitterness or hostility between the two sides which characterized race relations in some parts of Africa.

Leaders such as Julius Nyerere, Derek Bryceson, Amir Jamal who was of Indian descent, Dr. Leader Sterling and their colleagues argued that the future of Tanganyika as a nation and as a united country could not be guaranteed without racial equality.

And when some African members of TANU argued that people of other races should not be allowed to join the party or become citizens of Tanganyika after the country won independence, Nyerere made it clear that he would resign as a leader; a threat which brought others back in line to conform to the wishes of the majority of the TANU members who were committed to the creation of a truly non-racial society in which no one would be denied equal rights as explained by Nyerere and others during the campaign for independence.

Julius Nyerere, greeted by George Shepherd of the American Committee on Africa in March 1955 when Nyerere was at the UN presenting his case for Tanganyika's independence. Nyerere was in New York to address the UN Trusteeship Council that debated the third UN Visiting Mission's Report on Tanganyika. Six-and-a-half years later, Nyerere led Tanganyika to independence. He was 39 years old, the youngest leader in the world during that time.

Unlike West Africa, East Africa attracted a large number of white settlers for different reasons. One of the main reasons was climate. Another one was the fact that the largest number of British colonies in Africa were in East, Central and southern

Africa; which partly explains why a significant number of British settlers ended up in that part of the continent.

The largest number of the white settlers in Tanganyika and other parts of East Africa were not colonial administrators or rulers but ordinary citizens who simply wanted to live in Africa. Others went there because they had been offered jobs. Yet others felt that there was great potential for employment and economic development in different fields in those countries.

One of the areas in which British settlers in East Africa became deeply involved was commercial farming. East Africa is endowed with an abundance of fertile land, much of it at high altitude with a cooler climate, although still tropical. But it somewhat reminded the Europeans of the temperate climate back home in Europe, at temperatures they were comfortable with, and many of them came to settle in this region.

Much of East Africa is, of course, also hot, in fact very hot; for example along the coast, in the lowlands and in other parts of the region. But it also has more arable land, at higher altitudes, than West Africa does. For example, in an area where I come from called Kyimbila, there is a large tea estate called Kyimbila Tea Estate stretching for miles; we also grow a lot of coffee in our district.

The area of Kyimbila, including my home village of Mpumbuli, also has many pine trees. We even have some on our family property. These are the kind of trees which grow in temperate zones or in a cool climate.

Kyimbila Tea Estate is one of the largest tea estates in Tanzania, indeed in the whole of East Africa, and was originally established by the Germans. In fact, there was a German settlement at Kyimbila, about a mile and a half from our house, when the Germans ruled Tanganyika as *Deutsch Ostafrika* (German East Africa), and built a large church there, called Kyimbila Moravian Church.

There is also a large grave yard at Kyimbila where Germans are buried; I remember reading the headstones showing the deceased were born in the 1800s; they were born in Germany. After the Germans lost World War I, the British took over the tea estate.

When the British ran the tea estate when I was growing up,

they always had a British manager who lived on the premises. I also vividly remember one tragic incident that happened in 1956 when I was in standard one, what Americans call the first grade.

I was six years old then, and my schoolmates and I used to take a short-cut, walking past the manager's residence, going to Kyimbila Primary School about two miles from our house. I was the youngest in the group.

Everyday we went by, his dogs, a German shepherd and a Dalmatian, used to bark at us. They were not always tied, so quite often they used to chase us before being called back by their master or by his African servant who washed clothes and cooked for the British couple and cleaned up the house.

One morning on our way to school, both dogs were loose and they started chasing us. Although I was a fast runner, in fact a sprinter even at my tender age, my friends outran me that day. One of them was James Mwakisyala the closest neighbour I had in Mpumbuli village. His parents' house was only about 40 or 50 yards away from our house.

He was, and still is, a relative by marriage. His uncle, Brown Ngwilulupi who was also the elder brother of Weidi Mwasakafyuka whom I mentioned earlier, was married to my mother's first cousin, the daughter of the pastor of Kyimbila Moravian Church, Asegelile Mwankemwa. Both Brown and Weidi are now dead; so is my great uncle Asegelile Mwankemwa.

James and I were close as neighbours and as relatives-in-law when we were growing up. Years later in the seventies, he went to Carleton University in Ottawa, Canada, around the same time I went to Wayne State University in Detroit in the United States and we used to talk on the telephone quite often. He later became bureau chief of *The East African* in Dar es Salaam, Tanzania. *The East African*, a weekly paper, is based in Nairobi, Kenya, and is a sister publication of the *Daily Nation*.

And among all the pupils from Mpumbuli village and elsewhere who went to Kyimbila Primary School, he was also closest to me in age; he's only two years older than I am. We were also the same size in terms of physical stature. And both of us were small and slim. But he also outran me on that day which I vividly remember as if it was only yesterday because of what happened to me.

As the dogs kept on chasing us, I turned and looked back and knew I was not going to make it. So I dove under the tea shrubs, to my right, to take cover. The German shepherd went past me and kept on chasing the other children. But the Dalmatian saw me where I was hiding and came right under the bush and bit me on my right knee. I still bear a large scar on my knee more than 50 years later.

I almost lost my leg, and my life, on that day and came perilously closing to meeting the same fate on other occasions when we were being chased by the dogs. But something good came out of that. We all learnt to run faster, and longer. And quite often we took a detour on our way to school and back home to avoid the dogs.

Another incident I vividly remember had to do with my father when he worked as an assistant manager at a Shell BP station in the town of Tukuyu about four miles from our home in Mpumbuli village. He sometimes used to take lunch to work and one day he was told by the British manager of the petrol station that he could not put his lunch on the table used by the manager; it was *chapati* my mother had cooked for him on that day. I remember that very well.

My father was very bitter about the incident and told us what happened when he came back home that evening. That was around 1958 or 1959. My father, having secondary school education, was one of the few people in the area who knew English. And that was one of the reasons why he was hired as the assistant manager at the petrol station. He went to Malangali Secondary School in Iringa district in the Southern Highlands Province, one of the best schools in colonial Tanganyika and even after independence.

Before going back to Tukuyu, he worked as a medical assistant in many parts of Tanganyika - in Muheza, Tanga, Handeni, Amani, Kilosa, Morogoro - including the town of Kigoma, in western Tanganyika, where I was born.

He was trained as a medical assistant in the mid-1940s at Muhimbili National Hospital (then known as Sewa Haji and later Princess Margaret Hospital) in Dar es Salaam during British colonial rule.

He excelled in school and was supposed to go to Tabora

Secondary School for further education in standard 11 and standard 12 after completing standard 10 at Malangali Secondary School but couldn't go further because of family obligations, forcing him to seek employment early.

One of his classmates at Muhimbili National Hospital was Austin Shaba who, after completing his studies, went to Tukuyu to work as a medical assistant, and later became minister of local government in the first independence cabinet under President Nyerere. I remember my father saying Austin - they knew each other well - encouraged him to go into politics but he refused to do so.

Another classmate of my father at Malangali Secondary School who also went into politics was Jeremiah Kasambala. The son of a chief, he also became a cabinet member under President Nyerere and served as minister of agriculture and cooperatives in the first independence cabinet.

He came from the area of Mpuguso where I attended middle school in Rungwe District. He and my father had known each other for years and he equally encouraged him to pursue a career in politics. But, again, my father refused to do so although he was interested in politics and ketp up with what was going on in Tanganyika and elsewhere.

He listened to the BBC in English and Kiswahili everyday and had a profound influence on me. I also started listening to the BBC at a very young age in the fifties when I was under ten years old. I did not know English then, so I listened to the Swahili Service on the BBC and on TBC (Tanganyika Broadcasting Corporation) broadcast from Dar es Salaam more than 300 miles away.

And to make sure that I was paying attention, my father would sometimes walk away from the radio and then ask me later to give him a summary of the news. I already had a good memory and this exercise only helped improve it further.

I also remember the kind of shortwave radio we had. It was Philips, with an external antennae stretched out and attached to a pole, sometimes a dry bamboo tree, outside the house. All this reminds of the simpler life many people had in Tanganyika in the fifties. It had its inconveniences, and quite a few of them for Africans because of poverty, but still exciting.

It was also during the fifties that the campaign for independence in Tanganyika began in earnest. Like in most parts of Africa, it was a non-violent campaign unlike in neighbouring Kenya where it became violent during Mau Mau. Although I was very young when Mau Mau was going on, I remember seeing pictures of Mau Mau fighters in some newspapers published in Kiswahili. The most vivid image I still have of these fighters was their hair style, what they call dreadlocks nowadays.

The main Kiswahili papers during those days were *Mambo Leo* and *Mwafrika*. And I remember others: *Ngurumo*, *Mwangaza* and *Baragumu*. Although *Baragumu* was published in Kiswahili, it was not sympathetic to the nationalist cause articulated by TANU during the struggle for independence. It was, instead, used by the United Tanganyika Party (UTP) to promote its agenda among Africans by telling them that the country was not ready for independence and that supporting TANU would not serve their interests.

UTP was founded in February 1956 with the encouragement of Governor Sir Edward Twining as a counterweight to TANU in order to maintain the privileged status of the white minority settlers and was one of the three main political parties in Tanganyika before independence. It supported a multi-racial constitution but rejected universal suffrage without which genuine democratic representation is impossible.

The other party was the radical African National Congress (ANC) formed by Zuberi Mtemvu in 1958. Mtemvu and his supporters broke away from TANU because they were highly critical of Nyerere's moderate policies advocating equality for all Tanganyikans regardless of race.

The ANC argued that the interests of Africans were paramount even if it meant sacrificing the interests and well-being of whites, Asians and Arabs. Nyerere was resolutely opposed to that and won overwhelming support from the vast majority of the people in Tanganyika for his policies of racial tolerance and equality.

One of the organs he used to articulate his views was a Kiswahili newspaper, *Sauti Ya TANU* (Voice of TANU) founded in 1957. He edited the paper himself.

The main English newspaper was the Tanganyika *Standard*, the oldest English newspaper in the country founded in 1930. And it had a lot to do with my life only a few years later.

The future was never meant for us to see, and had someone told me back then in the late 1950s that my life would somehow be influenced by that English newspaper, I would not have believed it even at such a tender age.

But that is exactly what happened. About 10 years later, I joined the editorial staff of the *Standard* in Dar es Salaam. I was first hired as a new reporter in June 1969 when I was still a student at Tambaza High School, formerly H.H. The Aga Khan, in Dar es Salaam. I was 19 years old and the youngest reporter on the staff. I was hired by David Martin, the news editor, and Brendon Grimshaw, the managing editor.

David Martin was also the deputy managing editor of the *Standard*.. He died in Harare, Zimbabwe, in August 2007 where he went to live after Zimbabwe won independence in April 1980.

After completing Form VI, I joined the National Service which was mandatory for all those who finished secondary school and high school. After National Service, I worked briefly at the Ministry of Information and Broadcasting in Dar es Salaam as an information officer before returning to the *Standard* which was renamed the *Daily News* after it was nationalized in 1970.

And in November 1972, my editor Benjamin Mkapa, whom we simply called Ben Mkapa, helped me to go to school in the United States for further education. My trip was financed by the newspaper. They bought me a plane ticket and gave me a travelling allowance.

Years later, Mkapa was elected president of Tanzania and served two five-year terms.

Had I not joined the *Standard* as a news reporter, I may not have gone to school in the United States. And you probably would not be reading this book or any of the others I have written.

Although the *Standard* was a colonial newspaper in the fifties and articulated the sentiments of the white settler community and defended colonial policies, it provided ample coverage of political events during the struggle for independence even if such coverage was not always balanced and quite often reflected official thinking of the colonial authorities.

I remember when I was a news reporter at the *Standard* before it was nationalized in 1970, our rivals at the militant newspaper,

The Nationalist which was the official organ of the ruling party TANU, used to publish stories, editorials and feature articles in which they said we worked for "an imperialist newspaper" and sometimes even called us "imperialist agents"!

We simply ignored them, and even laughed at them, whenever we came face-to-face covering the same events. There was no hostility between us. They were simply articulating the ideological position of the ruling party which owned the paper they worked for.

And although the *Standard* defended white minority interests during colonial rule, it did not ignore what was going on in those days, even if it wanted to, and the leading African nationalist during that time, Julius Nyerere, had his views published in the paper many times, although not always the way he had articulated them.

There was usually a slant in favour of the colonial government, since the paper was its organ even if not officially so.

And as a moderate who was also committed to building a multiracial society, Nyerere was seen as a responsible leader who was not a threat to the interests of racial minorities in the country. He also sought to achieve his goals by constitutional means. Therefore ignoring him, or refusing to report what he said at public rallies and in interviews would have been counterproductive and not in the best interests of the white settlers.

Julius Nyerere, left, at Jangwani Grounds in Dar es Salaam with Bibi Titi Mohammed, right, in 1957 during the campaign for independence.

Although Nyerere was committed to non-violence to achieve independence, he could not guarantee that some of the people in Tanganyika would not resort to violence as some, especially the Kikuyu, did in neighbouring Kenya. As Robert A. Senser, an American journalist and editor of *Human Rights for Workers*, recalled what Nyerere told him when they met in the United States in 1957 in his article, "Remembering A Visitor from Tanganyika," published in *Human Rights for Workers: Bulletin No. IV-22*, December 1, 1999, not long after Nyerere died:

> The other day Ed Marciniak, once a Chicago colleague of mine in editing a monthly called *Work*, mailed me the obituary of Julius Nyerere, president of Tanzania from 1964 to 1985.
> Stapled to the clipping was a note from Ed saying: "I still remember your interview with him in *Work*."
> After all these years, I also remember that interview one evening 42 years ago, when Nyerere had dinner with my wife and me in our small apartment on Chicago's South Side.
> Nyerere, 35, then president of a political party in a British colony in East Africa called Tanganyika, had just come from London, where the British colonial secretary had rejected his case for Britain loosening its hold on the colony.

"It's a tragic state of affairs," Nyerere told me, "because the British government has an attitude that in effect says, 'There's no trouble in Tanganyika--no Mau Mau there or anything of that sort. So why bother with it?"

That quotation is from a yellowed clipping in an old scrapbook of mine--a page one article in the January 1957 issue of *Work*.

Its headline, based on Nyerere's prediction, was: "Africa: Free in 30 Years."

As I wrote my article, Nyerere quickly added that the prediction "sounds absurd to many, especially to the white settlers in Tanganyika."

History Can Outpace Human Expectations

In fact, of course, freedom came much quicker than even Nyerere expected. In 1962, only five years after we spoke, Nyerere, head of the Tanganyika African National Union, became Prime Minister of the newly independent Tanganyika and then, three years later, after his country's union with nearby Zanzibar, President of the new state of Tanzania. He retired voluntarily in 1985.

In the article I mentioned Nyerere's early career as a teacher in a Catholic secondary school in Dar es Salaam, the capital, before he started devoting full time to politics. The obituary, from the *London Tablet*, emphasizes that throughout his adult life Nyerere "never ceased to be a teacher by temperament, mission, and title: he was always Mwalimu." After citing his political successes and failures, and his many talents (he translated two Shakespeare plays into Swahili), the article concludes with this tribute:

"It is, nevertheless, Nyerere's moral example which made him so exceptional, the image of a President standing patiently in a queue waiting to make his confession at the cathedral in Dar: a humble, intellectually open and ascetic teacher, the true Mwalimu. Unlike almost all the other successful political leaders of his generation in Africa, he was uncorrupted either by power or wealth....Gentle, humorous, radical, persistent, he remained the icon of a truly ecumenical Christian approach to politics and human development."

Although Tanganyika won independence and was therefore no longer under British colonial rule, not everything changed overnight.

There were some whites who did not accept the change and refused to treat black Africans and other non-whites as equals even in public places. They were a minority but they did exist.

Andrew Nyerere, the eldest son of President Julius Nyerere and my schoolmate at Tambaza High School in Dar es Salaam from 1969 to 1970, told me about one such incident when I was writing a book, *Nyerere and Africa: End of an Era: Expanded Edition*, after I contacted him to find out if he had something to say that I could add to the book. As he stated in his letter in 2003:

> As you remember, Sheikh Amri Abeid was the first mayor of Dar es Salaam. Soon after independence, the mayor went to Palm Beach Hotel (near our high school, Tambaza, in Upanga). There was a sign at the hotel which clearly stated: 'No Africans and dogs allowed inside.' He was blocked from entering the hotel, and said in protest, 'But I am the Mayor.' Still he was told, 'You will not get in.'
> Shortly thereafter, the owner of the hotel was given 48 hours to leave the country. When the nationalization exercise began (in 1967), that hotel was the first to be nationalized.

But in spite of such incidents, and they were rare, race relations were good in general, in fact very good sometimes, as they were before independence.

For the vast majority of Tanganyikans of all races, including non-citizens, life in general went on as before as if no major political changes had taken place in the country ending colonial rule.

Even during the struggle for independence indignities of colour bar experienced by Africans now and then, here and there, did not fuel animosity towards whites among Africans to make them rebellious.

There was potential for revolt just like in any situation, anywhere, when people are demanding basic human rights and those demands are not met. But in the case of Tanganyika, conditions were no close to what they were in apartheid South Africa; nor was land alienation as serious or widespread as it was in Kenya, especially in the Central Province where the Kikuyu revolted against the British.

There were, however, incidents in Tanganyika which clearly showed that fundamental change was needed if the different races were to live in harmony.

Nyerere himself was involved in one such incident in the fifties (and there were others) just before he formally began to campaign for independence; he was already, even by then, the most prominent African leader in Tanganyika as president of the Tanganyika African Association (TAA) which was transformed into TANU in 1954. As Colin Legum, a South African of British descent who knew and interviewed many African leaders including Nyerere and Nkrumah, stated in a chapter, "The Goal of an Egalitarian Society," he contributed to a book, *Mwalimu: The Influence of Nyerere*:

> I was privileged to meet Nyerere while he was still a young teacher in short trousers at the very beginning of his political career, and to engage in private conversations with him since the early 1950s.
>
> My very first encounter in 1953 taught me something about his calm authority in the face of racism in colonial Tanganyika.
>
> I had arranged a meeting with four leaders of the nascent nationalist movement at the Old Africa Hotel in Dar es Salaam. We sat at a table on the pavement and ordered five beers, but before we could lift our glasses an African waiter rushed up and whipped away all the glasses except mine.
>
> I rose to protest to the white manager, but Nyerere restrained me. 'I'm glad it happened,' he said, ' now you can go and tell your friend Sir Edward Twining [the governor at the time] how things are in this country.'
>
> His manner was light and amusing, with no hint of anger.

This incident demonstrates one simple truth about Tanganyika in the fifties and throughout the entire colonial period under British rule.

It was not a rigidly segregated society; and whatever racial separation existed was in most cases voluntary and not strictly enforced even by convention.

There were no laws against racial integration. Had there been such laws, Colin Legum would not even have thought about going to the white manager to protest against what happened to his African colleagues whose glasses of beer were taken away by an African waiter at the Old Africa Hotel in Dar es Salaam.

Had this been apartheid South Africa, or had Tanganyika been a segregated society in the legal sense, separating the races, Nyerere and other Africans who were with him on that day would not have entered the Old Africa Hotel without being arrested. And their sympathetic friend, Colin Legum, who had invited them, would have been arrested as well, not only for defying convention but for breaking the law.

But the incident also showed that without fundamental change in the system, there would be trouble in the country even with Nyerere as the leader of those campaigning for independence.

After independence, Nyerere remained restrained in the conduct of national affairs and earned a reputation as a tolerant leader. But he also had a reputation of being tough and uncompromising on matters of principle especially involving equality.

One of his major achievements was containing and neutralizing radical elements in the ruling party who wanted to marginalize racial minorities in national life, forcing them to live on the periphery of the mainstream.

There were even those who would have resorted to outright expulsion of these minorities, if they had the power to do so, the way Idi Amin did in Uganda ten years later when he expelled Asians including Ugandan citizens of Asian origin. Nyerere was the only African leader who publicly denounced Amin and called him a racist because of what he did.

Fortunately, there were no racial tensions in Tanganyika after independence, earning the country a reputation as one of the most peaceful on the continent and tolerant of racial minorities.

But although the people celebrated independence and were glad to be masters of their own destiny as a nation, they did not see any dramatic improvement in their lives as many of them had expected.

Such changes don't come overnight, yet there were many people who had very high expectations, thinking that their lives would dramatically improve soon after the end of colonial rule. But that was not the case.

However, this was offset by the fact that there was a major achievement in one area, "overnight." The prophets of doom who had predicted racial conflict or some kind of civil strife soon after independence were proved wrong.

I remember a few years after independence that there were still some signs on toilets saying "Africans." I remember one very well at the bus station of the East African Railways & Harbours Corporation in Mbeya. No one took it down. It was simply ignored.

Although it reminded one of a bygone era and symbolized the subordinate status of Africans during colonial rule when they were not welcome in some places including a few hotels and clubs which had signs saying "Europeans," it did not inspire the kind of outrage - if any - some people might have expected from Africans after Tanganyika won independence.

There were Africans who simply accepted the status quo

during colonial rule; there were those who simply ignored it; and there were, of course, those who were determined to change it.

But even those who sought changes in the status quo were no more hostile towards whites than those who did not after the country won independence. And that was one of the biggest achievements of the independence struggle, making it possible for people of all races to live in harmony.

Many whites who left Tanganyika after independence did so for economic reasons mainly because of the economic policies which deprived them of their property and even means of livelihood especially after the country adopted socialism in 1967 and not because they were targeted as whites.

Many Africans who owned a lot of land and even more than one house for rent also lost most of their property and were equally bitter because of such stringent measures designed, rightly or wrongly, to reduce income disparities and gaps between the rich and the poor in the quest for socialist transformation of the country.

It was the most ambitious exercise in social engineering in the history of post-colonial Africa launched only five years after Tanganyika won independence. But it also proved to be a disastrous failure in terms of economic development as the economy virtually came to a grinding halt in the mid- and late seventies, less than 10 years after the government enunciated its socialist policies embodied in the Arusha Declaration of February 1967.

Socialism and Africanization were some of the main reasons why many whites left or were forced to leave Tanganyika and later Tanzania.

When Tanganyika won independence in 1961, it had about 22,000 white settlers, mostly British; a significant number of Germans, some Dutch including Boers from South Africa and others. And Kenya had about 66,000 whites, mostly British including members of the British aristocracy, at independence in 1963. It also had a significant number of Boers, or Afrikaners, from South Africa who founded the town of Eldoret in the Western Highlands in the Great Rift Valley.

Robin Johnson, whom I mentioned earlier, was typical of the British settlers who had established themselves in East Africa, determined to make it their permanent home as civil servants working for the colonial government or as farmers or something else.

In fact, a significant number of them were born in Kenya or Tanganyika. Some came from South Africa and others from as far away as Australia and New Zealand. And many, or their children and grandchildren, are still there today in different parts Kenya and what is Tanzania today.

Some of the settlers who acquired large tracts of land were members of the British aristocracy, probably the last people who would think of relinquishing power to Africans one day. Johnson himself gave up his job as a civil servant and took up farming. He was the District Commissioner (D.C.) of Kongwa in the Central Province in Tanganyika during the ill-fated groundnut scheme that was intended to produce groundnuts on a commercial scale. The scheme was a disaster. He was later assigned to Arusha in northern Tanganyika, what was then called the Northern Province:

> Robin himself was becoming increasingly interested in Tanganyika's long-term future. He felt if he became a farmer, like his father before him, and thereby rooted in the soil, he could play a more permanent role in the country's development than permitted to a transitory civil servant.
>
> He had met David Stirling, the founder of the Capricorn Africa Society, and felt that his policy of common citizenship and a multi-racial form of government might well be the answer for the East African states where Africans, though still backward, must soon begin to move politically, and there was a small settled European and Asian community.
>
> He resigned from the Colonial Service in 1951 when he was alloted one of the Ol Molog farms [in Arusha in northern Tanganyika]. His colleagues thought he was quite mad. Surely every diligent Administrative Officer only had one goal in life - to be a Governor finally. How irresponsible of Robin carelessly to throw that chance away.

Just as some white settlers were planning to turn East Africa into their permanent home dominated by whites, Africans were at the same time proceeding on a parallel path towards mobilization of political forces transcending race in their quest for independence and did not, for one moment, believe that the multiracial government proposed by some of the more liberal members of the settler community would ever include them as equal partners. And they spoke from experience.

The multiracial Legislative Councils, known as LEGCO,

which existed during colonial rule were dominated by whites. And whatever was proposed by the colonial authorities for the future would have proceeded along the same lines. Universal adult suffrage, a cardinal principle cherished in every democratic society, was totally out of the question in this dispensation.

Many of the settlers were, of course, aware of the political awakening and agitation that was taking place but did not believe that the people of Kenya and Tanganyika would demand or win independence within a decade or so. Even some of the African leaders themselves said their countries would not win independence until the 1980s.

The British colonial office suggested that if independence ever came to Tanganyika, it would be in 1985. Britain had to have some kind of timetable - although only theoretically - since Tanganyika was not a typical colony, like Kenya, but a trusteeship territory under UN mandate, with Britain playing the role of "Big Brother" to guide the country towards independence on terms stipulated by the United Nations.

Yet the UN itself was not seriously concerned about freedom and independence for Africans without being pushed by African leaders who included Julius Nyerere as the pre-eminent African leader in Tanganyika.

In fact, political awakening among Africans had already been going on for quite some time long before the "halcyon days" of colonial rule in the 1950s. And Julius Nyerere played a critical role at a very early age in galvanizing his colleagues into action, despite his humility. As Chief Abdallah Said Fundikira, who became one of the first cabinet members after independence, said about what type of person Nyerere was in those days: "If you want the truth, one did not particularly notice Nyerere."

He was talking about the time when Nyerere entered Makerere University College at the age of 22 after attending secondary school in Tabora, in western Tanganyika, the hometown of Fundikira, chief of the Nyamwezi tribe, one of the largest in Tanzania with more than one million people today.

Chief Abdallah Said Fundikira (2 February 1921 – 6 August 2007). He was appointed member of parliament by President Benjamin Mkapa in 2005.

It was when he was at Makerere that his leadership qualities came to be noticed when he formed the Tanganyika Welfare Association intended to help the small number of students from Tanganyika to work together as a collective entity for their own well-being. It was not a political organization but had the potential to become one.

The welfare association soon forged ties and eventually merged with the Tanganyika African Association (TAA), an organization founded by African civil servants in Tanganyika in 1929, to address their problems. But they had to operate within prescribed limits, as defined by the colonial authorities who said the association could only deal with welfare problems; nothing political.

Nyerere and his colleagues wanted the association to fight discrimination against the African civil servants who were being paid less than their European counterparts. It was a "welfare" problem, but with profound implications, hardly indistinguishable from political demands. He later described these "welfare" demands as "the politics of sheer complaints" which did not address the fundamental problem of inequity of power between Africans and Europeans.

But he wanted the colonial authorities to pay attention to demands by Africans in order to bring about fundamental change in this asymmetrical relationship that had existed since the colonialists took over Tanganyika before he was born. As he recalled those days: "When I was born, there was not a single person who questioned why we were being ruled. And if my father had heard that we wanted changes, he would have asked me, 'What do you think you can do, you small silly boy?'"

But nothing could dissuade him from his commitment to justice, no matter what the cost. And much as his father would have been apprehensive of the situation, had he lived long enough to discuss the matter with his son after he became mature, Nyerere knew that nothing was going to change until Africans themselves did something to bring about change. His mother was equally apprehensive and probably even more so. She was quoted as saying:

> I began to know about Julius' activities when he was teaching at Pugu College [St. Francis College] in 1952. Everyday, a man called Dossa Aziz came to our house and he would talk with Julius for a long time. One day I overheard them talking about taking over the government from Europeans.
>
> I became afraid. Later I asked Julius if what I heard was true. When he said yes, I became more frightened. I told him what he was doing was bad. God had given him a good job and now he wanted to spoil it. But he said that what he was doing would benefit not only us but everyone in the country.

Nyerere had just returned to Tanganyika in October 1952 after three years at Edinburgh University in Scotland where he was admitted in October 1949. He earned a master's degree in economics and history, and also studied philosophy.

The fifties was a critical decade in the struggle for independence in Tanganyika. It was the decade when TANU (Tanganyika African National Union), the party that led Tanganyika to independence, was formed.

It was also the decade in which the colonial government tried to neutralize TANU, as much as the British colonial authorities tried to do to KANU (Kenya African National Union) in neighbouring Kenya when they arrested and imprisoned Jomo Kenyatta and other leaders in 1952 And it was the last decade of colonial rule in both colonies.

Before the 1958-1959 general election in Tanganyika, the British colonial government launched a harassment campaign to discredit and if possible destroy TANU. Nyerere was banned from making public speeches; he was accused of libel and put on trial; and twelve branches of TANU were closed down.

The banning of Nyerere came after a highly successful campaign across the country to get support for TANU and for his campaign for independence. He travelled to all parts of Tanganyika, to every province, in a battered Land Rover which belonged to his compatriot Dossa Aziz who gave the vehicle to TANU to help with the independence campaign, and was able to build, with his colleagues, the party's membership to unprecedented levels. Just within a year, TANU had 250,000 members.

It was during one of these campaign trips that I saw Nyerere for the first time when he came to address a mass rally in Tukuyu in the late 1950s; riding in the same Land Rover that had taken him to all parts of Tanganyika before.

I remember that day well. He wore a light green shirt and rode, standing, in the back of the Land Rover, waving at the crowd that had gathered to welcome him when he first arrived to address a mass rally at a football (soccer) field in Tukuyu one afternoon.

Although he was committed to non-violence, the colonial authorities claimed that some of his speeches were highly inflammatory; but, to the people of Tanganyika, they were highly inspiring. And because of this he was banned, in early 1957, from making public speeches.

Yet he remained unperturbed. As he told a correspondent of *The New York Times* in Dar es Salaam, Tanganyika, on March 31, 1957: "I am a troublemaker, because I believe in human rights strongly enough to be one."

Earlier in the same year he had written an article published in the *Tanganyika Standard* which two district commissioners (D.Cs, as we called them, and as they also called themselves) complained about, claiming Nyerere had libelled them; twelve years later, I became a news reporter of the same newspaper.

Nyerere during the sixties as leader of Tanganyika.

Nyerere also said although TANU was committed to non-violence, the nationalist movement would resort to civil disobedience to achieve its goals; and, by implication, to violence if necessary, if there was no other option left in pursuit of independence. And his trial gave the colonial authorities the opportunity to learn more about him.

The trial was a turning point in the history of TANU and of the country as a whole. A reporter of *Drum* magazine was one of those who covered the trial. He had the following to say in the November 1958 edition when the proceedings took place in Dar es Salaam, the capital:

> The sun has not yet risen but hundreds of people are already gathered round the small courthouse in Dar es Salaam.
>
> Some have come from distant villages, with blankets and cooking utensils as if for a camping holiday. They have been in Dar es Salaam for more than a week at the trial of the president of the Tanganyika African National Union (TANU), Julius Nyerere, on a charge of criminal libel. It was alleged that Nyerere wrote an article in which two district commissioners were libelled.
>
> Police constables line the streets round the court and a riot squad stands ready nearby in case of trouble. As the time draws near for the court to open, the crowds jostle and shove for the best positions.
>
> The trial has been a mixture of exciting arguments, explosive surprises and hours of dullness.
>
> Mr. Pritt - Nyerere's counsel - insisted that the two commissioners should

be called to give evidence. He accused the government of prosecuting Nyerere without investigating his allegations. The government was telling the world that if anybody said anything against a district commissioner, he could be put into prison for saying what was true.

When Nyerere gave evidence, he took full responsibility for the article and said that he had written it to draw the attention of the government to certain complaints. He was followed by three witnesses who spoke of 'injustices' they had suffered at the hands of the the two district commissioners.

Halfway through the proceedings, the attorney-general appeared in court in person to announce on behalf of the Crown that it would not continue with the counts concerning one of the commissioners.

Now, on the last day of the show, the stars begin to arrive: Mr. Summerfield, the chief prosecutor; Mr. N.M. Rattansey, defence counsel who is assisting the famous British QC, Mr. D.N. Pritt. Mr. Nyerere, wearing a green bush shirt, follows later. He smiles and waves as members of the crowd cheer him.

The curtain goes up with the arrival of Mr. L.A. Davies, the magistrate. The court is packed. Everyone is tense and hushed.

The magistrate sums up then comes to judgement - Nyerere is found guilty!

The magistrate, in passing sentence, says he has formed the impression that Nyerere is an extremely intelligent and responsible man. He fines Nyerere Pounds 150 or six months. The money is raised by locals and the Kenya defence fund.

In the election that followed in 1958 - 1959, TANU won a landslide victory. It won 29 out of 30 seats in the general election. As Nyerere said after the victory, "Independence will follow as surely as the tick birds follow the rhino."

In March 1959, Sir Richard Turnbull, the last governor of Tanganyika, appointed to his 12-member cabinet five TANU members who had been elected to the Legislative Council (LEGCO), the colonial legislature which was established in 1926.

In 1958 Sir Richard Turnbull had succeeded Sir Edward Twining as governor of Tanganyika. He had previously served as chief colonial secretary in Kenya during the Emergency, which was during the Mau Mau uprising, and had witnessed first-hand the violence and bloodshed which resulted from the colonial government's refusal to address the grievances of the masses over land and working conditions and from its unwillingness to accept demands by Africans for freedom and independence. He did not want to see that happen in Tanganyika when he became governor.

Initially, the colonial government in Tanganyika wanted only three ministerial posts to be filled by LEGCO members, but

Nyerere insisted on having a majority from his victorious party, TANU.

During the election, TANU had sponsored an Asian and a European for each seat, besides its own African candidates. The two also won.

Governor Turnbull conceded and appointed three Africans, one Asian and one European to the cabinet to represent TANU and the majority of the voters who had voted for TANU candidates.

It was also in the same month, March 1959, that Nyerere was interviewed by *Drum* and spoke about the future of Tanganyika after it won independence, which was almost three years away:

> Tanganyika will be the first, most truly multiracial democratic country in Africa.
>
> When we get our freedom, the light of a true multiracial democracy will be put high upon the top of the highest mountain, on Kilimanjaro, for all to see, particularly South Africa and America.
>
> Tanganyika will offer the people of those countries free entry, without passports, to come and see real democracy at work.
>
> As long as we do not have a popular government elected by the people on democratic principles, we will strive for freedom from any kind of domination.
>
> We regard the [UN] Trusteeship as part of a scheme to keep Tanganyika under the British Crown indefinitely. The greatest enemy of our vision is the Colonial Office.
>
> But Tanganyika cannot be freed by drawing up resolutions or by tabulating long catalogues of the evils of colonialism. Nor do we find it enough to tell rulers to quit Tanganyika. It will be freed only by action, and likewise the whole of Africa.
>
> Continued colonialism is preventing investment in this country. Germany, for example, cannot invest money as long as the British are still here.
>
> I agree that the country lacks technicians. So what? Shall we give the British another 40 years to train them? How many have they trained in the past 40 years?
>
> As far as money for a self-governing Tanganyika is concerned, Tanganyika has not been receiving much money from the British taxpayer at all. For the past 11 years, Tanganyika has only received Pounds 9 million. I can raise 100 times that within a year if it becomes necessary.
>
> I believe that the continued, not existence, but citizenship of the European would be taken for granted had not the white man created a Kenya, a Central Africa [the Central African Federation of Rhodesia and Nyasaland], a South Africa and other similar places and situations.
>
> African nationalism is not anti-white but simply anti-colonialist. When George Washington fought the imperialists, he was fighting for the divine right of Americans to govern themselves; he was not fighting colour.

> The white man wants to live in Africa on his terms. He must dominate and be recognised by the rest of the inhabitants of this continent as their natural master and superior. But that we cannot accept. What we are after is fellow citizenship, and that is exactly what is frightening the white man.
>
> The question is not whether we must get rid of whites, but whether they must get rid of themselves. Whites can no longer dominate in Africa. That dream is gone. Africa must be governed by Africans in the future.
>
> Whether an immigrant African will have an equal part to play in this free Africa depends upon him and him alone. In Tanganyika, we are determined to demonstrate to the whole of Africa that democracy is the only answer.
>
> We are being held back, not by local Europeans, but by the Colonial Office and, I believe, by Europeans in neighbouring countries, who are frightened of the possibility of success in Tanganyika.

A month later in April 1959, after the interview with *Drum*, Nyerere went to Zanzibar to attend a meeting of the Pan-African Freedom Movement of Eastern and Central Africa, popularly known as PAFMECA when I was growing up in Tanganyika, and of which he had previously been elected president.

One of the most prominent Tanganyikan leaders of PAFMECA was John Mwakangale from my home district, Rungwe. He was also one of the TANU members who was elected as a member of the colonial legislature, LEGCO.

Mwakangale was also the leader who was assigned by the government of Tanganyika to receive Nelson Mandela in Mbeya when Mandela came to Tanganyika for the first time in 1962, soon after we won independence from Britain, as Mandela states in his book, *Long Walk to Freedom*.

While in Zanzibar, Nyerere played a critical role in forging unity between some Africans and some Arabs, bringing their political parties closer together in the struggle for independence and for the sake of national unity.

Speaking at a meeting of PAFMECA in Nairobi, Kenya, in September 1959, he made it clear that Europeans and Asians as well as others were welcome to remain in Africa as equal citizens after independence was achieved.

The following month, in October, he gave a speech in the Tanganyika colonial legislature (LEGCO) in which he uttered these famous words:

> We will light a candle on mount Kilimanjaro which will shine beyond our borders, giving hope where there is despair, love where there is hate, and

diginity where before there was only humiliation.

In December 1959, Britain's new Colonial Secretary Ian McLeod announced that Tanganyika would be given virtual home rule towards the end of 1960 under a constitution that would guarantee an African majority in the colonial legislature, LEGCO. However, Nyerere criticized the retention of income and literacy qualifications as eligibility criteria for voters and for membership in the legislature.

He was also critical of the reservation of a specific number of seats in LEGCO for the European and Asian minorities. But he saw the concessions by the British colonial rulers, including new constitutional provisions guaranteeing a legislature with an African majority, as a step towards independence in the not-so-distant future.

In the elections of August 1960, TANU again won by a landslide, 70 out of 71 seats, its biggest victory so far and less than a year before independence.

Nyerere was sworn in as chief minister of government under a new constitution, but the governor, Sir Richard Turnbull, continued to hold certain veto powers, although rarely exercised, if at all, since it was now inevitable that Tanganyika would soon be independent.

Tanganyika's first independence cabinet in December 1961. Some of the cabinet members I (the author) can easily identify are, in front row from left to right: Job Lusinde, Oscar Kambona, Rashidi Kawawa, and Julius Nyerere. Also standing behind between Kambona and Kawawa is Derek Bryceson; and behind Bryceson is Amir H. Jamal.

Nyerere's status as the leader of Tanganyika was formally acknowledged even outside the colony, for example, when he attended a meeting of British Commonwealth prime ministers in London in March 1961, although Tanganyika was still not independent.

But in his capacity as prime minister of Tanganyika since the colony won internal self-government, hence *de facto* head of government in lieu of the governor, he joined other African leaders in denouncing the apartheid regime of South Africa and its racist policies and declared that if South Africa remained a member of the Commonwealth, Tanganyika would not join the Commonwealth; a position he had articulated earlier in August 1960 when he said: "To vote South Africa in, is to vote us out."

Julius Nyerere soon after independence with his secretary and personal assistant Joan Wicken. She died in Britain in 2004.

South Africa withdrew from the Commonwealth, and many people attribute this to Nyerere's uncompromising stand on the apartheid regime and his threat to keep Tanganyika out of the Commonwealth had South Africa remained a member.

Following a constitutional conference in March 1961, Colonial Secretary Ian McLeod announced that Tanganyika would have internal self-government on May 1, and full independence in December in the same year.

On 9 December 1961, Tanganyika became independent. A few days later, it was unanimously accepted as the 104th member of the United Nations. Nyerere was 39 years old and, at that time, the youngest national leader in the world.

On 9 January 1962, Nyerere resigned as prime minister and appointed Rashidi Kawawa, minister without portfolio, as his successor. He said he resigned to rebuild the party which had lost its focus and to give the country a new purpose now that independence had been won.

But with independence came responsibilities. It was no easy task. So much lay ahead.

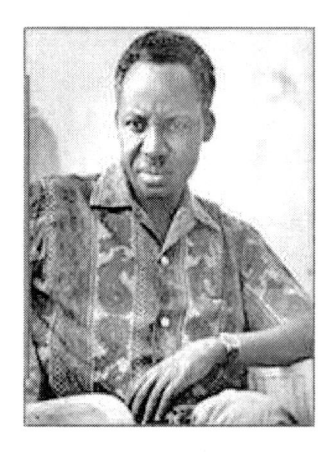

President Julius Nyerere, official portrait, 1965. He died in a London hospital on 14 October 1999. He was 77. Under Nyerere, Tanzania was the first country in Africa to have universal primary education. It had the highest literacy rate in Africa, more than 90 percent, and one of the highest in the world.

Rosemary Nyerere, one of President Nyerere's daughters who once served as a nominated member of parliament.

Charles Makongoro Nyerere, one of Nyerere's sons, also a member of parliament. He was once elected and later nominated as a member.

Nyerere in his latter years as president of Tanzania.

Mama Maria Nyerere, widow of President Nyerere, receiving blankets for orphaned children in the village of Butiama, Nyerere's home village, in Mara Region. Nyerere refused to have Maria Nyerere addressed as the First Lady and said she should be simply addressed as Mrs. Maria Nyerere. He also refused to be addressed, Sir, and said people should simply address him as Mwalimu, meaning teacher, since he was a former secondary school teacher before he went into politics.

Part II:

Narratives from the White Settler Community and Others in Colonial Tanganyika in the Fifties

THIS part of the book is a compilation of narratives from different individuals who lived in colonial Tanganyika in the fifties.

Some of them lived in Tanganyika even before then, in the forties and even in the thirties. And there are those who lived in Tanganyika in the sixties after independence. But they all have one thing in common. They lived in Tanganyika in the fifties, and almost all were members of the white settler community. Back then they were simply called white settlers.

Also almost all of them were British since Tanganyika was a British colony. Technically, it was a UN trusteeship territory over which the British had the mandate to rule and "guide" the indigenous people to independence. Tanganyikans who were colonial subjects included people of Asian and Arab descent.

Although Tanganyika was a trusteeship under the United Nations, it was nonetheless, for all practical purposes, just another British colony like neighbouring Kenya and all the other British territories on the continent which were under British tutelage.

The people whose narratives are presented here lived in different parts of the world when I got in touch with them to ask them how life was in colonial Tanganyika in the fifties, a decade which is the focus of this study and which was an integral part of my formative years when I was growing up. I was under ten years old then.

Almost all of them have fond memories of that period in their lives, although some of them differ in their perceptions and interpretations of the nature of colonial rule and the kind of impact it had on African lives.

I found them in Britain, Australia, New Zealand, the United States, Canada, South Africa and other parts of the world including Italy where they migrated after Tanganyika won independence. I found both men and women.

The fields in which they were involved covered the entire range or spectrum of professional life. Some of them were professors, scientists - I remember one entomologist in Australia and an airline pilot in the UK; consultants, businessmen, executives, historians, writers, accountants, and computer experts, to name only a few among the various fields they were involved in.

Some were still working when I got in touch with them. Many others were retired, among whom were two or three who told me they were writing their memoirs.

But they all remembered the years they spent in Tanganyika and other parts of Africa, especially East Africa. Many of them were born and brought up in Tanganyika.

And there were those who never left. They stayed in Africa. The ones who stayed migrated mainly to South Africa and what was then Rhodesia, which is Zimbabwe today. South Africa attracted the largest number of white immigrants among all the African countries.

But there were those who never left Tanganyika permanently. Some of them are still there today. And there are those who moved to Kenya, a neighbouring country with a significant number of whites, mostly of British origin including some members of the British aristocracy. Some may have moved from Tanganyika to Uganda, another neighbouring country, but for those who wanted to stay in East Africa, Kenya was their favourite destination and new home.

Some of those who left Tanganyika returned to Africa at different times through the years even if they did not stay there. Many continue to do so, visiting friends and the old places where they once lived and called home during those days of colonial rule.

And many of them were nostalgic about "the good ol' days" when life was simpler, and the people, friendlier. But as members of the white settler community in a country which was under British colonial rule, and with most of them being British themselves, life was simpler for them in another respect and not just in the "spartan" sense. They enjoyed privileges Africans, and sometimes even Asians and Arabs, only dreamt of in a country ruled and dominated by whites.

Many of them had vivid memories of the places they lived, and the schools they attended, and even the playmates they had when they were growing up in colonial Tanganyika.

They lived in places such as Lushoto in the Usambara mountains in northeastern Tanganyika; Moshi close to the slopes of the majestic Mount Kilimanjaro also in the northeast; Arusha in the north; Mbeya in the Southern Highlands Province; Nachingwea in what was then the Southern Province; Kongwa and Dodoma in the Central Province; Urambo in the Western Province; Mwanza in the Lake Province; and Dar es Salaam, the capital, in the Coast Province, among other places in this vast East African country.

And they attended schools which were almost exclusively white, except for a few Asian students in some of the schools. The schools they attended included the famous St. Michael's and St. George's in Iringa in the Southern Highlands Province; Lushoto Prep School, Kongwa School, Nachingwea School, Mbeya School, Arusha School, and St. Joseph Convent in Dar es Salaam. There were other schools they attended in Moshi, Mwanza, Dodoma and Tabora.

Some of them were also taught at home. And many of them were also sent to Britain for their education and further studies not available at the European schools in colonial Tanganyika. They were also sent to Britain for other reasons as well, including cultural, to be immersed in the culture of their mother country and to get better education in British schools which, rightly or wrongly, may have been considered to be academically superior to the ones in colonial Tanganyika and whose teachers were British themselves. And the school in Tanganyika were patterned after British schools as were those attended by Africans before and after independence.

In my search around the world, I found many ex-Tanganyikans (as many also call themselves) who were around my age and therefore couldn't remember much about colonial Tanganyika in the fifties the way they would have had they been older. I also found those who were old enough to be my parents.

I asked them a number of questions and told them they were free to say whatever they wanted to say without fear of offending anyone.

The purpose is to show how life really was in colonial Tanganyika in those days from their perspective as Europeans or whites who, by virtue of their race, were also members of a privileged class even if they were not colonial rulers themselves, as indeed most of them weren't.

Whether or not they succeeded in doing so is for the reader to decide. What is presented here is what they said in their own words in response to my questions. It is reproduced verbatim. Nothing has been edited.

Here are the questions I asked them. There were other questions I asked them individually when I was communicating with them and you will be able to see some of them in the letters included here.

But they all revolved around one central theme: how life was in colonial Tanganyika in the fifties, as has been elaborated in the following questions:

*How would you describe life in Tanganyika in the fifties or in any period during colonial rule?

*What is it that you particularly miss about those days? Can you give a few examples?

*What was the level of interaction between the Europeans and the indigenous people, black Africans?

*What was your overall impression of colonial Tanganyika in terms of life? Was life good? Or was it hard? How did you view the colonial authorities? As oppressors or benevolent rulers?

*Was any kind of racial integration allowed anywhere? There were signs in Tanganyika and Kenya saying, "Europeans," "Asians," and "Africans," in compliance with government policy sanctioning racial separation or what was also known as colour bar.

Were there many Europeans who were opposed to this? What was the general attitude among a significant number of them towards racial separation?

*Did you detect any hostility, overt or covert, towards whites on the part of Africans in general and among some of the indigenous people you or some of the people you knew interacted with? For example, house servants, co-workers even if subordinates.

*Was there any or much sympathy among a significant number of whites for the nationalist aspirations of the Africans in their quest for independence?

*What was the general attitude among many whites towards the native population? Paternalistic, compassionate, indifferent, hostile, overtly racist or what?

*Were there any or a significant number of whites who felt that the colonial government was not doing or had not done enough for the people of Tanganyika, especially native Africans, in the areas of health, education, infrastructural development, and political representation at the local and national levels?

*How do you remember those days? With fondness, nostalgia or not? And why?

*What was it that you liked the most about Tanganyika?

*When political agitation and the campaign for independence started, how did members of the white settler community feel or react?

Were they shocked or surprised? Did they accept it as something inevitable that was bound to happen one day anyway?

*Were you and many Europeans apprehensive about their future in an independent Tanganyika under African leadership even if it included whites and Asians as Nyerere did in his independence cabinet and thereafter?

His cabinet members included Derek Bryceson and Dr. Leader Stirling, of British origin; his secretary and personal assistant throughout his tenure as president of Tanganyika, later Tanzania, for almost 25 years, Joan Wicken, was British; Tanganyika's attorney-general soon after independence and thereafter, Roland Brown, was British. He also had Tanzanians of Asian and Arab origin in his cabinet, including Amir H. Jamal of Indian descent. Those are only a few examples.

*Did any of that allay fears among many whites that they would not be discriminated against under predominantly black leadership?

*What was the biggest fear among Europeans in Tanganyika after the country won independence? That they would lose the privileges they had always taken for granted during colonial rule or that they would become victims of reverse racial discrimination after Africans took over at the end of colonial rule?

*Were racial disparities in the standard of living, employment, wages and political representation a matter of concern among a significant number of the white settlers in colonial Tanganyika? Or did most of them see this simply as the way things ought to be for racial and other reasons?

*What vivid memories do you have of the places in which you lived in Tanganyika, and of your interactions with Africans?

Can you give some examples including stories of such

personal experiences or encounters? And of some of the exciting or trying moments you had including hardship?

And feel to share whatever other experiences you may have had in those days which I can include in my book, if you want me to.

Also let me know if you want me to use your name and mention where you live without necessarily naming the city or the town in which you currently reside. I can mention only the country or nothing at all. It's up to you.

Some people were uncomfortable or were not interested in addressing political subjects about Tanganyika during the colonial era. Most of the people whom I got in touch with were too young to know anything about politics. Many of them were around my age. I was under 10 years old in the fifties and was no more politically conscious than than they were.

But to accommodate everybody, I had to come up with other questions dealing with subjects I felt most of the ex-Tanganyikans living in different parts of the world wouldn't mind discussing with me and sent the following letter:

I have changed the focus of my work and am concentrating on stories of human interest, although not to the total exclusion of political commentary, since some people want to address that aspect as well; it's up to you.

This is what I have re-written; it includes some details about me and the project I'm working on:

I come from Mbeya Region in the Southern Highlands and would like to know how you remember Tanganyika in the fifties. I now live in the United States and have lived here for 33 years. I am a published author.

I was born in Kigoma in western Tanganyika on 4 October 1949 and lived in other parts of the country including Ujiji, Morogoro, Mbeya, and Rungwe District near Tukuyu when I was growing up.

Before I was born, my parents also lived in Amani, Handeni, Muheza, and Kilosa. My father worked as a medical assistant for the colonial government.

I'm writing a book about Tanganyika in the fifties which is partly autobiographical since those were my formative years, as were the early sixties. I want to include other people's perspectives on how life was back then to complement my narrative and analysis. I want this to be an authentic record of what people remember about those days, written in their own words.

Whether your recollections are those of an adult or a child, it makes no difference. They are equally important to me. If you were only a child in the fifties, share those memories with me on how you remember Tanganyika.

How was life in Tanganyika in the fifties? What fond memories do you have? Can you give some examples? Do you also remember some of the unpleasant experiences you had? Where did you live in Tanganyika and where did you go to school?

How would you describe life in Tanganyika in the fifties in general?

What is it that you particularly miss about those days? Can you give a few examples?

What was your overall impression of Tanganyika as a country and in terms of life and its people? Was life good? Or was it hard? Do you remember some of the inconveniences, for example lack of electricity, plumbing, etc., and how they affected your lives?

How do you remember those days? With fondness, nostalgia or not? And why?

What was it that you liked the most about Tanganyika? What vivid memories do you have of the places in which you lived in Tanganyika, and of your interactions with Africans, Asians and Arabs, if any and where - at home or other places? Can you give some examples including stories of such personal experiences or encounters? And of some of the exciting or trying moments you had including hardship?

Feel free to share any other experiences you had in those days.

I would also like to use some of the old photos you may have from those days if you can scan them and email them to me. They should be no bigger than 6" x 9", the size of my book.

Also let me know if I can use your name, and mention where you live, or if you want the information to be published anonymously.

Asante sana.

Kwaheri.

Godfrey Mwakikagile

***

From Anne Vanessa Maher, Italy, 15 March 2006:

Dear Godfrey,

Thank you for your letter and your very interesting and searching questions.

I have been trying to think how to reply and find it very difficult, partly because it takes time and specially as it is hard to make a selection of memories for someone else's publication.

Probably you have nearly finished your book. If you were interested and the deadline has passed I could try anyway to answer you later on for your own interest and mine.

I was at Mbeya, Kongwa and Iringa and was born in Kitale, Kenya, where my father was in the colonial agricultural dept, set up a Soil Conservation Service and trained African and British technical officers for it against considerable opposition from his own dept.

In Tanzania he worked for the OFC to wind up the(failed) groundnut scheme, making about 10,000 staff redundant including himself. Later he leased land to farm for a few years in
Uwemba, near Njombe, and then our parents left Tanzania for a job in Iran. (We stayed on in school for O-levels and at prizegiving shook hands with Julius Nyerere).

The kind of experience we had as children is certainly coloured by all this and my father's " liberal" views but they were colonial times so there is a lot of making sensc of things to be done.

It is difficult to select of one's own experience what is publishable and in what context.

Anyway, I wish you all the best with the book.

Yours sincerely

Vanessa Maher

-----Messaggio originale-----
Da: godfrey [mailto:godfrey@...
Inviato: venerdì 13 gennaio 2006 19.53
A: vanessamaher@...
Oggetto: Tanganyika in the fifties

Dear Vanessa,

I come from Mbeya Region in the Southern Highlands and would like to know how you remember Tanganyika in the fifties.

I now live in the United States and have lived here for 33 years. I am a published author.

I found your name and address when I was doing some research on the Internet about Mbeya School and St. Michael's and St. George's and about Tanganyika in the fifties. I stumbled upon a web site, www.iringa.org, where I found your name and email address.

I was born in Kigoma in western Tanganyika on 4 October 1949 and lived in other parts of the country including Ujiji, Morogoro, Mbeya, and Rungwe District near Tukuyu when I was growing up.

Before I was born, my parents also lived in Amani, Handeni, Muheza, and Kilosa.

My father worked as a medical assistant for the colonial government. When he was at Amani, he worked at the Amani Research Institute. As you probably know, it was established by the German colonial rulers and became world-famous as a tropical research institute.

I'm writing a book about Tanganyika in the fifties which is partly autobiographical since those were my formative years, as were the early sixties.

I want to include other people's perspectives on how life was back then to complement my narrative and analysis. I want this to be an authentic record of what people remember about those days, written in their own words.

Whether your recollections are those of an adult or of a child, it makes no difference. They are equally important to me. If you were only a child in the fifties, share those memories with me on how you remember Tanganyika.

How was life in Tanganyika in the fifties? What fond memories do you have? Can you give some examples? Do you also remember some of the unpleasant experiences you had?

Where did you live in Tanganyika and where did you go to school?

How would you describe life in Tanganyika in the fifties in general? What is it that you particularly miss about those days? Can you give a few examples?

What was your overall impression of Tanganyika as a country and in terms of life and its people? Was life good? Or was it hard? Do you remember some of the inconveniences, for example lack of electricity, plumbing, etc., and how they affected your lives?

How do you remember those days? With fondness, nostalgia or not? And why?

What was it that you liked the most about Tanganyika? What vivid memories do you have of the places in which you lived in Tanganyika, and of your interactions with Africans, Asians and Arabs, if any and where - at home or other places? Can you give some examples including stories of such personal experiences or encounters? And of some of the exciting or trying moments you had including hardship?

Feel free to share any other experiences you had in those days. I would also like to use some of the old photos you may have from those days if you can scan them and email them to me. They should be no bigger than 6" x 9", the size of my book. Also let me know if I can use your name or if you want the information you give me to be published anonymously.

Best regards,

Godfrey Mwakikagile

***

From Rosemary, 15 March 2006

Hello Godfrey,

Thanks for your prompt reply and for the info on the new book.

When I was driving home last night I was thinking about what you wrote regarding the economy in the seventies and eighties.

I left TZ in 1961 but I have been back for a few weeks in 1964, 76, 77, 80, 86 and 89/90.

In 1980 one couldn't even find the basic necessities such as soap, toothpaste, light bulbs, etc.; these items, however, could be found on the black market.

The Kenya border was closed due to the break up over the East African Community but nevertheless even simple bibis became ingenious. Just to give you an example, some women I knew would make some kind of fried pancakes, melt the Swiss chocolate which I had brought out from Europe, and glaze some of the pancakes with the chocolate.

They would set off early Saturday morning, cross the border on foot and sell these pancakes at the market. The ones coated with chocolate would obviously be more expensive. With the Kenya shillings they earned, they would buy the basic necessities in the Kenyan village, cross the border again on foot and then return home in the afternoon.

Anyway, coming back to the time limit, I think 2 weeks should be sufficient. I can only write in my spare time (which isn't much).

Is that OK?

Best regards,

Rosemary

***

Pam Sparrow, Gloucestershire, UK, 1 May 2006

Dear Godfrey

This is a set of reminiscences from a 90 year old Dick Crow. I scanned it, but could not edit so have re-typed them as he typed them except I have corrected a few points of grammar and punctuation.

You may well get some from a Les Ottoway in New Zealand as I sent him all the details and he said he would see what he could do and send them directly to you.

I am trying to get someone else to provide some along with his wife, but not sure if he will in fact play ball. Am seeing John and Peggy next Sunday to see what he has to say then.

I am still formulating mine, I was hoping to be able to get quite a few early photos but that ------- brother of mine refuses to let me have any of Dad's photo albums, so will have to rely on the odd few that I have of my own.

I don't know what sort of system you have for accepting attachments etc but I can only send a max of 10MB so maybe Dick's with the cartoons will have to come in bits. The cartoons may not transmit well as the copies he gave me are not good and are in blue, I have had to adjust the brightness etc. Let me know and if necessary I will have to get the originals from him and scan them myself here. Total attachments are within my allowance.

Hope all is well.

Kind regards

Pam

***

From Pam Sparrow, 6 May 2006

Dear Godfrey,

Just had an e-mail from Dick asking for a paragraph (attached) to be inserted to what he has already provided. I remembered it just in time to save it as rtf.

He wants it inserted AFTER the para starting "Cricket was a

popular game ... ending ... the many Asian teams." and before the para starting "In the days just after the war...

Also, he has quite a large website with various memoirs, the Merchant Navy Officers' website, and he has sent these latest ones off for inclusion on that and has asked me to let you know what he has done.

If you go to merchantnavyofficers.com you will find all his writings and also there you can view some of his paintings. He has given me a couple though not of ships and he has just painted 2 using 2 photos I sent him as a base.

Hope you are able to enjoy the w/e and relax. Now I am retired w/es don't have quite the same relevance as before. Spring has arrived and everywhere is looking nicely green at last after a very long and very cold winter. Thursday was unbelievably hot though today it is distinctly chilly.

Must off to bed.

Hope all's well.

Regards

Pam

Tanganyika in the 1940s/50s

By Richard Crow

Reminiscences of a marine pilot serving initially with the Tanganyika Railways and Ports Services which, after amalgamation with the Kenya and Uganda Railways, became the Tanganyika arm of the East African Railways and Harbours, mostly in the port and capital, Dar-es-Salaam, but also in the port of Tanga during the late 1940s and 1950s.

Between the wars and until the early 1960s Tanganyika was a U.N. Trust Territory administered by Great Britain.

It was run on the conventional colonial paternalistic pattern headed by the Governor from Government House in the capital at Dar-es-Salaam.

Between the wars it was a very much male-orientated society as very few of the junior officials or commercial staff were accompanied by wives. This was reflected by the type of housing provided both by

Government and commercial firms for their ex-patriate staff.

The East African Railways and Harbours was a quasi-Government organisation, the ex-patriate officers were recruited through the Colonial Office and enjoyed salary scales and service conditions, i.e. three year tours of duty and home leave, similar to Government officials yet dealt on a commercial basis in the port department with the ships of many nationalities that traded with Tanganyika and their Agents, so that they to some extent bridged the gap between the Official and Commercial communities.

The Government officials were mostly British and the commercials comprised mostly of British and other Europeans and many Asian traders. The work force was predominantly African with European and Asian supervision.

Whilst English was the official language Swahili was the lingua franca of the country and for government officials a degree of proficiency in it was necessary for promotion.

A series of topical cartoons by Geoff Green were published in the 1950s in the local newspaper, the *Tanganyika Standard* which highlighted and reflected every day life as seen from the Government and Commercial view points.

The trials and tribulations suffered by Government officials swotting for their Swahili examinations, offset by the award of a Cost of Living Allowance to Government salaries, and the romantic repercussions occasioned by Flag Showing visit of a R.N. ship were all grist to the cartoonist's mill.

A few typical cartoons are attached and some of the figures depicted could, at the time be related to well known personalities in the communities.

For example, the toga clad figure wearing an official plumed solar topee presiding over the arena in which the Commercials are being fed to the Cost of Living lions bears a striking resemblance to His Excellency Sir Edward Twining, the then Governor of Tanganyika.

Membership of the Dar-es-Salaam Club was restricted to European males and even in the 50s ladies were only admitted to parts of the club on special occasions and then as far as some of the "old timers" were concerned on sufferance.

Many of the single Europeans, or those whose wives were on home leave, would use the Club's facilities for lunch and dinner etc. The Gymkhana Sports Club with its cricket, tennis, golf and other sporting facilities had a more liberal attitude and allowed ladies as members. Cricket was a popular game, the Europeans had the country-wide club of the Tanganyikan Twigas (giraffes) matched by a similar Asian club, the Tanganyikan Tembos (elephants), whilst at a local level the European Sports Club and the Railways and Harbours Clubs fielded teams that played the many Asian teams.

In those days, just after the war, such luxuries as refrigerators and other electrical appliances, new cars and many other manufactured goods were often in short supply. It must have been quite a shock for my wife when she arrived in 1949 from the UK to such conditions, especially as she found that, as a junior pilot our quarters were across the harbour entrance at the Signal Station and had no electric power or lighting.

We were dependent on a wood fired dover stove for cooking although our African "mpishi" (cook) did very well with it. However, my wife bought herself a Valor kerosene oil cooker but it was not very successful as the sea breezes at the Signal Station kept causing it to "blackout" covering everything with oily smuts.

She did produce some rock cakes with it once, but unfortunately they were true to their name and when I dropped one it nearly cracked the cement floor. We gave it to our dog who received it with delight, but when she thought we were not looking went and buried it in the garden.

Lighting was also by kerosene Alladin pressure lamps (which gave out a lot of heat in the hot season) and of course we could not have electric fans.

Our first motor car was a 1938 Morris 12 which had been cannibalised with lorry door handles and Standard car wheels. It sometimes refused to start, broke down at inconvenient moments and on one occasion the steering wheel came off in my hand, but my wife and I, and the dog, had more fun with that old car than any of the new models we had later. It cost just £100 in 1949 and we sold it for £75 two years later when we went on home (UK) leave, so it was certainly also value for money.

The local butcher's "duka" (shop) was painted red, presumably to hide the bloodstains of the animals slaughtered in the early hours and in the days before we had a refrigerator we used to buy our fresh meat at daybreak. The meat was still warm and the joints were often unconventional cuts although we found fillet steak was usually a good buy.

There were no such things as T.V., videos etc and the old-fashioned wireless, or radio, was the only contact with the outside world and often a not very good contact at that, so people were in general dependent on making their own entertainment.

As was to be expected in a tropical climate, sailing and swimming were popular past-times catered for by yacht clubs and organised outings and picnics to off-shore islands and other beaches were popular at the week-ends. Friends within their own circles and level would give, and reciprocate, with small dinner parties or with children's outings and such occasions often helped to make useful official or commercial contacts.

I recall that at one such dinner party my wife was complimented on the flower arrangement of her dinner table."Oh, that was Ali, (our house-boy) he got them for me" she replied. "And I can guess where he got them from," one guest remarked, "Government House has masses of those flowers in their gardens".

Horrified, my wife denied that her Ali would steal from G.H., but next week she was mortified to find that the truth was even worse. Going for a walk with a friend who was staying with us, they passed a small Missionary Cemetery nearby where some of the graves were decorated with the self same flowers.

Even in the ports of Dar-es-Salaam and Tanga there was a certain amount of wild-life. During my first tour of duty as the junior pilot we lived in the Signal Station flat at the other side of the harbour entrance and a large baboon took up residence in our garden one week-end.

On another occasion my wife was advised to stay indoors, and keep her dog in too, as a lion had been reported in the area, this was just after a resident only a mile away had his dog seized from the verandah of his house by a leopard. Snakes were usually quickly and effectively dealt with by the Africans.

One year when the rains failed hippopotami were found in the south creek of the harbour at Dar-es-Salaam and we had one in our garden at the port entrance. The following day whilst servicing the channel leading lights I was startled by a hippo-potamus rising up out of the water at the edge of the reef in front of me.

That afternoon I was piloting an American ship to sea and remarked to the Captain, "There's a hippo in the channel just here". Right on cue, disturbed by the beat of the ship's propeller it stood up again.

A fair-sized crocodile was shot in the harbour at Tanga while I was there. My wife, convalescing up-country at The Lawns Hotel, Lushoto, shooed away what she thought was a large ridgeback dog from outside her banda (hut/room), but when it turned round and looked at her she realised that it was an adult lioness. She quickly retreated to her room and spent the rest of the night there.

One of the principal exports of Tanganyika in those days was sisal, especially through the smaller northern port of Tanga. The sisal plants, after being decorticated and processed, were baled in large oblong bales for shipment.

The sisal industry was controlled by the Tanganyika Sisal Growers Association and Mr Hitchcock was the President. The only other name I recall in that connection was Bennett of the Amboni Estates near Tanga. Each year they held a grand *white*, or at the very least *black* tie dinner function at which senior Government officials and the managers of the main commercial firms were guests.

When I was Pilot i/c Tanga in 1952 or 3 I was a guest at the dinner which was held that year aboard the British India Steam Navigation Co brand new passenger vessel, the "S.S. Kenya". His Excellency Sir Edward Twining, Governor of Tanganyika, was the guest of honour on that occasion and Captain Hamley, the Superintendent of Ports, was the senior representative of the E.A.R. & H.

Coffee grown in the Arusha area was another export from Tanga.

The ill-fated Groundnuts Scheme after WW II did provide a welcome impetus to the trade of Tanganyika and a new port, Mtwara, was built in the Southern Province.

Until the 50s Dar-es-Salaam port had no deep water quays so that vessels had to be manoeuvred under their own power and anchored in the harbour to discharge and load their cargoes by lighters.

In the early 50s, after the amalgamation of the railways and ports into the East African Railways and Harbours, a ship handling steam tug was provided for Dar-es-Salaam which greatly expedited ship movements and enabled moorings to be laid in the south creek to accommodate larger vessels and an oil tanker berth for the importation of fuel oil for the railways.

By the late 1950s deep water quays had also been built at Dar-es-Salaam thus providing the port with all the up-to-date facilities expected of a modern port.

The central line railway to Kigoma provided a link to the Belgian Congo from Dar-es-Salaam via Lake Tanganyika which allowed trade to and from the Congo to a Belgian enclave, "The Bel Base", in the port of Dar-es-Salaam.

Dhows from the Persian Gulf have traded with the west coast of India and the east coast of Africa since biblical times. "Dhow" is really a generic word similar to our "ship", but there are many different types. On the Indian coast you will find "baggalas" with more pronounced and ornate poops, influenced no doubt by the 18th century European ships then familiar to those waters.

In East Africa the large sea-going dhows were usually "booms". They were of a more traditional design with one or two masts and lateen sails. The larger ones with their raked stems and sterns could be well over 100 feet in length. Originally they would have sailed down from the Gulf with the northeast monsoon and return with the first of the southwest monsoons. Nowadays most of them are fitted with diesel engines.

They would bring from the Gulf such goods as Persian carpets, (I still have one such at home bought from an Arab dhow in Dar-es-Salaam) and return with biriti poles (there is little timber in the Gulf) and no doubt in the old days a full quota of slaves.

Bagamoyo, a road-stead port some miles north of Dar-es-Salaam used to be the principal port of the area before Dar was established in the 19th century. It was also at the end of one of the slave trails to the interior and when my wife and I visited it in 1950 the remains of the slave pens could be clearly seen and there was an abundance of mango trees planted, we were told, by the slavers to feed their unfortunate captives.

Tanganyika was, I think in general more rural and African than neighbouring Kenya with its larger towns, commercial atmosphere, tourists and numerous white settlers.

Life in Tanganyika seemed to be lived at a slower pace and the Tanganyikan Africans were also, in my experience less sophisticated, more rustic and more susceptible to old traditions and superstitions than their more city-dwelling counterparts in Kenya. For example, one day our shamba (garden) boy and some of the younger boat boys did not turn up for work and Kombo, the head signalman, told me that they were afraid to leave their village as they were frightened that the *Mumiani* would get them.

He explained that the *mumiani* were bloodsuckers who originated long ago in the days of the Portuguese occupation of the East African coast. (The standard Swahili/English dictionary defines "mumiani, a dark coloured gum-like substance used by some Arabs, Indian and Swahili for medicinal purposes"). I was later told that the scare was started when the Sewa Haji Hospital sent out a team seeking volunteer blood donors to replenish its blood bank. Q.E.D.

On another occasion a rather deadly snake of, I believe, the mamba family was killed at the Signal Station. The Africans cut its head off and buried it and the body separately quite some distance apart otherwise, they told my wife, the two parts would join up at sunset and chase them for killing it.

In the circumstances I suppose it is not surprising that after the amalgamation of the Railways and Harbours our colleagues in the big port of Mombasa used to refer to Dar-es-Salaam as "The Sleepy Hollow".

***

From Pam Sparrow, 8 May 2006:

Dear Godfrey,

Glad the insertion arrived safely and await to know when the book is on Amazon. I use Amazon quite a lot.

If you go to www.womens-institute.org.uk/gloucestershire our website, Who's Who, and scroll down you will see a picture of me if you are interested to see what the typist is like! Not quite the best photo.

Pam Sparrow

I have only just gone on to the County Executive cttee, March, and when I volunteered to go on no-one told me that I would have to be chairman of a county sub-committee, so it came as rather a shock.

At the election meeting I was nominated for Public Affairs and am quite happy with that as I am interested in the environment etc., but don't chair my first meeting until next Monday and will be glad when it is under the belt.

I was on another sub-committee for a couple of years but have come off that now I am on P.A. as it is too much to be on 2 plus Exec.

Hope the attached photo arrives OK, taken on my self timer digi camera on 23rd April in Bournemouth. It is my latest toy and this was the first self timer picture I had taken. I bought it to complement my film SLR camera as I am going to Greenland in July for my retirement holiday to me and need to have lots oif pictures as next February am giving a talk to a W.I. on the trip.

L-R: Tony Pike, his sister Pam Nightingale, Dick Crow, Kevin Patience, Bill Brummage, me on the floor. We were all in EA so had a wonderful curry chakula cooked by Pam with much chatter and reminiscences.

Must away to bed another busy day tomorrow, you are probably just finishing work now, do you work or are you retired too?

Kwaheri, salaams

Pam

***

From Pam Sparrow, 9 May 2006

Dear Godfrey,

The attachment I sent with this e-mail originally was a photo of the 6 of us in Bournemouth on 23rd April and I think was jpg so don't think I can do it as rtf.

So, if you cannot open that, if I scan any old EAs photos I have you will have the same problem.

Perhaps I could compress the attached picture or re-size it, would that help?

Don't mind you using the photo of me in the book but is not perhaps the best, will send a picture of me taken when about 2 and then you can compare the intervening 60+ years! I have the latest one on the computer so if you have a problem taking it off the website I could send that.

Will look at my albums and see what suitable photos there are and perhaps include them in my write up.

Another damp drizzley day here again, no chance of getting the washing hung out and dried. Bother.

Must away and collect up everything for my class.

Kind regards

Pam

From: godfrey <godfrey@...
To: pam sparrow <pamsparrow44@...
Subject: Re: General
Date: Mon, 08 May 2006 19:15:08 -0400

Dear Pam,

Thank you for very much your email. The insertion arrived safely and I'll definitely let you know when the book is on amazon.com.

But I have the same problem with the attachment you sent me today: unable to open doc. Please send it as rtf so that I can use it in the book.

I went to the web site and saw your photo. It's beautiful! Can I use it in the book?

I can copy it from the web site and paste it in the manuscript. And I'm sure you have been doing a wonderful job as chairman! They saw talent in you right away!

It's nice to know that you're still active in your retirement years. I'm also "retired" but in a different way. I work full-time as a writer but still have a long way to go in terms of success! Most writers have other jobs. They need the income. So do I. But I have taken chances to be self-employed and work at home as a writer.

If you have some old photos from Tanganyika, feel free to scan and send some of them to me so that I can include them in the book, but only if you want me to. Otherwise, memoirs by themselves - the text - are fine. I don't have to have the photos but it would be nice to include them in the book.

It's around 7 p.m. here in the US (EST - Eastern Standard Time) and I have quite a few hours to go before I go to bed.

Best wishes,

Godfrey

***

From Pam Sparrow, 12 November 2006:

MEMORIES OF AN EAST AFRICAN CHILDHOOD TANGANYIKA AND KENYA 1944-1954

Pamela Sparrow nee Mostyn

"Why were you born in Africa?" asks my friend and I thought she was intelligent, to which I answered, "Well, my parents were there". However, I did really understand what she meant to say.

My Mother, Muriel Teitlebaum, was born in Essex, UK and went to Africa as a result of joke. Someone on her behalf answered a job advertisement for a dispenser in Dar-es-Salaam and Mum was the successful applicant.

So, in 1940 she set sail for East Africa travelling via The Cape and so running the gauntlet of the U-boat hunting packs in the Atlantic. She arrived in Durban and there had to wait a month before there was ship northbound for Dar-es-Salaam where she was to work in the dispensary of the Sewahaji Hospital which was the African and Asian hospital.

I remember the hospital as being a yellow building near a railway level crossing with a huge tree (probably a mongo tree) nearby and I know the hospital still exists but no doubt in a new location.

The pharmacist was Sydney Cox and after his wife Dorothy joined him from the UK the two families remained friends for over 50 years until after Sydney's death. I was the oldest of the 4 children.

My Father, Nigel Mostyn, was born in North London and in the war was called up, joining the North Staffordshire Regiment and was posted to Ethiopia to fight the Italian campaign. The regiment was attached to the KAR (King's African Rifles) and when de-mobbed in 1945 he joined the East African Railways & Harbours in the Stores Department being posted to Dar-es-Salaam, Tanga, Mombasa and Nairobi and remained in the department until he finally returned to the UK in about 1964

As was usual during war-time when service personnel away from home had leave, social events were arranged for them and local women were asked to volunteer as partners for the arranged dances etc.

The designated partner for my father was unable to fulfil this particular engagement and my Mother took her place. They were married in August 1943 and years later looking at the wedding photographs I felt so very sorry for Mum as all the guests were Dad's male army colleagues.

It must have been a sad day for Mum in a way not having her parents or sister with her on such an occasion and she did not even have any girl friends from Africa to be with her either.

Fifteen months later I was born in the German-built European Hospital along Ocean Road in Dar-es-Salaam for what was going to be a happy, carefree and privileged childhood until the age of ten.

With my father being away in Abyssinia I was about 4 months old before he saw me for the first time. Thirteen years later I had my tonsils removed whilst on a school summer holiday from the UK and the ward I was in was the labour ward when I was born

My first recollection is when I was about 2½ in Tanga and was nearly a tragic one. As was usual the ayah (nanny) was taking me and my brother, who was then about six months old, to the beach in the afternoon and we were walking on the inside of a right hand bend with a hedge and a sheer drop down to the beach to which we were heading. A lorry came round the bend towards us, the brakes failed and my brother, who fortunately was lying down in the pram, went underneath the lorry.

The Africans tried to extricate him from the tangled wreck of what had been the pram only to succeed in catching his legs against the hot exhaust pipe. As luck would have it our next door neighbour who was the doctor drove passed and was able to prevent the situation from being really tragic. I used to look at the photo of the pram and wonder how anyone could have survived in it.

Houses and gardens

We lived in many houses, at least 4 in Dar-es-Salaam alone because each time Dad was given promotion it meant the standard of the house improved along the quality of furniture.

On the coast the houses were mainly bungalows with deep overhanging eaves to keep out the sun and so keeping the building cool. The floors were red cardinal polished concrete with just a central rug or carpet and the dogs found this heaven as they would lie on the concrete on their stomachs with their legs stretched fore and aft trying to keep cool.

The windows were not glassed but were covered in what we called XPM, expanded metal. This was a largish diamond mesh of very strong metal which was secure from the point of view of preventing someone accessing the property but was nothing against the pole cat burglars. The thief would have a long pole which would easily go through the diamond mesh because at its widest it was about 2" and this would then be used to grab articles from the room.

So, it was always necessary to ensure small removable articles were either not in sight or within reach of the pole.

The only house we lived in when in Mombasa was in fact a two story one and the sitting room was upstairs with a balcony. Whether it was because the Tanganyika houses were pre-First World War German-built and the Kenya houses British-built, between the two wars and post 39-45, but the windows had horizontal louvered glass.

We lived in one house in Nairobi up a hill which we called El-Shack because of its construction. The house was built of corrugated iron and when it rained the noise was deafening and of all the houses we lived in it was the darkest, all the others being very light and airy. Being on a hill the front of the house was about 6' above the ground with a flight of fairly steep steps up to the veranda, thus making the underneath of the house a perfect play area for me and my brother.

Heaven alone knows what dudus (insects) and other livestock inhabited this area but we seemed to survive unscathed.

My father had obviously moved up the promotion ladder because our next Nairobi house was a bricks and mortar one, a lovely L-shaped bungalow with parquet floors which our poor dog found lethal as my brother and I would throw balls for her to chase along the passage and she slipped and slithered unable to gain a purchase on the polish and came to a Tom and Gerry halt to much laughter from us. In the sitting room there was a live fire because Nairobi is at an altitude of 5,500 feet and in the winter at night it became really quite cold.

All the houses had big gardens, though none of ours I seem to remember looked like an English garden even in Nairobi where the climate was more suited to horticulture. The grass was generally a very tough, almost spiky, sparse rye type and the flowers I remember most are the beautiful bougainvillea, the bright purple being the natural one, the delicate sweet smelling deciduous frangipani tree with its white four petaled short trumpet flowers with yellow centres. The "wood" of the frangipani is very soft and spongy thus making it a totally unsuitable tree for climbing.

There were the yellow trumpet flowers, hibiscus, cannas with all their rich earth colours and of course roses. With having such large gardens there were of course trees and I remember in Mombasa we had a huge mango tree but do not ever remember eating mangos from it. We also had a paw-paw tree just outside the kitchen door and what a joy it was to eat paw-paw for breakfast that had been picked only half an hour earlier.

Another fruit tree that also grew in the Mombasa garden was a guava and my mother went ballistic one day when she discovered that I had stripped the tree of all the fruit and eaten every one. I still love guava today.

In the Nairobi bungalow garden we had a banana palm but that never seemed to produce fruit or perhaps I was not there when it did and there was also a variety of blackberry which grew just outside my bedroom window. There was another shrub, the name of which I do not know, but it had the most wonderful small florets of exquisitely multi-coloured flowers and when each flower was over it turned into very hard round small green seed which we used to put into the ends of our bicycle pumps to use as pea-shooters. Probably highly dangerous but once again we survived unscathed.

Food

Food was always "fresh" as distinct from frozen as there were no domestic freezers in the 40s and 50s so shopping was done almost on a daily basis. There were of course refrigerators which were the size of large wardrobes as everything that was of a perishable nature had to be kept there. Other non-perishable foodstuffs were kept in meat safes. These were large cupboards covered in a fine wire mesh to protect against the flies on high legs which usually stood in containers of water to stop the ants climbing up the legs.

However, the water had to be regularly changed to prevent mosquitoes from breeding.

Other non-perishable items such as flour were kept in airtight containers but this did not prevent the flour weevil from penetrating and taking up residence so regular inspections had to be made and many a pound of flour was dumped because of an infestation.

There were of course the meat, grocer and green grocer shops etc usually run by Asians, but there were also the markets where all the foods could be purchased.

Meat could be questionable as to it variety and age and in Mombasa there was a notice outside a butcher announcing "Shoats" and no-one really ever discovered exactly what this specie was. Meat was not often naturally tender and we often used to say it had walked to the abattoir and to soften it the mpishi (cook) would have beat it tender and cook it for a long time.

There never seemed to be a shortage of local vegetable and the one thing I remember is the delicious smell of roasting mealie (corn cobs) on the braziers set up along the pavements by the Africans. Fruit was always plentiful with a wide variety of local fruit though of course there was little English fruit and I remember pleading with my mother to be allowed to eat an unpeeled apple.

One of the fruits that was regularly bought was ndimu (lime) and Mum would squeeze dozens of these so we could have fresh squeezed lime drink.

We lived off bananas, guava, pawpaw, mango, pinepapple, oranges and probably many other fruits.

Living on the coast of course there was plenty of samaki (fish) which boys would hawk around in baskets made from banana palm leaves on the backs of their bicycles and I remember my mother going through these baskets looking at the gills to see which were the brightest pink before buying.

Eggs were also hawked from the back of bicycles and I can see my mother now with a large jug of water dropping egg after egg into it to see which floated and which did not in order to get a dozen fresh ones. At two houses in Dar we did keep chickens but they had to be kept in large wire pens as protection from hawks and other birds of prey and were also prone to attacks from snakes.

One day my mother heard anguished cries from the Africans shouting "nyoka, nyoka" (snake, snake), there was one in the tree in the chicken run. Not one of the Africans would go near the run, Mum had to despatch the reptile

Water for consumption had to be boiled and filtered and it my mother's Sunday afternoon job to boil up gallon upon gallon of water which then had to be filtered in a large ceramic cylinder with 3 filter cones in it. However, before it could be filled with fresh water these cones had to be cleaned of the debris that had accumulated from the previous batch.

There was always plenty of water kept in the fridge for drinking and water for consumption included teeth cleaning. The only time raw tap water was used was for bathing.

Education

The academic year followed the calendar year and I remember in the January after I was 5 my mother asking me if I would like to go to school and replying that I would not. The reply I received was that I was going whether I like it or not, so that was that.

At that time we did not own a car and we lived on the outskirts of Dar, but our next-door neighbours owned a bull-nosed Morris with a dickie seat and Lady Muck was duly perched in said dickie and taken into Dar for school at the Burton Street primary school.

This building was a fine old colonial 2 storey one with a veranda around both floors. In the grounds at the back were other school "rooms", one was no more than a polished concrete floor with poles round the edge holding up a conical "makute" (I think makute is dried banana leaves) roof. This was in fact my first class room though there was another walled-in room which was subsequently another of my class rooms.

The one I remember most clearly is in the house itself because of one incident that took place.

We were I think all seated on the floor and the question asked was how many days are there in a year. I shot up my hand and Miss Cameron-Walker asked me for the answer which was incorrect. To my dying day I shall never forget her vengeful rebuke to me for putting up my hand when I did not know the correct answer and not to do it again unless I knew the answer.

In Mombasa the school was a modern one built as an open-centred rectangle with the corridor running on the inside of the open square. I was only there for little over a year as Dad was posted to Nairobi from Dar in June 1953 for a few months and then down to Mombasa from where we sailed just before Christmas 1954 for the UK where I was sent to boarding school for the rest of my school-days.

The school day started early because of the heat and then we all went home for about a 2-hour lunch and returned for a couple of hours. During this time there was "homework", we had little notebooks with all the words listed we had to learn to spell and my mother loved having her hair brushed, so I would brush her hair while she tested me on my spelling.

Sports days were always fun with many of them now considered old-fashioned activities such as the sack race: the egg and spoon race and the three-legged race, biting the bobbing apple hanging from a string. Of course the best was the Mums' and Dads' race.

Entertainment/Recreation

In those days entertainment was self made and as children I never seem to remember being bored. Television was still in its infancy even in the UK, and of course it was non-existent in Africa and to us children we had not heard of it.

My father had a colleague called Mr Tavee (I assume that is the spelling) and one day I was reading a paper magazine which I think was called something like *Picture Post* and on the front page was a large blurred photograph with the headline "T.V. goes under water for the first time".

"Oh look Mummy", I said, "Mr Tavee has gone under water". She then had to tell me about T.V.

We would listen to the wireless on the big Marconi set to the various children's programmes like Children's Hour and some being broadcast from the UK. Of course with the climate being as it was it was very much an outdoor life. On the coast of course there was plenty of swimming and in the afternoons the ayah would take us to the beach where we would meet up with all of our friends and play making sandcastles and swimming.

I remember in Dar-es-Salaam on Sunday afternoons the whole family would go out to Oyster Bay crossing on the way a small inlet crossed by a low bridge called Selander after a pioneer engineer and I loved to hear the whoosh-whoosh-whoosh as we sped passed the low pillars of the balustrade and today if I have the car window open I listen to the same whoosh sound of the oncoming cars and remember those journeys over Selander Bridge.

At Oyster Bay there was a small concrete swimming pool made into the rocks and we would play around in it followed by a picnic. When the tide came in the water would wash over the walls of the pool and so there would be a change of water.

In Mombasa there was the Florida Swimming Club which had a big pool built again into the rock and we used to sit on the high wall with our feet dangling over the sea.

There are two particular moments I remember at the Florida, one was when a few of us swam in the rain and is the only time I remember being blue with cold in Africa, what fun it was though being wet in the water and out of it.

The other was when I lost my bathing costume; my mother had made me a navy blue with large white dots 2 piece with rather voluminous pants and as I dived so these pants filled with water like a balloon and they floated to the surface where I hastily retrieved then when I surfaced.

In Nairobi play was rather different and it was a world of make-believe and we made our own games.

As Mombasa is a coral island there were no beaches and so people had to cross to the mainland either on the ferry south to Whitesands Hotel or north over the exciting floating bridge to Nyali. This bridge would be almost like a switch-back depending on the tide and it was always a thrill to hear the wooden slats of the bridge rattle as the car made its slow way over the humps created by the movement of the sea below.

The ferry was equally exciting as it was just a pontoon supported by a collar of oil drums making it float, there was no form of power other than manpower and hope that it would in fact reach the designated ramp the other side. Many a time the current carried this pontoon way off-course and then there was mayhem to get back to the correct position. There was even greater panic and mayhem when this drifting pontoon was in the way of an approaching ship either entering or leaving port. Getting on and off this ferry was an adventure in itself if in a car due to the fact that tide ruled how far up or down the concrete ramp the ferry rested.

If the tide was high then the ferry would be far enough up the ramp so as there not to be much of an angle as the cars drove onto the pontoon. However, if the tide was low it meant the angle for the cars was much steeper and sharper and many a cars scraped and crunched front and rear ends. Today there is a modern ferry with an engine.

Of course in Nairobi our Sunday afternoons were spent in the National Park when sometimes it was a rather unexciting visit if the animals decided not to show themselves, other times it would seem we had seen all the animals there.

In Dar I remember visiting one friend and we made a house by turning the dining chairs over and resting the backs against the dining table and covered it all with blankets and other such coverings, somewhat dark and hot but we had great fun.

There were also Brownies, Guides, Cubs and Scouts and I was a Sandpiper when a Brownie. I was also a member of the Junior Red Cross and to this day still have my badge and certificate. Years later I was to be a member of the adult Red Cross for 12 years.

Bonfire night was not really celebrated and the only year that I remember it being marked was during the height of the Mau Mau so of course fireworks were banned.

The only thing we could have were sparklers and I remember standing on the upstairs balcony of our house waving these sizzling sparklers around making patterns in the warm dark

African air and being entranced by the sight and sound of these very simple lights.

We were living in Dar-es-Salaam when I had my 5th birthday and for it was given a Phillips 2 wheeler bicycle. In the morning I remember my father taking me to the front door, looking down the steps to this gleaming black and chrome machine and saying he wondered what it was doing there. We then descended the steps for a closer inspection and he pointed to the P of the Phillips and said it must be for me as it had a P for Pamela.

The Railway Club was just round the corner which had a tennis court and I shall never forget it as in the evening I learnt to ride it with Mum hanging on to the saddle running for dear life puffing and panting whilst I peddled furiously shouting, "Mummy, let go, let go" until she had to because she could no longer keep up the pace.

I was off and away.

There was the cinema and on a Saturday morning there would be the children's programme when we all went, Europeans, Africans and Asians and I remember being very annoyed when the Asian and African children would whistle, hiss and boo at the relevant scenes.

I don't really remember anything particular about Christmas which of course we did celebrate. Of course for us it was midsummer so there was no cold, no snow, just hot sunshine.

I do remember one particular Christmas and that was the only one we spent in Mombasa, though why that specifically I do not know. The hall of the house was large with a highly polished red cardinal floor and just inside the front door there was this huge Christmas tree, where it came from or what its real species was I do not know.

The one thing I do remember are the barley twist red candles in butterfly clip holders and the smell of resin from the needles as they were singed by the candles. I suppose highly dangerous, but I still am taken back to that wonderful time when I smell the smell of burning pine needles, alas not that often in this day and age and health and safety etc. and artificial and fibre optic trees. I remember nothing of the food but assume we probably had turkey etc.

Miscellaneous Memories

Whilst in Dar the news came through that the King had died and I well remember being in the Dar bookshop on the Askari roundabout and seeing the neat notice on the counter saying THE KING IS DEAD.

In June 1953 we were on the move again, due to sail to Mombasa for Dad's next posting, soon after Coronation Day and I can see Dad now with his head in wooden packing cases packing up and the last thing to be packed was the old Marconi wireless which crackled out the service from London.

In the event we had to stay another week or so as there was some problem with loading the ship and this meant that we were able to see the Coronation parade as it made its way along the harbour road (Secretariat Road) and the only particular memory I have of it was the Roland Emmet engine float and whenever I see a picture of a Roland Emmet engine my mind is always taken back to June 1953 in Dar-es-Salaam.

My idyllic and privileged childhood ended when we embarked in Mombasa on 20th December 1954 for the UK and it was during this voyage that I spent the happiest and most memorable Christmas of my life.

In the January of 1955 I was put into a boarding school and what a culture shock that was, not only the way of life, but arriving in a cold, damp, grey and miserable weathered country having three weeks earlier left brilliant sunshine and warmth.

Two of my life's great regrets are that I was not schooled in Africa and that I left when still so young.

***

From Pam Sparrow, 18 November 2006

Dear Godfrey,

I have re-edited the original draft as it needed honing and also I remembered more which I have added.

As you will see there are no photos in this one, but there are numbers indicating which ones relate to the paras., photos (hopefully) in a separate doc.

Let me know if both arrive OK, am doubtful about the photos though.

Don't know how you will have it set out, photos inc in the paras or together on separate pages.

Hope you don't think my ramblings are too long.

Regards

Pam

The following photos were sent by Pam Sparrow about her life in Tanganyika in the forties and fifties.

Aged 4 months with my father for the first time.

Aged 9 months with my mother at the Equator.

Aged 2 with my ayah (yaya) and Mitzi the dog.

Dar houses:

The house in Gerezani where I celebrated my 5th birthday.

12 Speke Street, Dar, 1959.

In 1971: The Kilimanjaro Hotel swimming pool is on the site of the house.

Mombasa: 1953 Kizingo Road.

1971

A garret loco.

Selander Bridge in Dar. On the right is the Indian Ocean.

The tennis court in Dar where I learnt to ride my new bicycle on my 5th birthday. (Photo taken in 1971 when visiting Dar).

The pontoon ferry in the 1950s without an engine.

The ferry now with an engine. Photo taken in 1971.

***

What A Life

Life in Tanganyika before it secured its independence was untamed and unpredictable, much like the children themselves, who were now being raised by their ...

The Evening Press, UK

First published Tuesday 4th Feb 2003.

JO HAYWOOD talks to Easingwold author Joyce Thackeray about her childhood in East Africa and the brutal slaying of her beloved mother.

"Just when I thought the good life would go on forever, my husband was told he had a year to live."

JOHN Thackeray died in 1997. After 35 very happy years together, his wife, Joyce, was understandably devastated. Her friends and family provided valuable support, but it was an unusual source of solace that really began to draw her out of her grief - her computer.

She decided to write a personal account of her life and soon found tapping out her thoughts on her new computer was a therapeutic pastime.

"You can bare your soul," said Joyce, of Apple Garth, Easingwold, whose autobiography, *The Woven Basket*, has just been published. "It's like talking to someone; a someone who is completely detached, who just sits and listens and allows you to cry without passing judgement.

"The experience was warming, exhausting and therapeutic. It helped me restore some emotional balance in my life."

And what a life it has been. Born in the Egyptian city of Alexandria, her father Basil was a strapping Coldstream Guard who, at six feet five inches tall, towered over her diminutive four feet eleven inch mother Matty, a Maltese woman five years his senior.

"She spoke seven languages fluently," said Joyce, "was fashionable and chic, and when she wore her elegant high heels she could just about make five feet two."

The family moved to East Africa when she and her sister Joan were very young. Her father had secured a post as a senior colonial prison officer at Kingolwira, near Morogoro in the foothills of the Uluguru mountains in southern Tanganyika.

Twins Martin and Mary expanded the expat clan in 1948 - the same year that tragedy struck with devastating swiftness.

During the afternoon of October 14, the children were out enjoying a breath of fresh air with their Ayah (native nanny) when they heard angry, raised voices in the house.

Joyce, then five, ran into the kitchen and found Luke, their head servant, clutching his chest with blood pouring between his fingers. As he sunk to the floor dying, he managed to say that

Joseph, a trusted prisoner allowed out to help with the gardening, had attacked him with a knife.

"His last words were for my mother," she said. "I ran towards the house and came face to face with Joseph, half naked and heavily bloodstained.

"I was unprepared for what I saw next. On the bedroom floor lay pools of blood, and in my eagerness to get to my mother's side I slipped and fell. Joan was at the top of the bed stroking Matty's hair."

Her mother had suffered severe face and throat lacerations. "Don't worry" were the last words she said to her girls before she died.

"It had not occurred to me at this point that she might die - mothers don't die," said Joyce. "I was sure my father would make her better when he came home."

The family returned to England for a while, but the lure of East Africa proved too strong and they set out on their travels again when Basil got a job at a new prison in Karanga.

Life in Tanganyika before it secured its independence was untamed and unpredictable, much like the children themselves, who were now being raised by their stepmother, Betty, along with their new brother, Peter.

"As children we were like the country we lived in, wild and free," said Joyce. "The loss of my mother was a traumatic experience in my young life, but the 1940s and 50s were generally wonderful.

"Growing up in the wild unknown, there was the freedom to travel and see wild game at close quarters before the advent of reserves and parks. My family grew up and experienced at first hand the warmth, culture and closeness of Africa's native people."

They also endured first-hand experiences with green mamba snakes, grunting warthogs, maniacal, laughing hyenas, and black centipedes which would fall dramatically into the bath after sneaking up the overflow pipe.

They saw many changes as Tanganyika struggled to gain its independence from the colonial power, changes that Joyce details in her book.

"My writing is not political, but it is interspersed with important political events," she said. "It is merely the story of a family growing up on the foothills of Mount Kilimanjaro, where we had the opportunity to meet many fascinating people, from island governors to tribal chiefs.

"It was a wonderful life, but not altogether an easy time. The wildness of the place brought its tragedies and sorrows, and there was always that feeling of trespassing into the unknown."

Joyce met John, her husband-to-be, when she was 14 and he was assistant superintendent of police in Tanganyika. He rejoined the RAF and they married five years later in England, before spending the next 22 years at various flying stations around the world.

They eventually settled in North Yorkshire, where Joyce trained as a nurse in the Friarage Hospital at Northallerton, John became a tutor at the Civil Defence College at Easingwold and their three sons were educated at Ashville College in Harrogate.

John never returned to East Africa, but Joyce managed to make a nostalgic 11-day trip "home" with her brothers and sisters in 2000.

She was perturbed to see how human habitation had taken over and the wild animals had been pushed into reserves and parks. But some things never change.

"The sight of the snow-capped peak of Kilimanjaro brought a lump to my throat," she said. "Perhaps there was not as much snow as I remember, but it was a magnificent and powerful sight nevertheless."

After such a childhood, service life, widowhood, the ups and downs of raising three boys and a successful foray into writing, what's next for Joyce?

"Funnily enough," she said. "I picture myself eventually looking out from some hotel balcony overlooking the great Rift Valley in Africa, watching the golden sunrise over the hill and uttering the words that Alice spoke in White Mischief, `Oh God, not another bloody beautiful day'."

Joyce Thackeray's autobiography, *The Woven Basket*, is published by Blackie & Co for £8.99. It is available at Borders in York, The White Rose bookshop in Thirsk, Northallerton Bookshop and Towlers in Easingwold.

***

Great North Road (GNR, Northern Rhodesia, Zambia) by Hurst and Blackett which was mainly about life in Tanganyika where he went after World War II as a public relations manager on the Groundnut Scheme. ...
www.greatnorthroad.org/bboard/archives.php?period=200506

Messageboard:

Tina,

I think there were two books titled *Lightest Africa* published around the same time (late fifties).
 That doesn't sound like a quote from my dad's book (*Lightest Africa* by Rodney Begg, published by Hurst and Blackett)which was mainly about life in Tanganyika where he went after World War 2 as a public relations manager on the Groundnut Scheme.
 It was a light-hearted account of life in Africa in those old colonial days, though I came across a copy recently and cringed at some of the stories, though I'm sure the racial overtones were not deliberate.

ZAdrian

Adrian Begg, Australia [Profile] [Contact]
Sunday, June 19th, 2005 at 08:02:29 (UTC)

Lightest Africa   Link
Reply
New

After Adrian's lively account I went looking for this book with the intriguing name and found the following quote from the author:

"I have called this book "Lightest Africa".
 When Stanley chose the title "Darkest Africa" for the accounts of his marvellous travels, he was thinking of the pygmies in the Ituro Forest and the immense herds of wild elephant and buffaloes in the limitless green savannah.

Nowadays the emphasis has been reversed and "Darkest Africa" implies the overcrowding and crime in the slums of Johannesburg's shanty town and the tragic plight of the Cape Coloureds, whereas "Lightest Africa" is concerned with the primitive unspoilt tribes in remote Karamoja, the snows of Kilimanjaro and the wonderful game reserves".

Tina Magee, United States [Profile] [Contact]
Sunday, June 19th, 2005 at 07:48:04 (UTC)

Sun, sardines and the Great North Road Link
Reply
New

Doug's mention of the sardine run kindles happy memories of a beach holiday at Isipingo, south of Durban.

It was 1950, I was nine, and we were living at Kongwa in Central Tanganyika. My dad, a keen but frustratingly inept fisherman, had read an article about the sardine run and the wondrous catches to be had as the big fish followed the sardines in to the Natal beaches.

Instead of going for our traditional holiday in England he rented a beach bungalow at Isipingo (straight out if Summer of '42) and we sailed on the BI ship, The Aronda, from Dar es Salaam to Durban.

We were going to get fit and bronzed in the South African sun, and live on fish. The sardines were there alright, and so were the big fish, but we weren't catching any.

The damned South Africans who were fishing alongside us--no doubt veterans of many a previous sardine run--were pulling in plenty. They would cast into the deep with a nonchalant flick of the wrist, sending their bait hundreds of metres out into the Indian Ocean, and moments later they would be reeling in another one for the record books. But not us. We didn't get any. Not one! Not even a sardine.

In the end dad got fed up and we went to stay at a resort in the Valley of a Thousand Hills, well away from the sea where there weren't any fish to tease us.

While we were in Durban dad bought an old Hudson

Commodore 8, a monster of a car, and decided that we would drive home to Tanganyika.

That was to be my first experience of the Great North Road though I came to know it well in later years when I was serving in the NRP at Nakonde, on the Northern Rhodesia/Tanganyika border.

In 1950 the drive from South Africa to Tanganyika was something of a foolhardy venture. Once you crossed into Southern Rhodesia the road was mostly unsealed except for tarmac strips in the centre, and we had a very old and overloaded car.

There were five of us (my parents, my grandmother, my brother and me) our luggage and several jerrycans of fuel. The Hudson was a thirsty beast and in those days petrol stations were few and far between.

After we crossed the Limpopo we drove through a bushfire that had already jumped the road a couple of times. Scary!

We made it safely and dad later related the adventure in a book he wrote called *Lightest Africa*. It was a long dusty, drive for a fish we never even caught but it was worth every minute of it for the experience.
Adrian

***

From Robi Rossi, Milano, Italy, 25 May 2006

Hello Godfrey.

I have to confess that I'm having a very difficult time getting through to you, for some unknown reason.

Message below is an example of what happens when I mail you. Have also tried using two other e-mail addresses of yours, found in you website, but it seems you don't receive those, either. Too bad.

This time around I'm mailing from my husband's email address and I really hope you receive this as it is my last hope.

Attached are my early, very early memoirs of life in Dar. I hope they will be of use to you. If so, you may use them as you will.

Just please let me know if you receive this, otherwise, keep smiling and all best.

Yours

Robi

First attempt at sending this to you failed, let's hope all ok this time around.

Robi Bertelé <robi_bertele@...> ha scritto: Data: Mon, 22 May 2006 18:01:14 +0200 (CEST)
Da: Robi Bertelé <robi_bertele@...>
Oggetto: Re: new book
A: godfrey <godfrey@...>

Ciao Godfrey.

I finally thought out a few points that may or may not be of interest to you. Please feel free to make use of anything you wish but I won't be offended if nothing gets utilised.

Going over those times has been such beneficial, therapeutic treatment for me as, other than snakes, I find I have only wonderful memories.

I'm sorry, I have no photos (no money in those days to buy cameras....).

You may also mention my name if necessary (Robi Rossi).

I still have not bought your book as I thought it best to get this out to you first, so as not to be influenced in any way.

Kwaheri rafiki. I wish you much satisfaction and success in your work.

All the best,
Robi

Godfrey <godfrey@...> ha scritto:

Hi Robi,

No problem. We all have things to do and sometimes don't even like doing things we have to do. We just want to relax. And sometimes we simply forget or just wait, and wait!

Thank you very much for your kind words and I hope that you'll jot down a few things for me. As I said, I'm going to write another book on the same subject including the sixties. But it won't be ready until next year.

Best regards.

Godfrey

Robi Bertelé wrote:

Grazie, Godfrey: you are too kind and generous over my laziness. Thank you also for updated info on book title and website.

All best

Robi

godfrey <godfrey@...> ha scritto:
Dear Robi,

Thank you very much for your response. I would have loved to have your input but that's no problem. I know you have other things to do. And you're not the only one who missed the "deadline." I didn't hear from a few others who had some information for me.

I hope that you'll contribute something towards completion of my next project. I'm going to write another book on the same subject. So if you think you can jot down a few things for me, go ahead and do that. But the book won't be ready until next year.

I would have waited longer but the book was getting too big and I had to stop. I had enough information for the first volume and am now ready for the next. This is a very interesting project and I'm very excted about it.

The link I sent you has just been updated.

Best regards.

Godfrey

Robi Bertelé wrote:

Godfrey, I feel very bad about having let you down by not sending an input for the book. I sincerely apologise and confess that neither do I have an excuse for this. I have just been unaccountably lazy.
Unlike me, it seems as though you have been inordinately busy and I am delighted that you have managed to obtain enough info to complete the book. I have'nt as yet been able to get into the site but shall keep trying.

I hope you forgive my remisses.

Yours

Robi

***

From Robi Rossi, Milano, Italy, 25 May 2005

My family moved to Dar es Salaam from Genova (Italy), in 1951 and we remained in Dar until 1967.
I was four years old when we arrived in Dar - very young, really, and yet some of the memories are so vivid. I shall jot down here what comes to mind, with attention given to the indications in your last email.

Unusual scent

Initially indefinable, but it permeated the air. Later we discovered that it was the aroma of spices, so characteristic to this part of the world. After all, Zanzibar, the Spice Island, is just a few miles east of Dar.

Even now, I could be blindfolded, kidnapped and taken to Dar or Zanzibar (I wish...!) and, upon arrival, would immediately recognise my whereabouts after my first breath.

(Expatriate) Men's day wear

This consisted of a white helmet (lined in green) and a white short-sleeved shirt and shorts. The shorts were stiff and wide and allowed just an inch of knee to appear before thick white cotton stockings took over the rest of the leg.

This was what the British had long decided was the right and practical "uniform" to be worn in the tropical heat of their African colonies. Most business men went around dressed like that during the day. Evening wear, of course, was very formal.

Hair

The colour and texture of my own straight, blonde hair elicited some excitement among Tanganyikan adults and totos alike.

Every time we ventured out of town, many of the natives would experience an irresistible attraction to come and "feel" my hair with their fingers. I would, of course, repay the compliment and stretch my own hand over their soft, woolly curls. The totos would love this innocent "touching" exchange.

Tanganyikans and Swahili

Our relationship with the local inhabitants, adults and totos alike, was easy-going and pleasant. Part of the reason for this I think is that Swahili, a delightfully musical language, is similar to Italian: words end with a vowel, a piece of cake for Italians to learn, as opposed to the British who never really mastered the pronunciation.

Most Italians spoke excellent Swahili, which made relationships with the Tanganyikans easy to knit and maintain.

When we lived in Mabibu, my Mother became the point of reference for many of the native families living around us, on issues involving family/medical/social aspects of daily life. Mum was asked to advise, to judge, to heal. She loved it!

Flora and fauna

Our family lived some miles out of Dar, in Mabibu, a place with a name and not much else, between Ubungo and Dar. The years that made up our life in Mabibu are an experience which will forever remain memorable.

There was a large house in Mabibu, surrounded by much land, which we rented and shared with another Italian family and, while the two Dads went out to work each day, the two Mums started a paw-paw shamba, employing shamba-boys armed with shovels and pangas.

The aim was to clear land and prepare it for the sowing of paw paw seeds and, once the seedlings appeared, keep these safe from the family of hippos that lived in the pond at the back of our house.

The hippos loved the paw paw seedlings and would come ashore on moonlit nights, invade the paw paw shamba and cause much havoc and destruction. So, we would often wake up in the middle of the night to shouts from our askari, "Kiboko! Kiboko!" and all the adults would run out armed with shot guns which they aimed in the air to frighten off the poor hippos.

We kids, forbidden to leave the house, would crane our necks from the burglar bars on the bedroom windows, hoping to catch a glimpse of the papa, mama and toto kibokos on the prowl. Great excitement!

The so-called paw paw plantation, however, was not a raving success.

When we first arrived in Tanganyika there was a huge demand on the pharmaceutical market for the white, milky substance that is produced by the green (unripe) paw paw, papayine. Once treated, the milky substance yielded a remedy for indigestion (something like Rennies, I suppose).

The clamouring demand for this product lasted right until our "manufacturing plant" was organised with (a) seedlings that finally bore paw paws (i.e. had not been attacked by happy hippos), (b) shamba boys that weren't too terrified of the snakes that infested our property, (c) special tools and instruments used to "milk" the green fruit and collect the milky substance, (d) a do-it-yourself oven to dry the paw paw milk and render it suitable for transportation, (e) a condescending Dad who would transport the product to the place of sale.

As I said, no sooner had we organised ourselves to perfection, the price for "papayine" dropped drastically and, much to the Mums' disappointment that was the end of that enterprise.

Mabibu was also the place where we obtained in-depth knowledge of mangoes. A large part of the property surrounding us had dozens and dozens of different species of mangoes and we quickly learnt the various ways of eating mangoes, depending on the particular species being dealt with.

The best way to savour the small, colourful peach-like species, is to bite the top off with your teeth and squeeze the whole bang lot into your mouth. If the fruit is of the proper degree of ripeness, you are left with the empty shell of the skin in your hands while the rest smoothly slithers into your mouth.

Naturally, it takes some practice to juggle the seed and flesh in such a way that the seed gets sucked clean without escaping the cavern of your mouth (or skidding down your throat).

But the joy derived from the release of the full, exotic flavour of the peach-mango is equivalent to seventh heaven.

We became very familiar with gecko lizards, ant lions, chameleons, bush-babies, monkeys and, unfortunately, snakes.
There were so many snakes whizzing around every which-where that we had to be very careful of where we put our feet both outside and inside the house.

Dad had given clear instructions on how we were to behave every time we came across a snake: remain absolutely still until the slithering creature decided to move on elsewhere. There was no danger that I would behave any different as every time I came across a snake I became petrified, literally, and would remain like that for a while.

I wasn't particularly fond of the iguanas that inhabited the large "hippo pond" at the back of our house, either. They liked to grab any of our dogs (of which we had many) who ventured too close to the pond, and try to drag them into the slimy waters.

Hardships

Being out in the bundu, Mabibu had neither running water nor electricity. However, because our parents never made a fuss about this, we never thought of it as an inconvenience.

Fresh, clean water was brought home once a week with a tanker-lorry. The water was poured from the lorry's tank into large metal drums sunk and buried into the earth inside our property (to keep the water cool). Only the tops of the drums were visible, and these had large, heavy wooden covers.

A pump was used to convey the water from the drums into the house for our daily needs (drinking water had to be boiled and filtered in a special ceramic filter prior to consumption). The pump, of course, ran on electricity which, in turn, was produced by means of a large, nasty, uncooperative machine. For a long time, we kids thought that the name of this machine was "Damnyouman".

You see, many attempts had to be made every night to get the generator running and, as mentioned above, it was always most disobliging in its start-up. Whichever Dad's turn it was to yank on the cord that started up the generator, he kept "coaxing" it on with colourful phrases, ranging from Italian to English to Swahili.

The "Damnyouman" mentioned above is a very polite translation of what actually flew over our ears as we crouched outside the generator room and killed ourselves giggling over our Dads' bad tempers.

School

School was the Primary School annexe of St. Joseph's Convent School, situated in Oyster Bay. Nothing particularly memorable about this except for this colourful group of children made up of an amazing number of races and religions that attended the school. It was wonderful.

For a long time I never understood anything that was being said around me, but then children are so inventive and sign-language became quite popular at least until we all became fluent in English.

"What was it that you liked the most about Tanganyika?"

You ask this, Godfrey, and my reply to this question was formulated a few years ago, AFTER having lived in various other African States:

Tanganyika in the 50s was a living paradise and the few of us who were priviledged enough to experience it, are all too aware of how much we owe to that country.

I attended high school in Kenya, met and married my husband in S. Africa, our sons were born in Zambia, we spent some years in Nigeria, but it is Tanganyika and its happy people I remember with most affection.

The standard answer to the question, "Habari ya siku minghi?" was, "Kazi minghi, juua kali, mshara kidogo", and it was always given with a big fat smile as if to say, "Well, it's all so difficult, but who cares? I'm alive and happy to see you".

How can one not fall in love with a Land that gives birth to such optimistic persons?

P.S. Please excuse all misspelling of Kiswahili terms. I learnt to speak the language by ear and such a long time has gone by since I last used it....

Robi

***

From Mark Evdemon, Pennsylvania, USA, 4 January 2006, in response to my email below:

Dear Mark,

I come from Tukuyu in what is now Mbeya Region. I also lived in Kigoma, Morogoro and Mbeya in the early fifties when I was under five years old. My parents lived in Handeni, Muheza, Amani, Kilosa and Tanga before I was born in Kigoma.

Can you tell me how life was in Tanganyika in the fifties and during colonial times in general? I want to write about those days focusing on the fifties. Any information even before the fifties would be helpful.

I learnt about you when I was doing some research on Mbeya school in the fifties.

Regards,

Godfrey Mwakikagile

***

Habari yako Godfrey.....I have forgotten most of my Swahili, not having used the language for some 45 years.

I have been to Morogoro, Handeni, Muheza,Tanga, Dar, Arusha, Moshi, etc.

About telling you of the colonial period of Tanganyika; maybe I will refer you to a brief page I made some years ago about some of my life. I made it mostly for my children to have something to see when I am gone. Any questions you might have, send them along.

I am from some 20 miles south east of Pittsburgh, PA. and have travelled all over the US. Last year I went to visit my brother for one month; he lives in the Pretoria area of South
Africa. Here's my memories page:
http://www.angelfire.com/pa5/markpa/

Keep in touch.........

Salaam.......Mark.

***

Mark Evdemon on his memories' page:
From Africa to the USA

12 February 1936 (Birthday)

I don't know exactly where I was born, whether in a hospital or at home. All I know is that we lived in Tanganyika (presently

Tanzania), East Africa.

My Father had a farm in the province of Mbugwe, in the district of Mbulu. Nice names, huh? Also, it was in darkest Africa. We walked around with lamps and flashlights. Not really; just kidding.

I had 2 older brothers, Photis and Panos (Pete) and younger sister, Stergia.

Anyway, the nearest town was Arusha, about 30 miles away.

My early memories are of a mud brick house, tamped dirt floor and a thatched roof. The kitchen area was an attached grass wall hut.

I recall one evening waking up to pots and pans banging around and all that noise was due to a hungry hyena scrounging around for food. There were lots of various wild animals and insects in the nearby bush country.

We slept under mosquito nets and took quinine pills to prevent malaria attacks from the swarms of mosquitoes.

The black people that lived in the area were generally friendly and several were employed by my Father for farm and house work.

My Dad had several guns and he often went hunting both as a sport and for financial reasons. One time as we were having lunch, we saw elephants uprooting some cotton plants and trampling a part of the farm. My Dad went after them with a gun and chased the elephants away by firing some shots into the air.

I didn't have toys to speak of. I played with whatever was handy and available. One of my "special" toys was catching dragon flies and tying a string around them and flying them about. They were my home made planes. Also, I was always interested in anything in the nature all around us.

One day a black man came to our home asking for help as he was attacked by a leopard and needed the wounds on his back treated with whatever medicines we had. My Mom took care of that and I am sure that he recovered well.

During one of the rainy seasons, a dry river bed flooded and sent a torrent of water all over the countryside. We had to have a small earthen dam built around our compound to keep the water out of the houses.

We did not have an automobile. The main road (a dirt road)

was several miles away and we had to camp on the side of the road and await a truck to come by in order to hitch a ride into town.

The first time I had a piece of chocolate, I was probably 3 years old, on a trip to Arusha. I thought that was a most wonderful treat.

There were a few other European-owned farms near us. One of them was a Greek farm and we would go over to visit and listen to their radio. It worked off a car battery. It must have been around 1940 as I recall the adults talking about the war in Europe and the Italians having a difficult time when they attacked Greece and were repulsed back into Albania. Probably why I have always had an interest in World War II history.

My all time World War II hero being Audie Murphy, the most decorated American soldier of all time. His book and movie "To Hell and Back" are both excellent accounts of his experiences.

When I was about 4, we were at some one's house and I had suffered a burn on the back of my left palm. I remember somebody riding me on a bicycle to a nearby clinic for several days while my hand was being treated. Near that house were ostriches and I would watch them and sometimes chase them around. I was lucky that they never attacked me. They say God takes care of stupid and drunk people but I was only about 4 years old.

At one other house that we visited, they had several wild animal pets and one of them was a buffalo. I was terrified of that large beast. I was lifted up by someone and was told that it was OK to pet it and I reached out and petted his horns and massive head.

One time I must have walked through some bushes and my legs were scratched. To stop the bleeding I rubbed some dust on the scratches, like using talcum powder.

The bleeding did stop and I suppose it's a miracle that my legs were not infected, or worse.

I had two Godfathers; one was Anthony Karaiskos and he gave me the name Marcos. I do not recall the other Godfather's name. He gave me my middle name, Constantine. I was asked which name I preferred as my first and I chose Marcos as Karaiskos was my favorite Godparent.

1941 - 1951

About May of 1941 we had moved to another place nearer the coast, between the towns of Tanga and Mombasa. I enjoyed the sea very much. At that time I was getting old enough to attend the Greek school near Moshi, at the foot of Mt. Kilimanjaro. That was approximately a 2 day trip by train. I was quite upset in having to leave home and stay in school for a 3-month term.

The school year was divided into 3 three-month terms and 3 one-month periods of home leave. Yep, they were boarding schools for most students. The school building apparently used to belong to some pre-war German organisation; there was a huge black swastika painted on the back of one of the main buildings. Tanganyika used to be an important German colony before and during World War I.

The school was surrounded by coffee and banana plantations. We lived in dormitories, about 120 boys on one side and 80 girls on the other side, separated by a large dining hall. It was grades 1 through 4, I think.

The food was not much to my liking, especially when we had to eat eggplants, okra and turnips. YUK !

One evening as we were getting ready to go to sleep, there was a strong earth tremor and we thought it was a lot of fun as our beds on wheels were bumping into each other like bumper cars in an amusement park.

We sometimes went swimming in a nearby crater lake called Duluti. It was a scary lake and it had leeches in it that we had to scrape off our legs when we exited the murky water. Slimy little things they were.

Another time while in school, there was a plague of locust swarms; millions of them landed on the playing fields and we would run through them. Some would fly up but most were too busy eating everything in sight and we stomped hundreds of them. The sky was almost dark when they finally decided to fly off and there were hundreds of birds feasting on them. What a strange experience that was!

One of our Saturday afternoon past-times was getting our "home made" slingshots out and using some firm round yellow berries called "ndulele" as ammunition. We would exchange fire with some black kids across a hedge that marked the perimeter of our school grounds. Nobody got hurt much during these exchanges and both sides enjoyed the duels. It did sting a lot when a berry hit home however.

I had a younger sister in school. Unfortunately she died there from malarial fever. That was a big blow and within a couple of months I was transferred to the English grade school in Arusha, some 50 miles away. That was around 1943.

I did not know much English, just good morning and good night and relied on some Swahili words for a while. Then I started speaking English as best I could and of course I was made plenty of fun of by many kids.

That led to several "fights" but that is how growing up in our schools was. Plenty of competition and scraps.

Life in the English school became quite good and interesting. They started me off in 3rd grade but was dropped back to 2nd for a spell until I was able to communicate after a few weeks. Most of the kids were English with a mixture of Greeks, South Africans, Germans, Italians and Polish (refugees from the war). Again, home was a long way away and we lived in dormitories for 3 months and went home for one month.

We would get on the train and travel 2 days between home and school. Others lived even further and it would take them 4 to 5 days of train and bus travel. The school was about 3 miles from the train station and when we arrived, they would line us up and walk us to the school. Our luggage was brought up by truck. We were assigned dormitories according to age groups.

Some weekends we boarded buses (more like cattle trucks) and they would take us on what they called Picnics. That was a lot of fun.

One time they announced on the public address system that they needed some volunteers for clean up duty. I and 3 others volunteered. They took us in a pickup truck to Ngorongoro Crater, some 50 miles away. This is supposed to be the largest crater in the world and is featured quite often on Television travelogs. Many animals live in the crater year round.

Another time, we were asked to get an OK from our parents for mountain climbing. I got the OK. There were about 12 boys and 3 girls in the group and we were bussed to a base camp on the slopes of Mt Meru. This is the 2nd highest mountain in Tanzania, at approximately 14,764 feet high.

About 3 in the morning we took off through the forest on our way to climb the mountain. We had an "Askari" (Swahili for soldier); he was to protect us with his gun from encounters with wild animals. Fortunately both there and back we only met up with wild boar and heard lions roar in the distance.

Half way up most of the climbers stopped due to fatigue and other problems. 4 boys and a teacher made it to the top. It was very cold and there were several small glaciers up there. We signed our names in a book that was inside a small stone hut and rested awhile, enjoying the vistas.

When the clouds obscured the views, we started on our return trip and met the stragglers as we descended the mountain. We finally reached our base camp about 2 AM and went to sleep. When we returned to school, they entered our names on a large plaque that was in the dining area, joining some other names that had preceded us on the Mt. Meru climbs.

Start of 1950 I left the grade school and went to the only high school in the area; it was in another country, Kenya. The school was located a few miles outside Nairobi. The name of the school was "Prince of Wales", an all boys school of European students.

Again, we had to board trains from our homes to attend the school. Now it took me 3 days of train travel, which included several lengthy stops. This was a large English school with 6 dormitories of about 120 students each.

Discipline was very strict and some seniors were appointed as "prefects" and they tended to play up their power and bully the new kids. They had the school authority of beating someone with a "taki"; this was a large tennis shoe that they used to apply 3 strokes to the victim's buttocks.

Many a student could not sit well for a couple of days. Also, more serious problems were reported to the Headmaster and he applied 3 or 6 strokes with a bamboo cane. That hurt even more. I personally experienced both the "taki" and the cane for minor insubordination, etc. Minor, huh?

Some weekends the school would take us on picnics to the Rift Valley and some lakes in it. Two of the lakes were Naivasha and

Nakuru and they both had large flocks of flamingos on them.

Some of us one time decided to walk around one of the lakes. It took us about 3 hours and as we trudged through the high reeds, we startled some water buck (large deer) and we came close to getting trampled by them. It was one of the many foolish things that we did and escaped unharmed.

About 1952 the Mau Mau rebellion was in full swing in Kenya, instigated by some of the Kikuyu tribe that lived around Nairobi. They mostly massacred the black people but also attacked whites whenever they had the chance. This caused the school to recruit the older students into fire brigades and to give us regular British Army uniforms and training.

On weekends we would go into the forest and bush country and train in ambush tactics and firing our rifles. We enjoyed that very much and typical of young people we were not afraid of possible dangers. We were about 200 strong and I am sure we were quite capable of defending our school from the Mau Mau. Fortunately we did not have to but we did assist the regular British Army in some terrorist sweeps through some villages.

About 3 miles from our school was a Catholic girls school and some weekends we would sneak over and go through the fence to visit the girls. The nuns were quite vigilant at times and would chase us away with a lot of unpleasant verbal remarks.

One day while in class, we heard a strange noise and our teacher knew what it was and told us to follow him outside. As we looked up where the sound was coming from, we saw our first jet planes, British Meteor fighters. That was quite an impressive sight.

End of 1953 the seniors were required to take our final exams, conducted by the University of Cambridge, in England. Mercifully I passed with Credits as indicated by my Cambridge Certificate in my Africa photo album.

After high school, I attended an Accounting school in Nairobi and lived at the local YMCA. My friend Tasso Ioanides and I went to school in the mornings and in the afternoon we worked at a car dealer repair shop, doing inventory and stock work. That paid for all our expenses of the YMCA and the school.

One weekend we were walking around town near the New Stanley Hotel and we saw Clark Gable and Ava Gardner; they were in the country to film the movie "Mogambo." I saw that movie about 2 years later.

On another weekend, we saw Princess Elizabeth and Prince Phillip, in a motorcade. Within a few days they flew back to England when the news of the death of King George VI was announced and Elizabeth became Queen.

Also another time we saw another American actor, Johnny Weismuller. He played Tarzan at that time.

When we completed the Accounting school, we left Nairobi and hitch-hiked back to Tanganyika. Our first ride was one third of our trip back home. Foolishly we left the village that we were dropped off at and started walking the dirt road, expecting to hike to Arusha on the next vehicle that came along. Unfortunately there was not much traffic that day and by nightfall we were still walking. We could hear lions and hyenas in the distance and we knew that we had made a bad mistake and it was too far to turn back by then.

Luckily around 7:30 we saw headlights approaching. As luck would have it, a Greek fellow who knew us stopped and picked us up. What a relief that was! He took us to my friend's house where we stayed overnight. Next day his Dad drove me to my home in Moshi, at the slopes of Mt. Kilimanjaro.

Time wise, this was early 1955 and fortunately I got an accounting job with Cooper Bros., a large English accounting firm. From time to time they would send a couple of us to another town to audit the books of various companies. It was a great experience staying at hotels and getting paid.

1956, my Dad died; he had a small grocery store. I left my job to look after the store. That was not a good decision but it was what happened.

One of my Mother's brothers was Uncle Gus who lived in the USA. He and his son Pano came to visit us and stayed with us for one month. They had a Polaroid camera and we all thought that it was a great invention, giving us instant photos. As they were leaving to return to the US, I said that I would like to come over and visit them.

About that time I heard that an American Olympic athlete was visiting Moshi. I found him on an athletic field. His name was Bob Mathias, a decathlon winner and he showed us various athletic skills. Very nice person he was and he told me some things about the USA.

The following week, I wrote to Uncle Gus and he told me to perhaps enter the USA on a student visa. I immediately started driving to the nearest American Consulate which was in Nairobi. I went for my visa, passport papers, etc.

On one my trips to the Consulate, I was driving and had to quickly stop the car when I saw a lot of dust on the road ahead. Turned out that a large herd of elephants was crossing the road. I waited about 40 minutes and proceeded to drive to my destination, having to zig-zag on that part of the road to avoid the large piles of elephant dung that they had deposited.

OFF to the USA

Summer of 1957 was time for me to fly to the US. It was sad leaving home and family but I was looking forward to a new adventure. My brother Pete and 2 of our friends drove me up to Nairobi to fly on Scandinavian Airlines. The plane was a large 4 engine propeller machine with nice comfortable seats and plenty of leg room, unlike some of todays arrangements.

The plane left in the evening and our first stop was Khartoum, Sudan, about 1 AM in the morning. We exited the plane and the heat even at night was overwhelming. We flew over Egypt and saw the Pyramids and the Nile. Fortunately, I had a window seat the whole flight to the USA.

The next stop was Athens, followed by Rome. There the plane was stopped for 2 hours and I had a chance to practice some of the Italian language that I had picked up while living in Moshi and going around with some Italian friends.

The plane took off and flew north over the Alps. That was quite a sight with all the snow covered mountains. We landed in Bern, Switzerland, and our next stop was in Frankfurt, Germany. From there we went to Copenhagen, Denmark. In the evening we took off, flew over the English country side and across the Atlantic.

Part way over the ocean, a German passenger had to be calmed down by the air hostess when he thought that the plane was on fire as he saw flames coming out of the exhaust of one of the engines.

Finally we saw the Statue of Liberty and New York City and we landed at La Guardia airport. Luckily Uncle Gus and Pano met me there and we went to stay at a hotel for 2 days.

We visited several sites and also went to the Empire State observation floor. My eyes were as wide as could be seeing America. I tasted my first hamburger, hotdog, fries and root beer. Also experienced pancakes with maple syrup and restaurants, cafeteria style.

We left New York in Uncle's car, a 1956 Dodge, and drove to Philadelphia where Uncle Gus had some relatives. We stayed at their house overnight. I saw my first Television show ever and it was the Ed Sullivan show. It was black and white TV but I thought it was wonderful.

We left Philadelphia for Toledo and travelled the Pennsylvania and Ohio turnpikes. It was interesting being shown around Toledo and the surrounding shopping centers. I met some of Pano's friends and they asked me about life in Africa.

After 2 weeks of trying to find a decent job, I gave up and went downtown to the Post Office to join the military. I was going to join the Marines. Luckily the recruiter was out for lunch and as I was looking at photographs of ships on the wall, the Navy recruiter started talking with me and before I knew it I was joining the Navy.

The next day I was put on a bus for Detroit. When I got there they asked me for my Social Security card that I never had. So off on the bus they sent me back to Toledo for a SS card and they bussed me back to Detroit. There were many other young peole at the Detroit staging area and after they processed us over a couple of days, they put us on a train for Great Lakes Boot Camp, near Milwaukee.

We arrived there about 1 AM. and were shown to the dormitory and our bunks. Finally went to sleep about 3 AM but by 5:30 they were waking us up with someone scraping a Coke bottle inside an empty corrugated garbage can. The noise was enough to wake up the dead and this "idiot" was shouting "Reveille, reveille, youz guyz get up right NOW!" All with a thick Bronx accent.

Well, to cut a long story short, we made it through boot camp and by November it snowed one night and all the Southern boys went running out into the snow. Even though this was my first snow, I stayed in the barracks.

We graduated amid several parades and were sent home for a week. The week before graduation they had given us various tests to determine our future Navy rating jobs. Some of us were given a test for Sonar, Radar and Radio. I scored best in sonar, then radar and last radio. In their wisdom, the Navy allocated me to Radio School in Bainbridge, MD. some 40 miles noth of Baltimore. Radio school was about 6 months long.

The winter of early 1958 it snowed heavily one weekend and all transportation shut down for a while. Radio school also closed up for a few days and since the base was running short of food, they offered liberty to all who wanted it. Some of us hitch-hiked to Lancaster, PA, some 30 miles from the base. We stayed at the YMCA at night and the USO in the daytime.

I finally graduated from Radio School and was given a week off before our next assignment. I had orders to report to Norfolk, VA. to a destroyer called the USS Beale, DDE-471. When the week was up, I boarded a Greyhound bus from Toledo to Norfolk. The bus stopped in Pittsburgh to pick up some passengers and apparently 2 girls boarded the bus there, on their way to vacation in Virginia Beach. This was summer of 1958.

Sometime during the ride, I befriended another sailor. I had previously spotted the 2 girls on the bus and I told him that the only way we could meet them was to split them up. One of them got up to go to the bathroom and that was our opening chance. I went and sat next to the one looking out the window. Her name I later found out was Isabella. She thought it was her friend returning to her seat until I said "want a lifesaver baby?" She was startled and in a smart mouth way said "I am not your baby and never will be" WOW !!!

Anyway, we talked for a while and by the time we had reached Norfolk, she had given me her address. I reported to the ship and quickly adjusted to my new surroundings.

First time out to sea was somewhat of an experience of mild sea sickness. It was very interesting being part of the Radio shack crew. All of our sea duties were for ASW (anti-submarine warfare). Our ship was part of Task Group Alfa and it consisted of an aircraft carrier, the Valley Forge or Randolph and 7 other destroyers and 2 submarines.

One time we ran into a hurricane named Daisy and it tossed us around causing damage to the carrier and the rest of the ships. Our ship spent about a month in dry dock in Portsmouth, VA., repairing damage and updating equipment.

That year I spent Christmas with about 12 other sailors on the base barracks; all others had left for home. For the New Year holiday, I hitch-hiked to Mckeesport to visit Isabel. We had been corresponding since our last encounter. We went to her friend's house for the New Year eve party.

Much of the rest of my time in the Navy was spent on the USS Beale. We visited some places like Bermuda, Jamaica, Guantanamo Bay, Cuba, Nova Scotia in Canada and other ports like New York, etc.

On one of our trips to New York, we were ploughing through rough seas in the north Atlantic and some young fellow was washed overboard by the waves . Unfortunately he was lost to the sea as by the time our ship turned around after a lookout raised the alarm of "man overboard" we were too far away to save him and the poor soul went under the cold seas and disappeared. That was a sobering experience.

Summer of 1960 I was transferred to another ship, a destroyer escort type that was smaller than the Beale. The name of this ship was the USS Brough, DE-148. The ship's base was Key West, Florida, and that was a pleasant change from Norfolk.

While in the Key West area, I decided to travel to the Miami Courthouse and get my American citizenship that I had finally earned, serving my adopted country. The ceremony was brief. It was myself and about 10 Cubans. I was the only one in uniform.

Some time in September of 1961 I lef the Navy, boarded a bus and went to McKeesport where on November 4th, Isabel and I were married. We took some days off for our honeymoon and travelled to Washington, D.C. and to Gettysburg, PA.

The economy was in a recession and I had trouble finding work. At one time I was selling hardware at Sears and Isabel worked at the Telephone company.

Our first born was Helen Christine, followed a year and a half later by John Basil and a year and a half later by Yvonne Marrie. In between we lived about 18 months in Dravosburg and then moved to McKeesport.

For about 3 months I attended a Computer school and landed a job at the Mellon Bank computer room in Pittsburgh. My previous job to that was at Continental Can but I was laid off one week before the Thanksgiving holiday and we had a slim Christmas that year.

Isabel left work and stayed home to raise the family. We never had much money but we always saved enough for weekend camping trips at Laurel State park and Prince Gallitzin camping areas. We also went on yearly 3 or 4 day vacations to Erie, Atlantic City, Gettysburg, Assateague on the Maryland coast, etc.

In 1973, December 21, we left McKeesport and moved to North Huntingdon; we didn't go camping anymore but still went on our yearly vacations like Dayton, Ohio, Michigan and Sandusky.

The kids got a small mixed terrier dog and we called him Duke. I don't know if that was after "Duke" Wayne or the Duke beer that I was drinking.

We bought an above-ground swimming pool and that kept us busy in the summer months. Helen graduated from High school and went to Clarion State University for one semester until she met Gary Todd and they were married in 1982.

John graduated in 82, attended Westmoreland Community College and then went to Indiana University, at Indiana, PA. Yvonne graduated in 1984, worked for a while at a super market and then attended Dental School for her work as a dental assistant. John finished college and his first job in the computer field was with AMS in Arlington, VA.

In 1995 I had a triple bypass and decided that I woud retire. Luckily Mellon Bank came through with an early retirement program and I retired in March, 1996. Isabel retired also and we have enjoyed the last years of retirement by taking yearly trips across the country and have visited 46 states so far and also took a trip to South Africa in 1998 to visit my brother Pete and his family.

End of story for now.........

***

From Godfrey Mwakikagile, USA, 6 January 2006

Hello Mark,

Thank you very much for the answers. Very interesting.

I'm learning a lot myself from you about my home country! On how things were back then when I was a child. I have very little knowledge and only a few recollections on how life was in the early fifties.

You have, for example, mentioned in your email a refrigerator running on kerosene. That's really new to me. I never heard of refrigerators running on kerosene back then, even when I was a teenager. To most Africans, any kind of refrigerator was a luxury item, anyway, and they weren't even familiar with it as you have pointed out.

And I didn't even know there were Africans working in banks and industries when I was a little boy. That's because I was too young back then to know about such things.

I was under five years old when we lived in Mbeya in what was then the Southern Highlands Province. The first provincial capital was Iringa. That's where the provincial commissioner, the main colonial administrator as you very well know, lived in those days. Later, before independence, Mbeya became the provincial capital.

The Southern Highlands was a very large province with many districts. I remember the whole country, which is more than 362,000 square miles, had eight provinces back then., as we learnt in standard three and standard four in primary school. I attended primary school in the late fifties. So I'm somewhat knowledgeable about those years.

But even at a very young age when I was only five years old in Mbeya in the early fifties, I can remember some things. For example, I remember seeing many Europeans in that town; at least what to me seemed to be many.

I remember one day when my father hoisted me up on his shoulders to see an elephant in town; it was some kind of circus going on that day in the town of Mbeya and there were many Europeans around, I believe mostly British.

I also remember very well when one of the performers, a white, had a snake wrapped around his neck entertaining the crowd. They said it was a cobra. And the performance was very exciting especially for children.

Later I heard that he was bitten by the snake, and died. But I don't know if it was just a rumour or not, may be just trying to scare children so that they shouldn't play with snakes.

When we moved from Mbeya to Rungwe District in 1955 when I was around five years old, I remember seeing quite a few Europeans playing golf and tennis in the town of Tukuyu which was the district capital. Tukuyu is about four miles from our home village of Mpumbuli which is close to a large tea estate know as Kyimbila Tea Estate, one of the largest in the Tanzania.

I went to Tukuyu quite often when I was a child, as many other children did, just to see what was going on and sometimes to buy things. The whites who played golf and tennis in the town of Tukuyu used to give us tennis balls now and then when we passed through there, where they played; which was very exciting to us as children.

I also remember when the governor of Tanganyika, Sir Edward Twining, visited Tukuyu in 1958 or 1959. He was one of the last two governors before Tanganyika won independence and it was a farewell visit when he came to Tukuyu.

I was there on that day and remember very well the white hat he had on. I think the rest of his attire was also white. He also had white gloves on. Soon thereafter, he was replaced by Sir Richard Turnbull who was the last governor of Tanganyika.

I'm glad I have been able to find and get in touch some people who lived in Tanganyika back then in the fifties and who are willing to share their memories with me on what went on in their lives in those days.

You are one of them. And I'm very grateful that you have made a significant contribution to this project which I have always wanted to do. You are one of the primary sources of this material about colonial Tanganyika in the fifties. And for that, I will always be grateful to you and the rest.

Best regards.

Godfrey

***

Mark Evdemon wrote on 6 January 2006

I will start with 2 of your questions.....

How would you describe life in Tanganyika in the fifties or in any period during colonial rule?

Being a European teenager at that time, I had it fairly "easy" and I was mostly concerned with getting good grades in school. I lived in various places, from a sisal plantation near Tanga, another near Mombo, a papaya plantation near Korogwe, a few other places and lastly in Moshi.

I am a "good" person (still am) and I treated ALL people nicely. We had several man servants at our home and many a time they invited me to share some Ugari, etc.

We travelled many miles by railway trains to our schools; grade school was in Arusha and high school we had to go to Nairobi. They were both mostly attended by European kids except for an occasional Indian.

At various times while at the sisal estates, my Dad employed many indigenous black people for harvesting the sisal. He treated them well but once in a while he would loose his temper with a lazy one and he would use Swahili curse words to get his point across. That's how I learnt my Swahili curse words (some education, huh?).

Sometimes we lived in primitive houses with no plumbing or electricity and other times we had good housing with modern amenities.

One time we had a refrigerator that ran on a kerosene flame; several local folks would come to look at it and marvel at how Europeans could make ice out of a flame. I would explain but not many understood.

Some black folks were educated, running the railroads, banks, industries, etc. but nowhere enough to prepare them for independence in later years.

What is it that you particularly miss about those days? Can you give a few examples?

I miss the many very good tropical fruits we had; going hunting and playing football (soccer) with both European and Black teams.

I do not miss the rainy season (masika), the malaria, the funji (funza) that got in our toes, the bad roads and sometimes the noisy hyenas at night.

***

More from Mark Evdemon on 7 January 2006

Here are 2 more answers to your questions....

What was the level of interaction between the Europeans and the indigenous people?

Briefly, the interaction was mostly on a business level with most people, as I saw it; an exception being some of us had Black friends from playing soccer together and drinking a few beers after the games.

However, when I was the only non-English member of the local Rugby team, I was given special permission to attend their strictly English club after the games.

We usually played rugby against other European teams and sometimes Indian teams. I sensed that many English people "looked" down upon non-English as FOREIGNERS. I imagine the indigenous people felt the same way about them. Not sure about that though.

I did witness some very rare interracial marriages but both Blacks and Whites frowned upon that.

What was your overall impression of colonial Tanganyika in terms of life? Was life good? Or was it hard? How did you view the colonial authorities? As oppressors or benevolent rulers?

My life was good; obviously as in any country, the poor had a tough life. We were not the privileged rich but life was still good.

We had our homes, our cars, etc.

The colonial authorities were definitely not oppressors. Most were like benevolent Dictators; I did run across some arrogant magistrates, etc.

Overall I would judge from reading History of other colonies like the Portuguese ones, the British were leaning towards the good side. Naturally, some Blacks might have had different opinions.

About the Asian population, I tended to favor the Punjabs (the ones with the beards and the turbans).

***

From Mark Evdemon, 9 January 2006

Was any kind of racial integration allowed anywhere? There were signs in Tanganyika and Kenya saying, "Europeans," "Asians," and "Africans," in compliance with government policy sanctioning racial separation or what was also known as colour bar.

Were there many Europeans who were opposed to this? What was the general attitude among a significant number of them towards racial separation?

I vaguely recall some of those "signs". Integration was allowed in all businesses, sports, buses and trains, but naturally a lot depended where you rode on the train by what one could afford. Some Europeans did not like the "signs" but it was not aggressively pursued.

Did you detect any hostility, overt or covert, towards whites on the part of Africans in general and among some of the indigenous people you or some of the people you knew interacted with? For example, house servants, co-workers even if subordinates. Was there any or much sympathy among a significant number of whites for the nationalist aspirations of the Africans in their quest for independence?

Yes, as in any multiethnic society, there are racial problems (maybe it's the old saying about "birds of a feather, flock together").

No excuses are being made by me. We had plenty of bigots on the white side and equal on the black side. Overall, I would say that both sides USED and tolerated each other.

As far as African independence aspirations, most whites accepted it that it was just a matter of time. The one good thing we had in Tanganyika was that there was no violence as there was in Kenya with the Mau Mau atrocities that were committed mostly by the Kikuyu on their own black tribesmen.

***

From Mark Evdemon, 10 January 2006

What memories do you have of the places in which you lived in Tanganyika, and of your interactions with Africans?

Can you give some examples including stories of such personal experiences or encounters? And of some of the exciting or trying moments you had including hardship?

I recall one time my brother and I were driving through a village on our way to Tanga when some chickens ran across the road and our car hit one of them. We stopped to see what happened and the owner of the chickens wanted us to pay for the "road kill".

My brother asked him what were the roads meant for, chickens or cars? The man said cars but still wanted money for his chicken. My brother told him that we would give him "shilingi mbilli" (two shillings) and we left.

Another recollection was when my car got stuck in mud on the road during the rainy season. Before long, half a dozen Africans came by and started pushing the car to get it free of the mud. "Harambee, ho" or something like that was the chant. After a while, the car was unstuck; I did not have money on me but I did have a case of beer in the car, so I opened up some bottles and we celebrated the event.

I feel that if something similar happened here in the USA, I would get mugged or worse by the black people. I have experienced several black racist feelings towards me here in the USA. The Africans in Tanganyika were generally very friendly people and I hope they still are.

What was the general attitude among many whites towards the native population? Paternalistic, compassionate, indifferent, hostile, overtly racist or what?

I think 2 words would describe the answer.....paternalistic and indifferent.

Were there any or a significant number of whites who felt that the colonial government was not doing or had not done enough for the people of Tanganyika, especially native Africans, in the areas of health, education, infrastructural development, and political representation at the local and national levels?

A significant number of whites felt that not enough education and political readiness was made for the future independence of Tanganyika, which was obviously evident.

However, there was enough apprehension about the day when independence would come to make us whites feel threatened. One of the reasons why I left Tanganyika in 1957. Others were that I wanted to improve my life and see the world. I did not want to have to deal with reverse discriminations, guilt trips, accusations and uncertainties.

***

On Mark Evdemon's identity in response to my email, 10 January 2006:

Hello Mark,

Thank you very much. I enjoy reading everything you write. An honest portrayal of how things were back then..
I remember what you said on your memories page that you were the only non-English member of the Rugby team. What's

your nationality or national origin? When you talked about the Greeks in Arusha, I assumed you were Greek. I could be wrong, of course.

Just curious.

Best regards.

Godfrey

Hello Godfrey....yep, my short term ancestry is Greek but long term ancestry, who knows. There were so many invasions, etc. all over Europe that one can only guess....I assume you belong to a certain Kabila but overall, you would not know either other than you are African.

One of our best "servants" that we had for decades was a tribesman "Wanyamwezi". I still remember his first name Saidi. He was like a family member and a fine human being.

I recall one time when he was going to get married, he said that his future wife had "matso kama njiwa" and he was quite proud of finding her.

For his honeymoon, my Mother gave him money and a month off so that he would go back and visit his village (I forget, maybe some place north of Dodoma).

Mark

***

From Mark Evdemon, 11 January 2006

Ogonile Godfrey...... I was not in Tanganyika when independence came so I do not have first-hand experience or knowledge.

However I have been told that many European-owned farms were confiscated with no restitution. A close friend told me that when he decided to leave Tanganyika, he was not allowed to take his money with him. He was only allowed a small percentage and the Bank would send him some money yearly. Several years later, the Bank notified him that his account was closed and his money was used to pay up his Bank fees, etc.

Now that was a lot of bull and as far as he knew, he had no recourse. In fact he lost his money regardless of international laws, etc. Much like what Mugabe has been doing in Zimbabwe. Mugabe has managed to destroy the economy of a fairly wealthy country when he inherited it. Zimbabwe was self sufficient in food stuffs and now they face starvation.

Anyway, Tanzania did not go that far but Nyerere's socialist policies did not help Tanzania in attracting businesses. When my friend visited Tanzania 3 years ago and went to his father's coffee estate, he found the farm in bad shape and the buildings in disarray.

I have heard that now there are many thousands of South Africans running a lot of the government in Tanzania. Have you heard of this? I wish I could corroborate a lot of what I hear. What do you think?

I wanted to visit Tanzania a few years ago but I was told that I would find some things have regressed instead of progressed and I would feel bad seeing some of these situations. What do you know for a fact?

Sure, I am an American citizen now and I love this country but I still have fond feelings for Tanganyika, my birth country. I am truly an African American but personally I do not like hyphenated identifications.

Citizens of the USA should consider themselves Americans regardless of origin. Sure, the past has been unjust to some due to racial problems, but I look to the present and I sense more Black racism these days than white racism. It is probably a never ending discussion so if we disagree, so be it but at least we can openly express our ideas, etc. without fear of offending.

The way I see it, one has to keep an open mind, and keep on learning and dismiss fiction from fact. People who get offended by sincere differences are not tolerant folks. What do you think?

The one thing I keep stressing to my grand kids, etc, is to keep an open mid and if some one else's ideas and ways are better than yours, do not be afraid to alter your ways. Be idealistic but tolerant of diverse opinions.

Last year I visited my cousin in the UK and while there he took me to meet an acquaintance of his from Tanzania. My cousin used to have a farm near lake Nyasa. His friend (English citizen of Greek ancestry) was for a while Nyerere's private pilot and he had interesting stories about his job. Unfortunately, I lost touch with him after several months of my return home.

If you have further questions or opinions, send them over. I hope I have contributed something to your writing of your book and wish you much health and success in your life.

Stay in touch.......an Internet rafiki,
Mark.

Author's note:
Mark Evdemon used a greeting in my "tribal" language, Kinyakyusa, in the preceding message when he said "Ogonile Godfrey." The actual spelling is "Ugonile."

I am a Nyakyusa, a member of an ethnic group of more than one million people who live in Rungwe and Mbeya districts in the southwestern part of the Southern Highlands of Tanzania on the Tanzanian-Malawian-and-Zambian border.

***

From Liz Crosbie, Cambridgeshire, UK, 4 January 2006

Dear Godfrey,

Thank you for your email.

I am sure you will have so much to write about as they were very interesting times. I am often amazed to think that when I was born in Nairobi that it was such a young city - about as old as I am now!!

My father went out there after the war when opportunities arose in Kenya for him to use his skills as a post office engineer. Britain was still in a sorry state after the war and the idea of bringing up a family in his mother-in-law's home and an adventurous spirit drew him to Africa.

It was the time of the Mau Mau and when my parents arrived at their small flat in Nairobi, my father, ever the engineer, decided to investigate a dangling wire in the living room and the emergency forces arrived on the door step as he had set the alarm off.

Both my parents loved Africa and the Africans and never felt anything other than a guest in a beautiful country but they survived the Mau Mau with typical British resolve and some understanding. They were both from Wales and Wales had suffered hundreds of years of domination by the English.

For me as a child, Nairobi was all I knew although we did come back to Britain on home leave for six months every 3-4 years. It felt cold and strange and I hated the cold more than anything and couldn't wait to get back to what for me was home.

My father was initially posted to Dar es salaam when I was 5 and I fell in love with it especially as we had a house by the sea and we spent many a happy hour by the sea and in it. However it was hot and very humid and to my mother's relief we were posted to Iringa and spent the rest of our time there. It was such a happy time.

My mother ran the girl guides and the rangers who were of all nationalities but I preferred to go out on the back of the post office lorry with my father and his African driver who had a hole in his earlobe which was just big enough to take a box of matches. I would sit on the telegraph poles in the back of the lorry and soon looked a sight as my hair would be sticking on end from the wind and the dust.

Elephants were the greatest cause of damage to the telegraph poles and my father's driver cum trainee engineer would stick his finger in the dung and tell my father how far away the elephants were before they set to work to repair the lines.

I went to St George's and St Michael's in Iringa and we have had a reunion in South Africa which was very emotional and a tribute to the very special feelings we have for Africa and the privileged childhood we had. We all said how unique our relationship was with the Africans who were and still are courteous, kind and everlastingly friendly.

Sadly although we have all contributed books and financial aid to our old school, I believe it has fallen into disrepair and recently suffered a riot.

I hope this is helpful to you and I will forward your email to some of the ex-Iringans for their memories.

Incidentally, the father of one has written a book entitled *60 years in East Africa* and his name is Voight. You may be able to track it down and I know you will find it interesting because it gives the German view of life in E.A. Good luck with your endeavours.

Liz

***

From Kevin Peters, 4 January 2006

Hello Godfrey,

Many thanks for your email.
I grew up in Kenya in the 50s which is probably somewhat different from Tanganyika in many respects.
I lived in Nairobi for most of that period but also experienced living on farms etc.
As you have probably gathered my interest is the military history of East Africa as well as the railways. If you can tell me what exactly you wish to know I may be able to help or possibly find some one who can.

Best.

rgds Kevin

***

From Jill Robinson, 4 January 2006

Hello Godfrey

I'm afraid that I would not be able to offer you any insight to that period of time as I was only 5-10 years old too.
Children have a much different perspective on their surroundings than adults do. For example - I didn't care that it was a Colonial period - Africa was home. My playmates were children of my Ayha (house maid also known as yaya in Swahili). We all

had the same thing in mind - just have fun.

Life was good. By the time I reached the age of 10 I was starting to understand that there were differences between white and black. Obviously I was influenced by the adults. However, I never experienced cruelty or downright rudeness from those adults to the blacks.

My best memories are when we went hunting - everyone including the support staff (blacks) had a wonderful time. I hated the hunting part - but the time around the camp fire was enjoyed by all.

From the age of 10 I moved to Nairobi and shortly afterwards the Mau Mau was upon us. Then the biggest differences came to light.

I miss Africa and home.

Good luck with your book.

Jill

***

From Jan van Someren Graver, Canberra, Australia, 4 January 2006

Godfrey

It will be a pleasure to discuss life in Tanganyika / Tanzania! However, I may not be the archetypal colonial that might you expect. I grew up on a coffee plantation at Lushoto with Kisambaa and Kiswahili as the first languages in my life and spoke German with my Mother in the house.

I have a number of friends with whom you might also like to make contact. One in particular lives in the US and has already made a real start in recording his life in Tanganyika / Tanzania.

I am a bit busy at this moment with a lot of work starting with the New Year and WILL get back to you because it is time that I put some of my early life on record and you have provided an impetus.

Meanwhile, allow me to wish you a very Happy New Year

with the expectation that it will bring you good health, peace and a success in your personal and professional ambitions.

Yours aye, Jan.

***

From Jill Ferguson-Rigg, 5 January 2006

Hello Godfrey,

Happy New Year.
Unfortunately most of my experience was in Kenya when growing up there during colonial times...we did visit Dar Es Salaam and other places in T but only for very brief periods but we never lived in T.

On my father's side his father served in the military and spent time out in T. but I don't have any family records either of that time.

It may be best to make trips to T. in order to do research....but there should be other people who visit Kenya Korner who would have lived during those times who may be best able to assist you.

Please do stay in touch. I've now lived 35 yrs in the Far East but still long for Africa. I always thought it was a cliche that "Africa remains in the soul", but I have now come to firmly believe it.

Good luck with your findings. The man who runs the KK site may also be of help to you. I would put a message out on the actual site expressing what you seek and from there you may well be able to connect.

Best wishes and kind regards,

Jill Ferguson-Rigg

***

From Russ Baker, Florida, USA, 4 January 2006

Godfrey Mwakikagile,

I am the father of Janice to whom you wrote an email requesting information. If you wish, I can try to be of help to you.

For your information, I am a *mzungu* (a white man or person); my parents went to Tanganyika in 1937 as church workers (missionaries) and I grew up out there. After coming back to the USA for studies, I returned as a missionary myself in 1956 - so was there in the closing days of the British rule and as Uhuru came in.

I speak both KiSwahili and KiSukuma; we lived in Mwanza Region and as a worker with the Africa Inland Church worked in the same area. Right now, nimestaafu and live in Florida.

Let me know your wishes; I will be glad to help if I can.

Russ Baker

***

From Tom Wise, 5 January 2006

Dear Godfrey

Thank you for your e-mail - always good to hear from an East African.

I was born in 1957 and left Tanzania in 1962 when I was just 5 years old, so you'll please excuse me if I tell you that I don't think that I would be a good source for you in recounting 'how life was in Tanganyika in the fifties and during colonial times in general'.

Perhaps some of the other participants in the Kenya Korner website may be more useful to you as points of contact.

Regards

Tony Wise

***

From Bill Hall, Northamptonshire, UK, 5 January 2006

Thank you for your message.

I'm afraid that my knowledge of Tanganyika is very limited. In 1956 I was in Dar es Salaam for a few months and then I moved to Tanga where I was for one and a half years.

I was shipping agent for the British India Line and my work was confined to the port so did not go upcountry much.

Although Tanganyika was technically a Mandate appointed by the League of Nations after the first World War, to the "man in the street" it was run very much like an ordinary British colony with a Governor, district commissioners etc.

The Asian community ran the majority of the retail trade and the import/export trade was almost entirely in the hands of British and Asian firms which of course was to the detriment of African aspirations.

However, British nationals and Asians from overseas could not enter the country without a work permit which, except for permanent residents, had to be renewed every three years, so there was no "carte blanche" for anyone who might want to exploit resources.

The Government encouraged the setting up of trade unions so that workers might have their say. In Zanzibar, where I was for a number of years, I was involved in the initial stages of the organisation of the port workers union there.

Having lived in Tanga, when I did go upcountry we always passed through Muheza and Handeni. We also used to go to Amani where there was a medical research unit (anti-malaria I think). A friend of mine who was a keen butterfly collector found many specimens in the forest near Amani.

Roads of course were sometimes a problem in those days (and perhaps still are?) and the only British car capable of withstanding them was Ford. Peugeoits and Volkswagens, and later Datsuns, and were the best.

My daughter was born in Tanga and later on, when we were in Mombasa, she went to school in Lushoto.

Initially there was only a small signpost on the border saying "You are now entering Tanganyika". After Uhuru there was a border guard who demanded to see passports.

I know that the British administration of East African territories has been criticized but people sometimes forget that when the British first went there (in the case of Tanganyika, the Germans) there was absolutely no modern infrastructure and that within the life span of one person (my father was born in 1885 and died in 1970) the country was running itself with modern towns, railways roads and trade etc.

Sorry that I can't be of more help but if there is any particular aspect that you would like me to comment on please let me know.

Best wishes.

Bill Hall

***

From (name withheld upon request), 5 January 2006

Hello Godfrey

How interesting to hear from you? How long have you lived in America and what took you there?

I would love to go back to Tanzania one day - it was a wonderful country from what I remember.

I first went there in 1956/7. My father worked for the police as radio communications officer, firstly in Dar es salaam. I went to St Joseph's Convent there.

Then he was transferred to Dodoma where we lived for 2 years. There I was educated by a little old lady who lived with her 96 year old mother. She was with the CMS Mission and we (6 of us) used to do our lessons around the kitchen table. At break time we used to play in the dry river bed and climb rocks - gosh when you think what children of today have to have to have fun!

From there we went to Mbeya until the end of 1962.

I then went to Scotland to boarding school until 1964 while my parents were sent to Mwanza. I used to fly home to them only once a year for the holidays - it was so far and the British Government would only pay one flight per tour which could be 2 or 3 years long and my parents couldn't manage more than one fare.

It was a dreadful two years. To go from the wonderful outdoor life in Africa to a cold grey Edinburgh and to be so far away from home. They were there until 1965 when they collected me and we went to Cape Town where we lived until I completed school in 1966 then we moved again, this time to Swaziland. My father again worked for the police there also doing their radio communications.

Please tell me more about yourself and how you came to be living in the US etc and I shall delve into the past and see what I can think of to tell you that may be of interest to you. What sort of info are you looking for?

Looking forward to hearing from you.

(Anonymous)

***

From Josephine McLaughlin, Australia, 4 January 2006

Dear Godfrey,

How pleasant to hear from a fellow former resident of East Africa.

I am afraid, however, that I cannot be much help to you as I never visited Tanzania and didn't really know very much about the country. I lived in Uganda and was at school in Kenya for a while.

As a young child I had no interest in politics and only slightly more in history. I was aware, as no doubt you are too, that while Uganda and Kenya were colonised by the British it was Germany that influenced your country and later there was a strong communist presence in Tanzania - mainly Chinese and Cuban I think though you have probably researched the history much more closely than me.

We did of course share a Lake.

I lived in Entebbe for several years in my teens and spent many happy hours messing about on the water. We also shared the sunshine, the wildlife and the huge horizons.

I have many happy memories and wish you the best of luck in

your aims. If I stumble across a website that may be of interest to you I will get back in touch.

If you ever come across a Nicholas McLaughlin (my long lost brother) I hope you will let me know.

All the best and I wish you a happy 2006,

Jo

***

From Robi Bertele, Italy, 5 January 2006

Godfrey, it's good to receive communication from a genuine Tanganyikan!

And the fact that you want to write about those years is of great interest to me. I have been asked over and over again by friends to do just that.

With regard to your request: I know nothing about that blessed land before 1951, when I arrived in Dar from Italy. I was 4 years old and, as you can imagine, my recollections are somewhat nebulous.

If you are not in a big hurry, however, I'd be happy to jot down a few notes that would be strictly related to life in my family, because I wasn't much into politics and local social aspects at that young age.

Just let me know if you can wait a couple of weeks or so because I'm presently working on a project that is taking up all my free time.

Kwaheri

robi

***

From Richard Mansfield, Australia, 6 January 2006

Dear Godfrey,

Thanks for your email - I will try to recall some of the days we had in Tanganyika in the 50s and 60s and get in touch with you again.
They were happy days with lots of happy memories.
Will be in touch in a few days with a longer detailed email.
Kwaheri Kwa Sasa (I still speak Swahili but its a bit rusty!!).
Talk to you soon.

Richard

***

From Richard Mansfield, Australia, 12 January 2006

Dear Godfrey,

Thank you for your email.
I have read your questions very carefully and I find them to be rather political.
For my part relations with all whom I met and worked with whether, African, Asian or European were both cordial and straight forward. Life was fruitful, enjoyable, fair and free from bias.
I wish you well in your future writing.

Richard.

***

From Hal Rogers, USA, 6 January 2006

Hello Godfrey,

Very nice of you to email.
My grandfather passed away many years ago but my father is still living and was a teenager in Africa. I can certainly ask him

questions if you have specific ones. I see him about once or twice a week.

However, I can tell you a bit based on what I have been told over the years.

My family loved living in Africa during those years..the late 1940s- mid 1950s. My grandfather had been in Africa during World War II with the British Royal Artillery. After the war, he got out of the military and went back to Africa and got a job with the Groundnut Scheme. There is a fair amount of info about this on the internet if you look it up on Google.

At the time, the management of the government and economy in the colonies was by the British. The Indians also accounted for a lot of commercial trade and economy. Of course, as an African the situation was different. Some Africans were not happy with the colonization by the British and wanted to remain like old times. This is what led to the Mau Mau uprising and also the movement that gave most British colonies their independence over the years.

Of course, the movement was not only against British occupation but also against other European powers that had colonies in Africa.

It is our opinion that the British colonial governments were not brutal like some other European countries. Although certainly some British policies or actions were not easy on the Africans.

However, there was a good portion of the African population that were very pleased with the British rule and enjoyed a better standard of living and better health care etc that wasn't possible before colonization.

Some however believed that the British should leave and that Africa could run itself better than the British for example. However, the independence of many countries turned out to be very self-destructive. Many governments became corrupt and still are corrupt. Infighting among different tribes is still a problem in some African countries. Some Brutal dictators like Amin in Uganda killed many thousands of people.

We have a professor friend here in the US that for many years took college students for summer research projects to Kenya to study elephants in particular. He found that despite the stability in Kenya it is still quite corrupt and can be very dangerous. In some ways, you might compare it to going to a major US city and walking the projects at night. It is quite dangerous. Only in Africa, there is a lot more projects and much more isolated areas where you have no protection if something goes wrong.

Also the infrastructure of roads etc is in terrible shape. I have heard people say that the roads were better under British rule.

My uncle returned to Kenya about 5-6 years ago. He had really looked forward to the trip. However, he said that the conditions were terrible there. As a teen, he felt safe travelling around. But that is not the case now. He was very uncomfortable travelling outside of the safe zones.

He says he will never return again despite loving the climate and countryside of Africa. The trip was actually quite depressing to him. He felt very overwhelmed by the level of poverty and fear.

On a positive note, Kenya probably is the safest place to be in East Africa. Other countries like Uganda are still not as well run.

Well I hope that this information will give you a little insight into the past with some comparison to the present.

Africa has an amazing amount of natural beauty and history. But unfortunately, until the governments are able to improve dramatically, they will have difficulty being at the level of the big European countries.

We certainly don't know the answers to solve this problem but we recognize that so much has to be done before people of the world can travel Africa freely and safely.

Best regards,

Hal Rogers

***

Continued from Hal Rogers, 6 January 2006

Also I meant to say that my grandfather, and my father, lived in Urambo around 1948-49 in Tanganyika as a part of the Groundnut scheme after WWII. They lived in a tent city for a time.

The tent city town was surrounded by a ring of cleared ground which was called the Tetsi(sp?)Belt to keep the flies out. The ring had thousands of sunflowers growing on it.

My grandfather purchased a bow and arrow from an old African (probably about 45 years old or so) and my father (about 10 years old or so) would take it out and use it out on the ring and hunt for whatever. Mostly killed snakes. He is amazed that he wasn't eaten by a lion or bitten by a poisonous snake.

One time he was up in a tree when a large lizard came almost eye to eye and was spitting at him. Needless to say, he got out of the tree in a hurry!

The Africans would also call my dad a "toto" and he would argue and say "I am a bwana" The Africans would all laugh of course at this young boy. It was a running joke with everyone.

The old African that I mentioned previously was a tall skinny man..someone you would think was very weak and feeble. However, he could draw that bow back and send an arrow straight through a cheap cement wall! Most white men couldn't even draw the bow completely back.

My father was one of the founding members of the Urambo Cubscout Group. It was opened up by the chief scout of the world at the time. His name was Lord Rowallen (not sure about the spelling on his name).

Urambo had a very flat countryside with little granite hills. You could go to the top of these hills and lookout for miles. It was a very beautiful site. Unfortunately, the British groundnut scheme was a real eyesore on the landscape since a lot of natural bush countryside was destroyed in that process of growing peanuts. My grandfather's job was overseeing maintenance of transportation vehicles such as trucks and land rovers.

My father was rather rough as a young boy in the late 40s and the Africans used to nickname him Simba. In the end, my grandfather sent him back to school in England to civilize him!

Do you know about bark cloth? It was a red rust color. I doubt it is made anymore.

Regards,

Hal

**

Response from Godfrey Mwakikagile, 6 January 2006

Hello Hal,

This is really interesting! Those are the kind of human interest stories I'm looking for. It's going to be in the book, for sure.

And please let me know if you have any photos from those days, if you can scan a couple or so for me to include in the book.

The groundnut scheme was indeed a disaster. I'm going to write about that also.

As a child, I lived in Kigoma and Ujiji (I was born in Kigoma on 4 October 1949); Morogoro and Mbeya before my parents returned to their home district, Rungwe, to live in a village about four miles from the town of Tukuyu.

My father worked as a medical assistant during British colonial rule. He was one of the few Africans who had secondary school education in those days. He went to Malangali Secondary School in Iringa. He also worked for Brooke Bond in Mbeya.

I have heard about the bark cloth but I have never seen one. And I don't know if some people still make it; an interesting item!

Have a nice day.

Godfrey

***

Continued from Hal Rogers, 6 January 2006

I was just talking to my dad and he remembered that while in Tanganyika my grandfather was given an African sword by a local chief in the Urambo area. He still has that today.

It has a carved wooden sheath, carved wooden handle, and the blade is probably about 2 feet long. It wasn't new when he received so it could be 70 or more years old by now.

Thanks again for your email and I hope that our thoughts will help you in your paper.

Regards,

Hal Rogers

***

From Alan Thompson, Nottingham, UK, 6 January 2006

Hi Godfrey,

Thank you for your e-mail.

I would be happy to share some of my childhood memories of the time I spent in what was Tanganyika in those days.

I spent the first year of my time in Africa in Nairobi. This was from 1954 to 1955. My dad was an engine driver for EAR&H and we then moved to Dar es Salaam. We stayed there until 1962 when we returned to the UK for good.

I can give you a lot more details but what specifically would you like to know? I have no information before the 1950's as I was only born in 1944!!

Best Regards,

Alan Thompson

***

From name withheld upon request, 6 January 2006

Dear Godfrey,

I read your email with great interest and also had a look at your website and looked you up on Google. It was fascinating reading.

I don't know if I can contribute much at all to your latest work. I was 6 when we moved to Tanganyika in 1956 from Nyasaland and went away to school when I was 12 only visiting Mwanza annually until 1964 when my parents left.

So my memories obviously are from a child's perspective and at that age one is concerned with school and playing, nothing too deep.

I know I did love school there and had friends from other race groups although I seem to remember Mbeya School having white and Indian children - I don't remember black children at all.

Also, from when I was 12 until 14 and away in Scotland, I was there on holiday having fun and parties with friends who were in a similar situation.

My life as an only child in Tanganyika was wonderful and I feel sorry for children these days brought up in large cities and in a world of computers, movies, video games etc etc. Life then, as you say, was so much simpler and people seemed to be so much happier, didn't they. I have lived in four African countries but Tanganyika was the country I loved most of all.

If you would like me to write down some details of the kind of life I, as a white child growing up in the colonial times led etc, then I would gladly try to do so. I don't know if it would be that interesting though or if I would be able to write much.

Political matters I obviously cannot really comment on as I was too young then to understand much. But I will give that some thought too.

I have printed out your email and will read your questions again over the weekend and delve into the past and see if I can come up with anything worthwhile for you.

I shall look through the photos but, unfortunately, through moving around such a lot, photos from those days seem to be few and far between. When my father died in 2000 I couldn't find his old album anywhere and I know he had quite a few.

Regards

Anonymous

***

From Nick Edmonson, Greater Manchester, UK, 7 January 2006

Good Morning Godfrey,

Most of the place names you mention in your email are familiar to me. But, considering that I left East Africa in 1953 they are very very distant memories.

Father, set out for the Groundnuts scheme in 1950 determined to give of his best. It did not quite work out that way. He was only interested in Education; politics never was particularly high on his agenda. Regrettably those in 'power' did not share his view.

He had hoped to be able to run the school in Nach as a white school for part of the day and as an African school for the rest of the day. I am not entirely sure of the contract that my father signed, but his hopes were not able to be realised.

What was life like? Brilliant.

Mind you I was only eight years old !

We were provided with an enchanting bungalow. The pit that was left from which soil had been taken to help with the construction of the walls became the bed for three banana plants. Bath water was channelled directly into that pit the plants never ever tasted of soap.

The main idea at the time had been the setting up of a Groundnuts scheme, officially to help the local population but also to line the pockets of those in authority. As is typical for many high-sounding schemes, the situation had not been properly investigated, so ended up being a monumental waste of government funds.

From a childish point of view the life was lovely. Constant heat and constant sunshine. Rain that was a totally new experience. Tropical rainfall has to be experienced, and heard, to be believed.

Father quickly earned the respect of those he took on as his African staff. Our cook, Severin, had been trained in a German Mission station. He was magnificent. Indeed he stayed with us during the whole of our stay in East Africa. Matayo [Sp?], our houseboy, was a master of the charcoal filled smoothing iron. He was tall and majestic in his white robe and fez.

To watch him in action with two irons going, using one and reheating the other, to my young and incredulous eyes, was amazing. There was a never ending stream of Africans arriving at the door seeking employment because Dad's fame as an employer spread far and wide.

--And no snow. At least not at ground level.

I well remember our first car; it was a huge Chevrolet with a split windscreen. It was apparently a swine to start and to that end Dad had several of the concrete pillars that houses were built on, laid flat and sloping so that the car could roll backwards and he could start it with out the starter button. Mother had trouble in the early days getting used to the heat out there.

So, Dad caused the left hand of the split screen removed. That was fine until it rained ! Plastic macs were in vogue by then, but it was not much fun for me getting soaked in the back seat. The joys of motoring Africa style ! !

My mother achieved her own recognition. She loved the hut called a rondavel (sp?). A thatched cone built on several wooden pillars round the edge with a taller central pillar. She had one built in the school playground. Here she would gather with young African mothers and teach them to knit.

This was a remarkable sight if only because of the way those children were carried on the backs of their mothers. Watching the little ones sway and move according to their mothers' actions was a delightful domestic sight. She would also talk to them about basic hygiene.

One of her greatest struggles was with the local witch doctor. Shoving orange peel into the ears of little ones suffering ear-ache is not a sound idea. But in the absence of any better information, that is what many mothers would inflict on their tiny offspring.

My father Norman Edmondson + unknown

Me- Nicholas Edmondson - aged 8

My mother Dorothy Edmondson feeding her beloved hens

Our Duka - built by Dad and the children, to learn how to shop!

One of my most abiding memories is of being at Ndanda Mission Station and watching a queue of African people that must have been 2 miles in length, waiting patiently for the Dispensary to open.

Their ability to remain patient and good natured was legendary. All too frequently the Mission Stations were the only source of medical attention available to most of the Africans.

The behaviour of the white settlers towards the Africans was not always as good as it should have been. Mind you, many of the white people were unsettled by the war, totally footloose and earning more money in East Africa than was possible back 'home'. Many should not have been given work out there. Too much money and not enough facilities to spend it on.

The Indians who ran the Dukas in Nach (Nachingwea), had a thriving scheme that many a white family fell victim to. They would be allowed unlimited credit, but, above a certain level, it would be necessary to surrender your passport. This was fine until your tour of duty came to an end. No passport - no possibility of returning to the UK. Countless families got themselves into bother in this way.

There is Godfrey, a great deal more, just give a pointer and I will try a gain to regress fifty odd years.

Good wishes for the New Year,

Nick

***

More from Nick, Greater Manchester, UK, 7 January 2006

Godfrey

Yoiks. You don't ask for much ! !
I shall really enjoy myself going back down memory lane.
Should you wish to use my name in any book that comes out of this, you are welcome.
My only stipulation is that I live in Greater Manchester, England. Please do not be more specific.
Over the course of the next few days I will assemble my thoughts in some sort of order and then get them off to you.

Cheers,

I'm going to enjoy this project.

Nick

***

From Nick Edmonson, Greater Manchester, UK, 9 January 2006

How would you describe life in Tanganyika in the fifties or in any period during colonial rule?

It was a wonderful life. Plenty of sunshine plenty of time to do whatever you fancied. The war was over. Money was abundant, servants were cheap. There never was any hesitation or excuse needed to have a party. The myriad of insect and animal life was fascinating.

What is it that you particularly miss about those days? Can you give a few examples?

The freedom to wander wherever. The ant hills, magnificent structures. While it was true that care had to be taken in case of wild animals, common sense prevailed. I still vividly remember the day some friends called me to come out to play, wearing only their swimming trunks. Within minutes I was to experience a tropical downpour for the first time. Rain falling as warm water, which was a novel experience.

Wandering off into the bush, finding your own nature trail. The peculiarly shaped Baobab tree. The baboons and their families.

What was the level of interaction between the Europeans and the indigenous people, black Africans?

For the most part the interaction was good. However, I remember being shocked to hear one European admit that he treated his dogs better than he treated his African staff.

Many of the Africans looking for work stated very clearly that they would only work either for a priest or a teacher. If work was not available then they would wander off in search of work elsewhere.

What was your overall impression of colonial Tanganyika

in terms of life? Was life good? Or was it hard? How did you view the colonial authorities? As oppressors or benevolent rulers?

Yes life was good, very good. Because of the nature of the work, the Groundnuts scheme was funded by the British Government. Therefore, there was a large amount of wastage of money.

Those in authority, in many cases, were newly promoted to their position so did not always do their job as efficiently as they could have done. They were mostly benevolent in their treatment of the Africans. But, there was always a minority who could be oppressive.

Was any kind of racial integration allowed anywhere? There were signs in Tanganyika and Kenya saying, "Europeans," "Asians," and "Africans," in compliance with government policy sanctioning racial separation or what was also known as colour bar.
Were there many Europeans who were opposed to this? What was the general attitude among a significant number of them towards racial separation?

I have no recollection of any segregation. Whites and Africans just did not mix.

The white population had their meeting places and the Africans likewise. I was not aware of any Europeans who were opposed to the status quo. Whites and Blacks just did not mix.
Except, that is, in Church. The Europeans sat on the left and the Africans sat on the right hand side of the little straw covered church. My mother was frequently the pianist at the services.

Did you detect any hostility, overt or covert, towards whites on the part of Africans in general and among some of the indigenous people you or some of the people you knew interacted with? For example, house servants, co-workers even if subordinates.

No, none that I ever came across. The House servants were a

vital part of everyday life; but were very firmly kept in place.

I did though, witness one distressing event. An African was walking along a town street, minding his own business, when an Alsatian leapt at him from the back if a pick-up truck.

The African was shocked and scared witless. He leapt out of the way and into the road. He landed in the path of an oncoming car.

The (white) driver of the car only just managed to pull up in time. He leapt out of his vehicle and punched the hapless African in such a way that his jaw was fractured. Dad took it upon himself to ferry the unfortunate man to the local hospital.

Was there any or much sympathy among a significant number of whites for the nationalist aspirations of the Africans in their quest for independence?

Hugely so. After all the Europeans had arrived and taken over the best land for themselves.

There was an overwhelming feeling that the African "so newly brought out of barbarism" was incapable of looking after himself without the benevolent eye of the European.

What was the general attitude among many whites towards the native population? Paternalistic, compassionate, indifferent, hostile, overtly racist or what?

For the most part White and African got on. Mainly this was because the African 'knew his place'. He was also happy to be earning.

Were there any or a significant number of whites who felt that the colonial government was not doing or had not done enough for the people of Tanganyika, especially native Africans, in the areas of health, education, infrastructural development, and political representation at the local and national levels?

Many Europeans were aware that not enough was being done for the welfare of the Africans, but were unwilling to say so for fear of disturbing their own newly acquired life-style.

My father had signed a contract to head a school for Europeans. He was not allowed to teach African children. The only Africans who got near the place were those learning to become office workers. They came to what was effectively night-school.

How do you remember those days? With fondness, nostalgia or not? And why?

With extreme fondness !

I was at an age when everyday presented me with a new experience. Yes, I would love to return there, but I have my doubts as to whether I might like what I found.

Remember I was very young, but I recall those days with happiness. With one crucial exception. My parents were also my teachers, therefore there was no such thing as school holidays for me.

What was it that you liked the most about Tanganyika?

This is a difficult one.

After all life was one long new experience. I was very fair skinned and blond in the eyes of an African. I therefore had some form of magical attraction to them.

Witnessing the wildlife was incredible. Being held up on a track by a family of lions. Although we were in a car, we dare not move. Wondering why the lions were not worried about us and then realising that the ticking over of the engine was a 'purring' sound to them.

On another occasion my parents and I were motoring across the Serengeti Plain and became aware that a flock of ostriches were over to our left.

Their leader suddenly took off and came running alongside us. Without warning the whole flock took a turn right across the front of the car. Although we rapidly slowed down, the last to leap over the car left a claw mark in the bonnet. You don't get that sort of behaviour in English safari parks.

When political agitation and the campaign for independence started, how did members of the white settler community feel or react?

Were they shocked or surprised? Did they accept it as something inevitable that was bound to happen one day anyway?

Before we returned for the last time to the UK we were living in Nakuru (Kenya). Dad was in the process of taking over Greensteds School. The positioning of the buildings was perfect, absolutely alongside the Rift Valley.

The Mau Mau uprising had just started. White settlers living away from civilisation were seen as easy targets. Many Europeans chose to carry guns. Father was told that he had to be issued with a revolver. This was kept under lock and key in the school safe. He never ever carried it with him.

As children we were taken once a week to a firing range and issued with 5 x 0.22 cartridges and expected to hit a tiny target. This I found immensely difficult. Because of the seriousness of the situation , the school was allocated a detachment of Africans from the 'King's African Rifles'. They patrolled at night.

Nothing ever happened that I got to know about, except that the local Police station was raided by the Mau Mau; they stole 30 African Police uniforms and got away without being spotted.

However, as term broke up for the Easter Break and all the boarders were shipped out back to their various homes throughout Kenya, father woke up to a very rude experience on the first day of the holiday.

The custom in those days was that all toilets were outside. Dad, taking his customary first walk of the day, was met by a large dark object blocking his way at the back door. An Askari [African policeman] had been strung up by the neck over the back door.

His lifeless body was rapidly removed. I never saw any of this.

We left the school within three days and my father booked a passage home by sea.

That in itself was a novel experience.

The general feeling amongst the Europeans was that all this

was a little local nuisance and that given time and a few strong-arm European tactics, the indigenous population would be subdued. As we all know that situation escalated.

Another of the silly aspects of the Mau Mau situation was that the colonial ladies took to carrying small pistols and had different coloured holsters to match whatever outfit they were wearing.

Were you and many Europeans apprehensive about their future in an independent Tanganyika under African leadership even if it included whites and Asians as Nyerere did in his independence cabinet and thereafter?

His cabinet members included Derek Bryceson and Dr. Leader Stirling, of British origin; his secretary and personal assistant throughout his tenure as president of Tanganyika, later Tanzania, for almost 25 years, Joan Wicken, was British; Tanganyika's attorney-general soon after independence and thereafter, Roland Brown, was British. He also had Tanzanians of Asian and Arab origin in his cabinet, including Amir H. Jamal of Indian descent. Those are only a few examples.

Too young to give a sensible answer to this question. Although I do remember my parents discussing the merits of the guidance of Leader Stirling.

Throughout our stay in Nach (Nachingwea), my parents were very friendly with the District Officer who lived in Ruponda. He was present, and officiated, at the formal transfer of power to the Africans as Independence was declared.

Full of self-fun he poked merriment at his uniform. Needless to say it was white, but he had to make his own official ribbons to create the appropriate official tassels as worn on these grand occasions. So, ever resourceful, these were created out of crepe-paper. Inevitably the rain arrived and the dye from the paper ran giving him a multi-coloured suit. He was amused that nobody appeared to notice.

Did any of that allay fears among many whites that they would not be discriminated against under predominantly black leadership?

The idea of being led by Africans was anathema to a great many Europeans.

What was the biggest fear among Europeans in Tanganyika after the country won independence? That they would lose the privileges they had always taken for granted during colonial rule or that they would become victims of reverse racial discrimination after Africans took over at the end of colonial rule?

We left Africa in 1953 so the question does not arise for me.

Were racial disparities in the standard of living, employment, wages and political representation a matter of concern among a significant number of the white settlers in colonial Tanganyika? Or did most of them see this simply as the way things ought to be for racial and other reasons?

Cheap labour was in the minds of most Europeans. I do recall that both the cook and the house boy were paid £3 per month. This was, to them, good money.

What vivid memories do you have of the places in which you lived in Tanganyika, and of your interactions with Africans?
Can you give some examples including stories of such personal experiences or encounters? And of some of the exciting or trying moments you had including hardship?

As a child I had a mop of red hair and a face and arms covered in freckles. Whenever we were out motoring through the countryside, if we came across a market we would stop to see what was being sold.

I can remember a sea of faces swarming towards us as we got out of the car and then divide to allow me through. I was something strange, possibly divine, to the eyes of the African because of my colouring. This experience took place many times.

Feel free to share whatever other experiences you may have had in those days which I can include in my book, if you want me to.

Also let me know if you want me to use your name and mention where you live without necessarily naming the city or the town in which you currently reside. I can mention only the country or nothing at all. It's up to you.

Soon after we arrived in Nachingwea, my father took a Land Rover from the motor-pool in the local transport office. The intention was to drive anywhere for a certain length of time and then drive straight back again. This we did complete with a picnic hamper.

We stopped in a small clearing alongside a river and the bridge over which we had just passed. The river bed was totally dry. This in itself was new to me. We enjoyed our picnic and the smells of the countryside, all very new to us.

After a while and with claps of thunder in the far distance Dad suggested that it would be advisable to cross back to the other side of the bridge, and resume our picnic there. This we did.

In the course of the next hour the thunder came closer and then I witnessed the birth of a river. In all too short a time a trickle of water down the middle of the river bed became a fast flowing torrent and the plank/tree-trunk bridge became unsafe.

Had we stayed on the wrong side of the river the route back home would have been horrendous. We had no map of the area.

The image of the birth of that river will stay with me always.

I would also like to know if you have access to any material written by the colonial administrators which contain and reflect their views on the colonial era in Tanganyika and its inhabitants; or if you know where I can get some of this information on the internet.

Sorry I can't help with this one.

Incidentally, though, I do have a further email address: nachingwea@ntlworld.com - just to remind me of my youth !

A further story to amuse:

A Catholic priest was out driving in the bush in a Chevrolet pick-up. It seems he had an accident, crashing his vehicle into a tree. As is required by law all accidents must be reported. Accordingly he made his way on foot to the local police station. There he was met by a very cheerful African.

"Jambo Bwana. I would like to speak to the European Police Officer."
"Sorry, he's away on holiday."
"May I speak to your sergeant ?"
"No. One of his wives is having a baby."
"Who are you ?"
"I'm the prisoner !"

Apparently that police station possessed a Victorian brass bedstead, the envy of many Africans. It did not have mattress, but that did not matter. Africans were known to commit minor offences in order to spend several nights sleeping on an Englishman's bed.

***

The father of one of the pupils at Nachingwea School had been rather a naughty boy during his teenage years. He spent much of his time in a Borstal [a type of boot camp].
He was delighted to have been able to get a job with the Groundnuts scheme in order to show the world that he was a reformed character and prove his own self-worth.

***

I'm sure that during your own school days, Godfrey, you were late arriving at school. You will have needed to find a plausible excuse quickly.

Try this:-

Two brothers arrived 1½ hours late one morning. Dad, looked at them and asked if they had a sensible excuse for being late.

They replied that they felt that the road being blocked by a herd of hungry elephants was excuse enough. It's not the sort of excuse you come across every day !

***

There was the story of the African who was given a cast-off hat by a European. The fellow was very proud of his new acquisition. Later that same day he was given a lift on the back of a flat-backed lorry along with several other Africans.

The custom was to hang on firmly to the top the woodwork behind the cab. Unfortunately, the wind blew the hat off the African's head. He went to retrieve it. He did not survive to tell the tale. It had been his first ever ride on any sort of transport.

***

My father was typical Englishman. He like a cup of tea. While out in the countryside one afternoon with the house-boy, Mataiyo(sp?), Father stopped in a pleasant spot and got out the primus stove and all the little gadgets needed to get the thing going.

Mataiyo had disappeared unnoticed and arrived back with a steaming brew for each of us just as Dad had got the Primus finally alight. Mataiyo was delighted to show us how he had found three small pebbles, two dry sticks and some tinder and had rubbed the sticks together to start his tiny fire.

If you were prepared to listen there was much that could be learned from the African.

***

From Angela Monkman Brushett, UK, 8 January 2006

Hello Godfrey...

I am just awaiting my visa to go out to TZ for three weeks!! Usa River. You have just caught me.

I have looked at your web site and now realise I am

corresponding with quite an amazing person - a privilege!

How on earth did you track me down? And through ExpertSearch too...???

May I preface any further communication by saying that I am NOT (nor ever have been) a political animal. I grew up, was brought up and was educated in TZ and in Kenya and to all intents and purposes was mtoto wa Africa - it was and still is in my heart, my home - so if you want political response there is little I can help you with.

But I am happy to give you commentary.

Best wishes,

Angela Monkman Brushett

***

From Angela Monkman Brushett, 9 January 2006

Schools in Tanganyika in early 50's, for Europeans, were:
Boarding - Lushoto, Mbeya and Arusha . Also Kongwa(all prep schools age range 7 to 12). I believe these were all government sponsored/approved.

Day - Junior European School in Dar (prep 7 to 12) which has become the basis of the current International School so I assume they will have the archives.

St Joseph's in Dar run by the White Fathers took some Europeans but was mainly Goanese Catholic.

There were no secondary schools for Europeans in Tanganyika at that stage although if my memory serves me correctly there was an attempt to establish one in Iringa.

These schools admitted British, Greeks, Germans, Swedes, Danish, Italians, South Africans, Poles, Russians, Lithuanians, Jews, etc. etc. as historically this was just after the second world war with its displacement fall-out. So they were amazing melting pots of little society.

I recall no others which fed into my secondary school in Nairobi from Tanganyika up until 1957.

Kenya was different, partly because it WAS a colony and

Tanganyika was not, only a protectorate under the League of Nations/United Nations and therefore must have had different educational statutes and directives.

Hope this is helpful.

Angela

***

From Mattew Primrose, New Zealand, 9 January 2006

Dear Godfrey,

Thanks for your e-mail.

Where abouts in the USA do you live and what do you do there ?

I have spent a few years in the USA (I was in the oil industry) at various times in New Orleans, San Francisco and Houston and have been up and down the west coast a few times, but never really explored the central or eastern states.

I was only a young child in the 1950's when we lived in Tanganyika, first in Dar es Salaam (1950-53), then Moshi (1953-59).

After that we moved to Kenya for a couple of years before my parents decided to return to the UK as my father was told his job would disappear with upcoming independence and Africanisation.

He returned to East Africa for two years on his own, while my mother, brother and I remained in the UK, and handed over several branches of the company he worked for to African managers.

During this time he was mainly in Tanganyika. In 1962, while he was for a time in Dar es Salaam, we joined him for a few weeks holiday during which we toured through Kenya and as far as the Murchison Falls national park in Uganda.

This was a sort of farewell to EA for all of us. My father's job finished in 1963 and he returned to the UK to rejoin the family. He had spent 25 years in East Africa, including a few years in Ethiopia and Somalia in the army during WW2. He died in 1982.

My childhood memories are mainly of living in Moshi,

boarding school in Lushoto, our few years in Kenya and our holiday in 1962.

I remember Moshi as a thriving town with a lively market and a number of major businesses serving the farms in the area. The company my father worked for sold farm and construction machinery and had the EA agencies for Caterpillar and John Deere form the USA plus Ransomes (farm machinery), Lister and Ruston (diesel engines, generators, pumps. etc) and British Leyland (cars and trucks) from the UK.

One of the few other European children of my age in the area was the son of the local Ford dealer that also sold cars, trucks and tractors. We also had friends whose father managed the Tanganyika Planters Estates at Arusha Chini. These were large sugar and sisal estates that stretched for miles.

My father's other clients included the coffee farms and other highland farms on the slopes of Kilimanjaro. Many of these were owned and managed by the Chaga tribe cooperatives, a few belonged to missions and some were in the hands of European farmers.

I started school at a kindergarten run in the hall of the Moshi Anglican Church.

As I said, there were few Europeran children those that there were came from farming, police, and professional families such as doctors, lawyers, etc. The only two other boys of around my age in town were sons of a chartered accountant, and whose mother worked part-time as my father's typist/secretary.

After a couple of years at the new European primary school, when I was just over 7 years old, there were insufficient children to justify a class in the school, so we (myself and the chartered accountant's sons) were sent to a boarding school in Lushoto in the Usambara mountains. This was still a small school of maybe 100 or so children from all over Tanganyika.

The only realistic alternatives were one of the very exclusive, and costly, preparatory schools in Nairobi or to be sent back to relatives in the UK to attend school there.

The Ford dealer's son and our friends from Arusha Chini were sent to schools in the UK at this time.

Boarding school was hard for 7 and 8 year old children (it was somewhat basic and austere) and the high altitude in Lushoto gave us our first experience of living in a cold climate for a few months of the year at least.

As we grew a bit older, school vacations back home in Moshi became a joy. I remember the climate as fairly even, not excessively warm (we certainly did not have air conditioning), and just cool enough for a fire at night for a few weeks a year.

It was a bit lonely though as there were never more than two or three other children of my age around at a time, including my younger brother and the older son of the chartered accountant. Consequently I spent a lot of time on my own, climbing trees and roaming the countryside exploring (to my parents constant worry as snakes were common and several pet dogs in the area were lost to leopards at one time or another).

I also spent many hours pestering our shamba boy, Andrea, who would show me many things I missed on my own such as the chameleons in the bouganvillia bushes and frogs in the ponds and irrigation ditches.

I have been told that I spoke Swahili better than English at one time, but I have just about lost it all over the years.

At weekends we would sometimes go ' up the mountain' for a picnic and to fish for trout in the streams. Occasionally we would visit one of the hotels on the mountain, mainly Marangu Lodge, that was used as starting points for tourists climbing Kilimanjaro. We would have Sunday lunch or tea and look at the monkeys and other animals they kept in cages for the tourists.

Another Sunday outing, only a couple of times a year, was the 50-mile drive to Arusha. We usually spotted quite a lot of game, mainly zebra and giraffe, but very occasionally an elephant, and of course lots of gazelle and antelopes of all kinds. We would also sometimes see Meru or Masai tribesmen with their cattle. They looked similar but there were definite differences in dress and appearance.

Most years we would have a vacation by the sea. We usually went to a beach hotel near Mombasa with our friends from Arusha Chini, whose children would be on summer vacation from school in the UK in later years.

My father only got ' home leave' to return to the UK every third year. I was too young to really remember our 'home' trips in 1953 and 1956 and in 1959 my parents decided to forego the trip to the UK in order to tour by car from Moshi to Capetown and back.

This was a wonderful trip through Tanganyika, the Rhodesias (as they were then) via the Kariba Dam and Victoria Falls, through central South Africa to Capetown and then back along the east coast of S. Africa to Durban before turning inland again to Johannesburg and back north to Moshi.

All this was done in a ' new' 1959 Austin Cambridge saloon car, nothing fancy or 4WD, with only a few punctures and no real other trouble.

Borders, politics and economic troubles in some of those countries would make such a trip much more difficult today and possibly quite dangerous for a family on their own.

Things have obviously changed with the years.

Shortly after I started working for Shell in the early 1970's, I met a geologist who had been in the Moshi area on oil exploration work. I mentioned my recollections of the area and our friends on the large sugar cane and sisal plantations at Arusha Chini. He knew Arusha Chini and said they had found a network of narrow gauge rail tracks in the bush, but nobody knew their history.

There was no sugarcane and the sisal had grown wild to be indistinguishable from the bush plants.

Nationalisation of the estates after independence killed off the incentive to plant new crops 3 to 5 years ahead of first harvest, and most of the estates died when the old crops had run their lifetimes. A great pity in a country of so much potential.

I trust this very biased *wazungu mtoto* account is of interest.

If you haven't already read it, I strongly suggest you find a copy of Elsbeth Huxley's *The Sorceror's Apprentice*. It is out of print but may be available in libraries or I have seen it on the internet from used book dealers.

It is a well written account of her travels through all 3 E African territories around 1947/48. She makes many observations about the history and political structures exsiting at the time, as well as first-hand accounts of observations and meetings with both African and European farmers and officials. When I read it, it gave me a real sense of understanding the background and foundations of the E. Africa that I experienced in the 1950's and early 1960's.

Regards

Matthew Primrose

***

From Sharon Bernhardt, South Africa, 9 January 2006

Hi Godfrey... I have only just received your E.mail.

Give me a little time and I will send you some info. I am also writing a book at the moment about my childhood growing up Africa.

I was only eight years old when I went to Mbeya boarding school, but I am happy to share an excerpt from my (proposed) book.

I hope you have a wonderful New Year.

Speak to you soon....

Sharon

***

From Gerald Beers, Berkshire, England, 11 January 2006

Dear Godfrey

I lived in Dar es Salaam, Kilosa and in 'the bush' as I was building and maintaining railways and harbours.

I have very happy memories of Tanganyika in the fifties. It was a nice country to live in, very peaceful and hardly any crime.

I never ever felt threatened in any way and never felt that I was in any danger. The people were very friendly and all in all it was a nice place to live.

Of course it was not a rich country and we never seemed to have any money but we were very happy.

Good luck with your project.

Regards

Gerald Beers

PS: I was reasonably fluent in Kiswahili but I am afraid I have forgotten most of it now. After all, it was 'zamani mwaka hamsini' (long time ago in the year 1950).

***

From Pam Sparrow, Gloucestershire, England, 12 January 2006

Dear Godfrey

I am not sure what sort of things you are wanting, but I was only 10 when I left Mombasa at the end of 1954 to be dumped at school in the UK.

My memories are probably more of Kenya as Dad was posted from Tanganyika there in the early 50's. I could only really tell you about life from a young child's perspective, if that is what you want I could try and do something for you.

Is is it specifically Tanganyika info that you are wanting because I am actually in contact with quite a few people, mostly of my parents' generation (now in their 80s/90s) and I know a couple of them were in Tanganyika with us so if I asked them they may write something which I could forward but first I would need to know from you a little more precisely exactly what it is you want so I can tell them.

How long have you lived in the States and where abouts are you there?

Probably from Kenya Korner you know I live in the UK in Gloucestershire which is sort of in the the south west, in Stroud which is not far from Bristol.

Salaams

Pam

***

From Dave Allen, UK, 13 January 2006

Dear Godfrey,

I'm afraid that I have so many memories of my time in school at Mbeya and Iringa and of course memories of Kondoa Irangi, Babati and finally Biharamulo which are the three places that I lived whilst in Tanganyika it would take me at least 2 weeks to put them all on paper.

I was born in Tanga and lived in Tanganyika for 14 years before my parents moved back to UK. I am very interested in where you got my name and the information about me having lived in Tanganyika. I will try and put something on paper for you.

Kind regards,

Dave.

***

From John Griffiths, UK, 13 January 2006

Dear Godfrey,

This will be only a short reply to acknowledge your e-mail until I have time to write a more detailed reply. May I request the reason for your interest?

I feel very privileged to have been brought up in Tanganyika, and still have a very strong feeling in my heart that there is a part which will always be African.

I was brought up in Kenya and also in Tanganyika, going to school in Nairobi, Mbeya, Kongwa and Iringa. Yes, I only have fond memories as mine was a wonderful childhood spent in a wonderful country.

Bye for now

John

***

Continued from John Griffiths, UK, 13 January 2006

Jambo Godfrey

Habari.

Alas my Swahili is not what it was, but some of my school friends are still very fluent and have more interesting stories about being born at the roadside in the bush and learning Swahili as their first language as they were looked after by an ayah (yaya, housemaid).

I will most certainly put together some thoughts and look through old photographs, and speak with fellow Iringans to direct their recollections to you.

My last six years in Africa were spent in Iringa, my father ran the telecommunications side of the post office and during the holidays. I used to ride out with him in the back of the pickup to visit the lines men.

The lines men were the only way of fault finding as elephants were fond of telephone poles to rub against, often bringing them down. For protection the linesmen had bows and arrows, so my father told me.

I am about to go out, so will contact again with some more memories.

Nice to meet you Godfrey
Best wishes

John

***

Continued from John Griffiths, UK, 13 January 2006

p.s.: in Iringa everything worked, no water shortage, there was always electricity and I don't recollect ever being without anything.

***

From Winnifred Colclough, USA, 14 January 2006

Dear Godfrey

How interesting to hear from you. As one has to be so careful I searched your books on the Internet and see you have written quite a few.

I was born 12 October 1944 in what was then Northern Rhodesia (Zambia) and moved to Mwanza in Tanganyika in 1946 when I was 2 years old.

My father, Hendrik S. A. Smit was in the British Overseas Civil Service and started as a land surveyor. He gradually worked his way up until he was the head of Town Planning in Dar es Salaam in the early sixties. He was on very friendly terms with Mr Nyerere.

We lived in Mwanza until 1949 and moved to Moshi where we lived until 1955 when we moved to Dar es Salaam. I was schooled at Arusha, Kongwa, Iringa and St. Joseph's Convent in Dar.

I have nothing but the fondest memories of my days in Africa and in fact about 70 of us students from Iringa are meeting in South Africa in September for a reunion. Many of us have not seen each other for over 40 years!

Of course, I realize now that my life was very privileged but when I was young I was not at all "political".

I would be delighted to share my memories and what few photos I have.

I am in contact with many people who lived in Tanganyika in the '50's and '60's. I have printed your e-mail and will respond to each "heading" at a later date. I am at work at present so can't do it now but I just wanted to respond to you.

Did you e-mail everyone on that Iringa website?

I will be in touch again soon.

Kindest regards.

Freddie

***

From Mike Mills, 14 January 2006

Hi Godfrey

Thanks your e-mail.
I would like very much to contribute but may take a little time.
I went to Tanganyika in 1949 with my parents, my father being employed by Lands and Surveys initially to survey the Central Province for the construction of dams.
During the period till 1975 we lived in Kongwa, Lushoto, Mombo, Manyoni, Singida, Shinyanga, Ngudu Kwimba, Mwanza, Tanga, Mbeya and DSM plus short-term living in Kondoa Irangi, Kwa Mtoro and numerous other small villages.
Enough for now. I will gather my thoughts and those of my sister, who was born in Kongwa, and get back to you.
Kwa heri kwa sasa
Cheers

Mike Mills

***

From Shiraz Shivji, USA, 14 Tanganyika 2006

Dear Godfrey,

I actually bought one of your books on Mwalimu Julius Kambarage Nyerere.
I was born in Tanzania in Iringa from an Asian family that were early pioneers and my father was born in Iringa as well. My grandfather came to Iringa at the age of 10!
When I was growing up I was fluent in Swahili and knew a few words of Kihehe of the local Hehe tribe. From your name it seems to me that your parents were probably from Tukuyu.
I do remember very fondly my early years growing up in the nineteen fifties. Of course, at that time the color bar was very strong and we had a tiered society where the whites were a very privileged class.
However as I was a little boy (I turned 13 in 1960) it did not

seem to bother me as much. It did affect all of us to a great degree. For example, the *Wazungu* (whites) had their own schools that were very well supported by the Colonial government. Others could attend the very few Mission Schools or start their own. Our community, the Ismailis, spent a lot of money building our own Aga Khan Schools in practically every town. These schools were open to students of every race and creed.

I had a lot of classmates that were Hindus, Muslims and (a few) Christians. After independence St Michael's and St. George's opened it's doors to 40 Asian and Black students in 1961. I attended this prestigious school the following year in 1962. I may be off by a year in my dates! I will check the exact dates later!

Like you I came here for graduate studies. I went to Stanford for a Ph.D. and have been here for more than 36 years. I do have some pictures from the fifties and early sixties that you may find useful.

Overall life in Iringa was quite pleasant. Of course the weather has a lot to do with this. We used to visit relatives in Dar Es Salaam, Morogoro and Kilosa. I used to love the tropical fruits in Kilosa especially the mangoes.

I had interactions with Indians and with Blacks but not much with Europeans. I found that the relations among the races were cordial except when the *Wazungu* (whites) wanted to show off their "superiority". During Ramadhan we used to exchange food for "futuru" across races. In fact we used to enjoy eating cassava cooked by our Black friends. In Iringa we did not lack for water or electricity (Tanesco).

Best regards,

Shiraz

***

From Farhan Yazdani, Tahiti, 14 January 2006

Dear Godfrey,

I would be delighted to help. I also have a lot of photos which are in France, and at the moment I am in Tahiti.

I am also sending your mail to my cousins in Brighton, UK. Their dad wrote his memories as a doctor in Dar-es-Salaam

Perhaps you can send your message to the Iringa school list and your book will become an encyclopaedia!

Where are you in the states?

Warmest greetings

Farhan

***

From Jerzy Krotiuk, South Africa, 14 January 2006

Dear Godfrey

Jambo, Habari gani?

I was born in Moshi on the 10th October 1948, went to school in Mbeya and Iringa, we have extremely fond memories of Tanganyika and can reminisce for hours, you will notice the Iringa web site is strongly supported.

My home nowadays is in South Africa and I work as an expatriate in Qatar, I get home once every 6 months. I was in Tanzania in 2000 and was involved in a contract to construct a powerline from Sumbawanga (Rukwa Region) to Mbala in Zambia, during this time I visited Mbeya & Iringa schools.

After a gap of 36 years I was quite shocked at the changes(I left Tanzania in 1964) We have a lot of photos and my father who is still alive is presently also trying to write a book about his experiences in Tanganyika after the war, believe me he has plenty!

I will only be home in June, maybe I can scan a few photos but obviously they have to have some relevance as to their history and would have to be described, trully a fascinating and nostalgic period of our lives.

Take care and keep in touch. I hope I can help in some way.

Kind Regards

Jerzy Krotiuk

***

From Sheila Cout, 14 January 2006

Dear Godfrey

I have just read your letter and I nearly cried. It's been forty-odd years since I left. I was seventeen then and I think about the place and our lives there practically everyday.

I thought by now we were completely forgotten. So your letter was wonderful.

Did we ever meet? I was born 1945 in Arusha. To me it is the center of the world. I went to primary school there and then to Kongwa and Iringa Secondary School. They were European schools and that was basically our downfall.

You see, we were set apart from everyone else and in a way we grew up thinking we were the only people that mattered and we owned the place. But at the time we had no idea life was great and the country was beautiful. I don't remember any inconveniences.

But we were never told or taught about Africa, its history, its people, its human richness. All that was ignored and we were taught about the Battle of Hastings. I did not have one black friend and that in a nutshell is what troubles me. We lived there but we were not a part of it.

Basically for us white kids life there was one long adventure. It was a dream that was shattered the day I left. I loved Mount Meru the most. It was my protector, my mother.

Our interaction with Africans and Arabs was minimal. Yet we used to spend hours talking and listening to stories with whoever worked in our house. We had our own communities, i.e. Greek, English, Afrikaans, Polish, etc., and we stayed in those areas. But funnily enough, the English made us Greeks feel second-class.

I think I will finish now. I could talk to you for days about the place.

Thank you, keep well, Godfrey.

Sheila.

P.S.: I want to go to Arusha soon. It's going to be my equivalent of going to Mecca.

***

From Pam Sparrow, 14 January 2006

Dear Godfrey

Thanks, now that gives me something to work on, but don't expect it all tomorrow, it will take me some time to think about, formulate, look for some suitable photos from the ones I have etc.

My brother has all Dad's EA family photos and for some reason, no matter how many times I ask, he does not seem to be forthcoming in letting me have them which annoys me as he does not remember as much as I do being younger and he has never had the same continuing interest in his roots and EA and has never been back like I have.

He's not interested in trying to trace people we knew and grew up with as I am. Families, who'd have them.

What is your proposed timescale anyway?

Do you still want me to ask my older friends for anything?

Salaams

Pam

***

From Judy Allen, Australia, 15 July 2006

Dear Godfrey,

We lived in Dar-es-salaam for about 5 years. My 2 sisters Patricia and Elizabeth went to Mbeya Primary school as boarders. Those memories for them were not very happy ones. Life was good. My father worked for EAR&H (East African Railways & Harbours Corporation) as an engineer. My mother worked most of the time for Stewart Stores.

We did not have any unpleasant experiences that I know of. Sorry I cant help you any more.

Best wishes with your book

Regards

Judy

***

From Carol Lee, London, England, 15 January 2006

Dear Godfrey,

Nice to hear from you.
I have written a fair amount about childhood in Tanganyika in my book, *Crooked Angels*, published by Century hb and Arrow pb a couple of years back and being republished by Parthian on Feb 1st. The ISBN number of the upcoming edition is 1-902638-67-0.
There is a little more about teenage years in Tanganyika in another book of mine, also to be published by Century, on May 4th this year, *A Child Called Freedom*, which comes out to coincide with the 30th anniversary of the Soweto Uprising in June.
Would you let me know the titles and ISBN numbers of your published work and I'll have a look too.
Also, who will be publishing your book of Tanganyika memories and if you have a working title for it yet?
Meanwhile, if you look at *Crooked Angels* (you may find the Century hb or Arrow pb of this still available via Amazon) you'll get a lot of info from there.
If you still want more, I'd prefer to do it on the phone.

Carol

***

From Christine Byron, UK, 15 January 2006

Dear Godfrey

Thank you for your interesting letter and request to hear from me about experiences in Tanganyika in the 50s.

It sounds a great idea to write a book like that. So often people talk about it but don't actually get around to doing it. I would be delighted to help you, although my contribution may be very modest.

But I think I would enjoy looking back and thinking and reminiscing about those times. I recently went back to visit Iringa school and the region with my husband. After 50 years away it brought back a lot of memories.

I am just about to go away for a short holiday, so am just acknowledging your letter for now, but will try to reply in some detail to your questions during February/March.

I hope this will be OK for you.

Very best wishes

Christine Byron

***

From Geoff Jones, 15 January 2006

Dear Godfrey,

Many thanks for your mail. This will have to be short as I am in the middle of some work but I will get back to you later in more detail.

In the meantime you may like to have a look at www.ntz.info/index html. This is a web site set up by David Marsh who also lived in Tanganyika during the fifties.

It is full of names and information which you should find interesting. It is made up of many memories and photographs entered by people who grew up out there.

Best wishes

Geoff

***

From Sheila Graham, Durban, South Africa, 15 January 2006

Hi Godfrey,

It was good to hear from you via Kenya Korner which site has been instrumental in us reconnecting with people we had lost touch with over the years.

I'm not sure that I will be of any use to you in passing on impressions of the then Tanganyika as I was only nine years of age when I first went there.

My Dad was seconded to the EAR & Harbours in 1949, and I know both he and my Mum loved Dar es Salaam where they spent five years, very happy years.

You can imagine that life there was a far cry from post-war England at that time. As a child I remember loving the life: the pleasure of going to the beach after school, the warmth and freedom we had.

As I recall, I don't think there was an official colour bar in force in those days but distinctions were rather along social and cultural lines so one's friends both for adults and children tended to come from similar backgrounds

After Dar my Dad was posted to Arusha for a couple of years. At that time Arusha was rather sleepier and not the international centre it appears to be today. Again, although vastly different to Dar in many ways, we had a super life there.

My Dad was posted to Kenya where he spent time in Voi and Maji Mazuri up on the western Rift - again, times which we all loved and enjoyed.

I went to England for my senior schooling, visiting home (both Tanganyika and Kenya) for holidays, and seeing my parents when they went back to England on home leave every two years.

Once I had completed my schooling and college I went back to Kenya where I worked in LegCo (the then Legislative Assembly) as a Hansard Reporter at the particularly interesting time of handover from British to Kenyan rule. It was a very stimulating time to be involved in the parliamentary process as you can imagine.

I met my husband, had both our sons in Nairobi before we left East Africa and settled down in Durban, South Africa.

We have thought about a trip back to revisit old haunts, but so far have done nothing. Both our sons and their families have settled overseas, one in Scotland and the other in Vancouver, so most of our spare time and cash is spent visiting them!!

I sorry that I'm not much help with giving you background on the Tanganyika of the 1950s, but children do see life through rose coloured spectacles and have no understanding of any social or political problems which may exist around them.

I hope you do manage to visit Tanzania and the many places your family live in so many years ago. It would be wonderful.

Regards,

Sheila

***

From Norman, South Africa, 15 January 2006

Hi Godfrey,

This is colito in answer to your interesting e-mail, 50s Tanganyika (sounds great).

I was there from 1957-59 so I can only help with 3 yrs. I arrived in Kenya in 1952 and went to Dar in 57 and stayed in TY until 1964 when in January my family was deported by the army in the mutiny. My father was seconded to the 1st Battallion Tanganyikan rifles at Colito Barracks 10 miles north of Dar from the Royal Artillery.

Another great source of information is Walter Gomez whom you will find on the St. Michael's (and St. George's) School list. He lived there all through the 50s. He is a Goan Indian from the Arusha area.

I only have fond memories of my favourite country . I loved it there and being expelled left a big scar on my life for yrs. I arrived in South Africa in '65 and have never left. I stay 32 klms from Cape Town .

I wish you all the best with the '50s TY book.
Kind regards.

Norman (senior)

***

From Maria Jones, South Africa, 15 January 2006

Dear Godfrey,

Thank you for this e mail.
I was born in Mwanza in 1944 and I have an older brother called Stephan who was born in 1943.
My parents were from Austria and my father was recruited by the British in Cyprus working with displaced people. No quite sure what he did.
My mother and he then went to Tanganyika where he was put in charge of an Italian Prisoner of War camp I think in the Mwanza area or somewhere near Lake Victoria.
After the war my father was appointed into the British Colonial Service by the British Government and worked mainly in the Public Works and Administration Departments in and around Lake Victoria.
My brother was born in the Mission Hospital in Bukoba.
I remember my father telling me that one of his tasks combined with the Italian Prisoner of War camp was to spread the word amongst locals that the Kaiser was dead, that Tanganyika had been handed to the British after the First World War and they were to stop creating problems for the few British troops in the country - i.e. don't ambush them they are friends.
Just before my 6th birthday (January) we lived in Biharamulo where there was an old German fortress type Boma. The lorries used for transport burnt wood instead of petrol. We did not have any electricity and my mother was the only female westerner for miles around. A trip for groceries involved a 250 to 300 mile round trip to Bukoba on dirt pot-holed roads.
Our kitchen had a big wood burning stove set in a separate building from the main house. It had a grass thatched-roof. I wanted to be important and decided to make my mother a cup of tea. I waited until the Mpishi (cook) went off for lunch and shoved as much wood as I could into the stove to get it really hot. The grass thatch caught fire and I ran into where my mother was

having a sleep in her bedroom - speaking only German and Swahili I shouted that jiko na choma (the kitchen is burning) in Swahili.

By the time my mother and the staff realised what was happening, the kitchen was a shell, together with our entire supply of groceries which had just been purchased. My father had left on safari to visit outlying areas and did not return for one month.

My first school was Arusha School. As I was not yet 6, my mother was appointed the Escorting Adult. We travelled to Bukoba where we caught a steamer with other children travelling to school and steamed to Jinja where we went by bus (I think) through the National Parks to Voi and then around Kilimanjaro to Arusha.

My poor mother hardly spoke English and was driven crazy keeping track of 30 assorted "children" of varying ages bent on mischief. She then had to face the harrowing experience of leaving me at school for the next 3 months and returning home on her own. I don't recall any trauma as there were many other German-speaking children at the school.

To me Mwanza was a civilised town. My father was stationed briefly in Geita and as there was no electricity at the Government "Station" we lived in a house on the mine. (Gold mine). This mine was owned by Williamson Diamond Mines and once a week a small plane flew in and landed on the air strip and picked up the weeks haul in the form of gold bars.

Once, as a joke, the son of the general manager of the mine decided to stage a "highjacking" of the gold as it was being loaded. We all joined in but then handed it over. We were severely reprimanded by the General Manager and lectured on the dangers of such pranks.

My second school was Kongwa near Dodoma where many of the "Iringians" were before St Michael's & St George's name of school at Iringa was built. From Mwanza getting to Kongwa involved two nights and one day travelling by train to Dodoma and then on buses to Kongwa.

Kongwa was the sight of the failed English groundnut scheme started after the war. (Some time ago in September 1989 I was in England and saw a full documentary on Kongwa including what had become of it - I am sure you can get a copy of this from the

BBC archives - you would be fascinated). There are many "fireside" stories of Kongwa.

On some trips there was no dining car and we had to take our own food or buy from the hawkers at the stations (dodgy !!).

I remember I had a bottle of juice in my luggage which leaked so I had nothing to drink for the duration of the trip and wet sticky clothes. I was probably 11 or 12 at the time. Occasionally one of the wheels of a coach would fall off the track and this involved many hours waiting for repair crews to jack it back on again.

In Kongwa we were housed in small individual houses, approximately 500 or more metres apart, of 10 girls with three of the houses forming a School House. I was in Wilberforce and then there was Curie, Palmer and Livingstone. These houses were surrounded by high fences of a needless cactus-type shrub.

Until Princess Margaret's visit to the school - the toilets were long drops some distance away and were an entomologist's delight in terms of insect life.

Hungry hyenas often came and knocked over the dustbins and on one harrowing occasion as we were all walking the 2 kms walk back from the school building after prep at about 8p.m. they swooped down and carried off this Alsation dog belonging to a teacher. The hyenas dropped the dog when several girls gave chase but the dog was so severely hurt it had to be put down.

We were allowed pets and many of us rode around on bicycles despite the terrible thorn strewn basic paths and tracks politely referred to as "roads". This was because of the distances to the dining room (coverted aeroplane hanger) and class rooms (a series of wooden buildings).

All the while, in the middle of Africa, we wore full uniform of brown skirts, beige blouses, green/gold/brown striped ties, closed-up black or brown shoes and white socks. We had to wear blazers too. Our "casual" uniform was gingham checked dresses in the colours of our various School Houses - yellow for Wilberforce, green for Palmer, blue for Livingstone and red for Curie.

The senior boys over the age of 18 were allowed cars and guns and encouraged to go hunting. Kongwa is very arid and the local tribe the "Wa Gogo" are nomadic and dress similar to the Masai. They often breached the water pipes to water their cattle and then we had no water until the breach was discovered only for the pipe to be breached elsewhere.

On Sundays we could request an "exeat" and sandwiches and go far out into the "bush" as long as we went in an odd number. This was a co-educational school and boys and girls were taught respect for each other. We were a very innocent bunch.

I have memories of walking for miles with my friends right out into the bush with no one else in sight and only the faint sound of the bells that the Wa Gogo hung around the necks of the first-born cow of the season competing with the sound of insects. This sound for me brings back wonderful vibes.

Part of my father's employment was for overseas leave every 2 or 3 years when he would take us on a slow passenger line to Europe and England.

It was not until I went to college in London in the 60's that I recall using an escalator or had the occasion to use a public pay phone.

Many of the Iringians are extremely successful high achievers. We had a reunion in South Africa two years ago and I was so impressed by what my fellow pupils had achieved. I don't recall many of them but these achievements were impressive.

Tanganyika was called the land of "bado kidogo" by ex pat teachers because of its laid-back life style and we were warned by many of these teachers that we were doomed to failure if we did not make a real effort at school.

At Kongwa we only went home twice a year. At Arusha we had three holiday periods a year and Iringa too.

Iringa is near the Zambian border so the trip there from Mwanza was also a three- to four-day affair (first to Dodoma and then on by bus) - depending on the efficiency of the trains and buses.

In the rainy season I often had to be taken home from Arusha across the Serengeti Plains by white hunters in their special landrovers as the roads were impassable from flooding rivers.

I'll wait for your reply. I'll look for old photographs. Hope you can pick up something from this screed.

Regards.

Maria Jones

***

From Bryan Ulyate, 16 January 2006

Hi Godfrey,

Thanks for your interesting mail, yes I will send you as much info that I can but will be in a couple of weeks as I would like to compile as much as I can, so bear with me.
Tanganyika was a fantastic place with lovely people no matter what colour or creed they were. Due to the Swahili language it united everyone so you never got tribal conflicts that I knew of. Sadly it was very badly managed by a government that end up ruining a wonderful country and bringing it to its knees.
Anyhow I will go into further details when I compile my memoirs for you, thanking you regards,

Bryan

***

From Barbara Laing, 16 January 2006

Hello Godfrey

I will do my best to put something together for you. I will also contact my brother and ask him to jot some memories down - he's a professor at San Diego State University.
I got married in Mbeya in 1964 - happy memories.
Regards

Barbara Laing

***

From Geoff Jones, 16 January 2006

Dear Godfrey,

At the moment I am supervising prep at the school where I

teach so I have a few minutes to put down a few thoughts.

My father decided to take the family to Tanganyika during 1953. After the war he had found it impossible to find a full time position in the church and he was teaching in Coventry England. Prospects were not great and the pay even less so, so when he saw the advert for a post as chaplain master to Arusha School he applied immediately.

In brief he was offered the post and we left for Africa aboard the MS Boschfontein in April/May 1954. I was really too young to appreciate the journey out but I do remember the excitement and one or two interesting moments during the three week voyage.

We landed in Mombasa and stayed in a Hotel for a few nights before catching the train up country. We were met in Moshi by the Headmaster, Cyril Hamshere, and driven the last 50 miles in the School Dodge Wagon.

We had a wonderful life living in the school, of course during term time we had many friends to play with and during the holidays the staff kids had all the school facilities at our disposal.

My brother, Huw and I were especially friendly with the Morgan boys Richard Mark and Brian. We got up to all sorts of mischief together and seemed to be out from dawn to dusk. They later moved to Dar es Salaam and later to Mbeya where their Dad Bill was Headmaster.

Arusha was a good place to live with a most pleasant climate and being on the slopes of Mt. Meru there was rarely a shortage of rain. It was a busy place too being the centre of tourist activity and the gateway to many of the Game parks. It was well served with good communications 70 miles of good tarmac road in every direction as well as an airstrip with connections to all parts of the country.

I don't recall any bad moments during my time there but that may be memory cutting things out.

We had friends who farmed south of the town and we spent many happy days with them.

When I think back now I appreciate how fortunate we were to live there. I went to school in Arusha and then went to Iringa in 1960, two years later I was moved to The Prince of Wales in Nairobi and remained there until I finished in 1966. I then left to return to the UK to train as a teacher.

Hope this is some use, if I think of anything more I will write again, or if you want more detail let me know and I'll dredge the memory banks again.

Best wishes.

Geoff

***

From Marion Gough, England, 16 January 2006

Dear Godfrey

Thank you for your email.
I went to Africa in 1950 to Urambo during the Ground Nut Scheme.

When I was little they lived in a tent, then made a little hut with tin roof. Some lions had been shot and Dad made me stand in-between them to take a photo and they were still twitching. I was really frightened!

One of the East African Railways & Harbours (EAR&H) buses used throughout East Africa in Tanganyika, Kenya and Uganda in the 1950s. I remember they were Leyland buses. Photo sent by Marion Gough.

I had an Ayah (yaya, house maid), called Celia who helped my mum look after me. When she was first in Urambo she used to bake bread on her kooni (kuni - firewood) stove and many people used to come to buy it. This helped make ends meet.

The Ground Nut Scheme folded and my father was offered a job with the EAR&H. Then in 1952 moved to Iringa when my Dad joined the EAR&H.on the Road Services Side.

I first went to Mbeya School in 1953 until 1959 when I then went to St Michael's & St George's School (now Mkwawa High School).

In the early days, when I was a very young child, my mother looked out in the garden or a friend and saw a cheetah 'attacking' me. She went hysterical until she was told it was their pet cheetah and he was only playing!!

I have very happy memories of Mbeya School. We worked and played hard. The teachers were very strict and we were all really scared of the Doctor, she was very unkind but made us better! I had a carbuncle on my wrist once, and she told me she had to lance it and I was NOT to cry!! Well you can imagine at about 8-9 years old not crying!

I remember playing British Bulldogs which is a very rough game but good fun. Being a boarding school, we had to 'fight' for any seconds of food as the prefects always took the best. The food wasn't bad.

We had some wonderful fancy dress parades. The sports were brilliant and I remember playing hide and seek amongst all the beautiful fir trees that surrounded the front of the school and down the drive. I always looked at Mbeya Peak and was always mesmerised with it.

We went scrumping once to get some fruit and suddenly one of the teachers went into the Orchard, we hid low then made a bee-line for the exit. We couldn't stop laughing afterwards.

Marion's father Doug Goulding in the Tanganyika rally in the late 1950s. The writing on the building on the left says Shell Lubrication. And further behind is the New Palace Hotel, Dar es Salaam.

We were allowed two weekends and three Saturdays off a term and my parents always arrived for those to take me out. My Dad used to be in charge of the School Buses with EAR&H. He once had to drive the bus home with all the school children in all the mud after the rains, we skidded all over the place but we got back safely.

Another time, I had whooping cough and, again in the rains, drove me to Dar es Salaam. He had to stop to remove a log in the way on the escarpment, and as he walked back to the car, it was sliding sideways towards the edge. Needless to say he saved the day!!

During quarantine times, i.e. Diphtheria and chicken pox, our dormitories were out of bounds to others and we were not allowed out. We did have some fun! That is when the Matron wasn't looking.

I also remember, bath times. We had to queue up for our turn. There were two to a bath and three lots went in. If we talked in line, we had the wet taccie (plimsoll) also if we talked during rest time. This was between 2 - 3p.m.

I missed Mbeya School when I left.

Life was quite relaxed in the 50's as far as I knew as a child. Dad worked very hard and had to check every vehicle accident and report on it. My mother was the Secretary of the Iringa Golf Club. Before that she worked for the Iringa Hotel. She also worked for Joyce McQueen's (A clothes shop) and Dr Shupla's Pharmacy.

Marion's father Doug Goulding as Santa Claus at the Iringa Golf Club during the late 1950s.

During the summer holidays, I used to ride my bike, walk in the forest.

Once when I went to watch the Rifle Club (target shooting) my friends and I went off around the back of the hill and I suddenly became uneasy and my hairs stood up on the back of me neck.

I wanted to go back, but the others said I was chicken. However, we got to a small cave and at the entrance was an extremely fresh spoor. This I knew to be of a leopard and knew it was watching us.

Needless to say we made a very hasty retreat!

I remember climbing the Big rock behind our bungalow at the edge of the town in the colonial area, I returned in 2002 and climbed up that hill again - happy memories.

Marion Gough's family. Photo taken in Majorca in 2001. From left: Dawn, 29; David, 25; Marion and her husband Rod; and Berveley, 32, a GB Rower who was a spare in the 2000 Olympics in Sydney, Australia.

We went to the cinema in Iringa, and watched films on a Sunday Evening at the Iringa Golf Club.

My father was Father Christmas once and came down in a Landrover from the golf course. It was all very exciting when you are children.

There was obviously no TV then. We used to listen to the radio and thoroughly enjoyed that.

We all played on our own, or sometimes with friends, we were never bored.

I used to ride my bike and Daniel, our houseboy, used to escort me with my bike until I was old enough to cycle alone. He used to teach me Swahili, as we weren't allowed to speak it at school, which I think is stupid.

I think it is imperative to learn the language of the country you live in. Mum and Dad spoke it well. Daniel was with us for nearly 9 years, we thought a lot of him.

I had lots of pets, at different times, dogs, cats a monkey in the early days, parakeets, rabbits, hares and chickens.

One special cockerel, Sooty, was blind but he knew my voice

and when he heard me he used to fly up towards me and I used to catch him and he used to balance on my arm.

Life seemed easier for all in those days, there were very few shanties and a lot of people were employed. The shops in Iringa were very busy, and so too, were the hotels.

The road services were efficient and the roads in good condition except for the dirt roads, they had corrugations.

The weather was generally better, fewer droughts, the shambas produced good quality produce and most people were self-sufficient.

Daniel lived in a little house next to ours, his wives were in a nearby village and they each had a little house of their own. Dad paid him every week but he also had meat, a few groceries and water.

My Mum had some Asian friends and they taught her to make lovely curries, which she passed onto me when I was old enough to cook.

I remember, during our holidays, we either went to the Serengeti, Malindi Beach, or Dar es Salaam to the Inn by the Sea. I went to try to find it, but it is now gone.

It had little rondavals for guest houses and when we went to the toilet, behind the rondaval it was covered from top to bottom with crab spiders, I know they are harmless but they freaked me out!! The surf in the dark, under the moonlight was fluorescent - magic!

I remember toast made on an open stove with butter and brown sugar. Silly things to remember.

I also remember diving through the waves and coming face to face with a Lion Fish. I ran out and asked Helen, the owner, to tell me what it was.

We used to look in all the little coral pools when the tide went out.

One day, I could see a massive rainstorm coming, so I ran out (whatever is in the mind of a child?) to save Mum and Dad getting wet on their way back from the beach.

The tide went out a long way, and they kept calling me back to see a jellyfish stranded. Hence we all got soaked - you get wet swimming!!

We were stranded several times because of the floods when

the roads were washed away on the way to Bagamoyo.

Jamat Street in Iringa in the late 1950s.

I went back there too in 2002. It is sad to see the buildings as they are, but I was happy to go back and had some lovely chats to some of the residents in Bagamoyo. One tailor made me a skirt in one hour, I still wear it.

Tanganyika was my home and is still very much in my blood. I try to get back as much as I can and am in the process of fund raising to help the building of an Orphanage. I have sent two shipments of text books, papers and pens to two different schools, together with several computers (used). I had such a happy, if not, lonely, childhood that I feel I must return the privilege.

My Dad was very much respected by all, African and Asians alike. There were very few Arabs in those days, in my recall. We got on very well with them, they really are easy to be friends/colleagues.

One of the mechanics in Iringa is the son of the Works

Foreman of the EAR&H and remembers his father talking about him. My father is now 87 years old and very frail.

I miss the freedom of those days, the sounds and lovely views. There was not the greed of today and material things didn't matter like they seem to now. People cared more then than they do now.

Jamat Street in 2002. It has not changed much since the 1950s. Photos sent by Marion Gough when she visited Iringa and the former St. Michael's and St George's School (now Mkwawa High School) in that year.

I think Tanganyika was a well-run country, fairly well fed. The people generally happy and friendly. Life was good to us; we tried to make life better for others.

Life was hard sometimes; Dad worked very long hours and had to go on safari sometimes to sort out accidents that had happened far away. It was lonely sometimes. We had very few power cuts, if we had them we just lit lanterns and cooked in the kooni (kuni - firewood) stove. We boiled and filtered all our water. It was a way of life you got used to and the character of the place.

I visited our old bungalow too in 2002 and the residents, two bankers, welcomed us into their home and were very hospitable.

They were delightful. We shall go again when we are next in Iringa. I shall also visit Mkwawa. I gather it is becoming a University now. What a wonderful achievement and this will help Iringa a lot. Iringa is now a far far bigger town than it used to be.

I think I may have bored you, but these are a few of memories that have come to mind. I left in 1963 a little after independence.

I love Africa and it's people and it will always be a part of me.
Nenda pole pole
Kwa Heri sasa

Marion

***

From Godfrey Mwakikagile, 17 January 2006

Hi Marion,

I just started reading what you sent me and saw your question on whether or not I'm working on a project with this material.

I'm writing a book about Tanganyika in the fifties. It's essentially autobiographical from my perspective as a child in the fifties complemented by memories of others who lived in Tanganyika during the same period I did.
Asante sana.

Godfrey

***

From Marion Gough, England, 17 January 2006

Godfrey,

Wow, that sounds brill. When you have finished it, let me know and I will buy it!

Did you know David Snowden, he and I have come in contact after 40 years! He has written a small book, unpublished, about his father's days in Iringa working for the EAR&H, he has put in

a few of my photos. Did you ever go to Iringa?
Kwa heri

Marion

Marion's father Doug Goulding at their house in Iringa in 1960

At home in Iringa in 1962. Standing in front of the car, Gwen, Marion, and Judy.

Marion on a scooter at home in Iringa in 1962.

Iringa Main Road in 1960.

Mbeya School in 2000. This is the former Mbeya School of the 1950s. Photo sent by Marion when she and her family visited Mbeya that year, including the house where she and her parents used to live in during the 1950s.

***

From Joyce Delap, Australia, 16 January 2006

Dear Godfrey,

How very interesting that you are going to write a book about Tanganyika in the 50s.

I got your email at home yesterday.

We do not go onto the computer on a regular basis, just now and again, so I have sent it to myself at work so that I can reply during a lull, which is now.

The Wattle Factory in Njombe, Southern Highlands, in the 1950s. Photo sent by Joyce Delap from Australia.

We went to EA in 1951 starting off in Jinja then on to Nairobi and then to Tanganyika. We went to Njombe in about 1958 (my father worked for the CDC (Colonial Development Corporation just in case you haven't heard of it) and was posted to the Wattle

Factory there where they made tanning extract and I went to St Michael's and St George's at the opening term of the school. A lot of the pupils came from the Kongwa School as it was being closed.

It was a beautiful school with so many facilities and a lot of pupils, most of us boarding. I do have fond memories of my time there.

There was one particular time that was not so good when it happened but on reflection you just have to laugh. There was a guava orchard just ouside the school boundary and a group of us used to go there to smoke! I tried cigarettes but at the time thought they were pretty disgusting but I still went with the gang because it was exciting doing something a bit naughty. Needless to say we got caught, got sent to the Headmaster and got into trouble but it was all OK in the end.

Getting to school was quite a saga. There was a bus which started in Mbeya. My parents had to drive me to Makumbaku (I don't know if the spelling is correct) Corner and I caught it there. It was quite a ride to Iringa.

Because I was only a school girl whilst we were in Tanganyika I don't have too many other memories of our time there. I was at Iringa for 2 years and then I went to England to school and by the time I left school my family had moved back to Kenya.

DC3 at Njombe airport in the Southern Highlands in the 1950s. Photo sent by Joyce Delap.

I remember we used to go out for weekends to visit the farms owned by our day pupil friends and have wonderful times. One of the weekends I remember we went to the Ruhaha River and had a picnic and swam in the river. I remember one of the high lights was when Julius Nyerere came to our Speech Day to present the prizes and I was a recipient and had to go up and shake his hand. He also organised for us to have a day off school which went down very well indeed with us all. I remember the cheer that went up.

I don't know if you know Njombe at all. It was a very small town. There were a lot of staff at the factory and the surrounding area because the CDC owned large tracts of land where the wattle trees grew. We lived in a row of houses near the factory where as far as I can remember the shift workers lived. My father was an Engineer. The office workers lived a little way down the road near the offices where my mother worked.

Dar es Salaam airport in the 1950s. Photo sent by Joyce Delap.

We had a duka in-between which supplied us with much of our daily needs. I can't really remember much about that, just that I used to ride my bicycle there to spend my pocket money. It was really good for us children there because it was so safe in those days. We did not really have any great inconveniences.

I remember we had to use powdered milk which did not worry me because I didn't drink it. My father did not seem to mind it much. We had to make our own bread which our cook did very well indeed. The cooking was done on a wood stove which I learned to cook on and quite enjoyed it as I remember. The reason for that was because electricity was supplied from the factory and was not on all the time. I remember that I was afraid of the dark for quite a while as a child and in Njombe I had a little tilly lamp.

My life in EA was a wonderful experience and I wouldn't have missed it for the world. It is a great pity we had to leave. My husband and his brother and sister were all born in Nairobi so would have been even more of a wrench for them. We were married in Nairobi and our son was born there. We have lived in Australia for 31 years now and we still feel very sad that we had to leave the 'Garden of Eden'. But things change and you have to move on.

I was 3 1/2 years old when we first went to EA so it was rather a long time ago and I have never had the best memory in the world. I will have a look thru my photos and see if there is anything that may be of interest.

I would be very interested to read your book when it is finished so I would appreciate it if you could let me know when it is and what it is called so that I can buy it. What else have you written? Hoping to hear from you again soon.

With best wishes for your success,

Joyce Delap

***

From Maggie Phillips, 17 January 2006

Dear Godfrey

Thanks for the explanation - and good luck with your book. I'd be grateful if you would eventually let me know the name of the publisher, so that I can order a copy in due course.

I lived in Dodoma, Central Province, until 1957. My father was in the colonial service, and was a Labour Officer. Dodoma was very small, and there were not many Europeans living in the town. There was a hotel, a club, and a golf course.

I went to a very small school just outside town. It was run by an old, retired missionary called Miss Read.

I rode there on a bike every day, and was always frightened by the cattle - those huge horns! I was also afraid of snakes and scorpions - and alarmed sometimes by the Wagogo tribesmen who carried spears. But my memories are of a very safe, happy time. Dodoma was in the Rift Valley - stunning scenary and a healthy climate.

Then we went to live in Dar es Salaam - much more exotic, interesting - and HOT! So humid - it was like living in a sponge. It's such a beautiful place - wonderful beaches, palm trees.

We had a boat. My father was still with the Dept. of Labour, and we went to live in Iringa for a couple of years, but spent most of our time in Dar.

I went to boarding school in Kongwa, Central Province. That school was based in the buildings that had been erected for the staff of the Groundnut Scheme - which failed. Kongwa School closed in 1958, and we all moved to St Michael's & St George's School in Iringa - a much more healthy climate in the Southern Highlands.

Life was very good in Tanganyika. Such a beautiful country. I would love to go back. I was last there in 1972. It was very different then from how it was when I left finally in 1966 to come to England, where I have basically lived ever since.

You might like to get in touch with my father, Frank Glynn, who is now living in England (83!). After Tanzania became independent he stayed on working as an adviser to President Nyerere, employed by the Ford Foundation. He was in charge of the "Africanisation" process. He then went to do the same job in Botswana - another lovely African country.

He had a book published last year about his experiences in Tanganyika: *Before The Winds of Change*. I think you can get it from Amazon.

Best wishes

Maggie Phillips

***

From Bryan Ulyate, 17 January 2006

My father's side of the family came to Tanganyika soon after the First World War when Britain seized it from the Germans. They then encouraged British citizens to emigrate to East Africa to help develop it. My father was born in Kenya as his father had property both in Kenya and Tanganyika, these were in the form of farms and hotels.

After finishing school my father trained as an aircraft mechanic in Nairobi, he was then given the opportunity of going to work on aircraft in England and accepted the offer, this was in the beginning of 1936.

I was then born in England where my father had met my

mother and got married in 1942. I had an elder sister at that time too.

After the war the family moved firstly back to Kenya in 1946 then moved to Tanganyika, this was in 1950 and I was then six years old.

We moved onto my grandfather's farm where I watched our house being built by my father. The house was made up from two very large wooden sheds which were about twenty feet apart and he linked them up with mud and sticks mixture. It was a very primitive house with no electricity but we did have running water, the floors were concrete and the roof was corrugated tin so when it rained you could not hear yourself as there were no ceilings.

The toilet was outside, it was a big wooden box over a deep hole, round the outside was a wooden shed as such. As a kid I was terrified of falling down the hole and when I was naughty my father used to threaten us with throwing us down the toilet.

Whilst living here my mother gave birth to my brother then my sister and I were then sent off to boarding school in the town of Arusha. Arusha School was the only school available to us, it was fifty miles from where we lived which was just outside the town of Moshi which then had no schools.

We were taken into Moshi and put on a steam train which went to Arusha, the so-called road between these two towns was so bad and the transport was not much better as it would take one the full day to drive the fifty odd miles through what was wilderness with all the wild game one could imagine.

On the farm I was looked after by an African nanny better known as an 'Aiya' (yaya, Swahili for housemaid). What I can remember of her was that she was a lovely caring person and I adored her. She would take me back to her own little mud and straw hut where there was always a fire burning in the middle of the room and she would cook her maize meal into a thick almost solid ball meal which was called ' Ugali ' I loved it and my mother could never understand why I was never hungry at our meal times. My father would get very cross when I refuse to eat and I would get whipped by him with a whip made from rhino hide.

I soon learnt to speak Swahili which I could do better than speak English, Swahili is a wonderful language and you could converse with anyone in the language, it bridged the gap between tribal people as well as Italians, Greeks, Germans and the English who did not understand the others mother tongues.

I went to school in Arusha from 1951 till the end of 1961 where I became head boy, although I used to battle academically apart from mathematics where I excelled and never got under 90%. But it was in sports that I did very well. Arusha school was a wonderful school and I enjoyed all my schooling there. In the later fifties they finally built a tarmac road from Moshi to Arusha which made life a lot easier to get around and our parents could come and take us home at half terms.

Life then was great with a great amount of freedom but it was also very hard, yes we had our hardships when with crop failures we used to live on maize meal only, known there as Posho and eggs as we had a good chicken run and plenty of eggs. For meat we lived a lot on wild game which was abundant and I used to go out with my father hunting for game which was exciting as well as scary.

The farm also had its fair share of snakes which were terrifying at times as they would get into the house and we always had to check out our beds before going to sleep that no snakes had crept in.

My parents could only afford to let us have shoes for school so in the holidays we ran around the farm bare-footed till one day my brother got bitten by a night adder and was touch-and-go whether he would live as there were no hospitals nearby, he nevertheless did survive.

Where we lived was on the slopes of Kilimanjaro and to see that mountain everyday was just magnificent. In later years I eventually got the opportunity to climb to the very top of Kilimanjaro an experience I have always treasured.

As for the people of Tanganyika, thy were lovely people always friendly and of good nature, a country where so many different tribal people lived in harmony together and this could be put down to the common language spoken by everyone in the form of Swahili, as I have said before and will say again a great language which unites people.

The climate in Tanzania is also great as nothing stops growing provided it gets enough water which in later years has become a serious issue due to the destruction of the forestry with poor management never replaced reducing the country to almost desert and drying up the rain falls.

The fifties were a great period with the country being a major exporter of maize, wheat, sugar, sisal coffee, citrus fruits, beans and many other produces. Sadly with independence coming along instead of utilising the knowledge of the "foreigners" who were there the new government got rid of us all and with it the country collapsed to its knees. A very sad thing for a country with everything to offer.

I will leave you on this note for the time being but if I think of anymore or you want to ask me more don't hesitate.

Regards,

Bryan

***

From Tony Sellick, Canada, 17 January 2006

Hello Godfrey,
Wow, a voice from the past!

I have been in touch with a few people from the Iringa web site and it has been interesting re-living some of those wonderful years.

I was born in England and moved to Tanganyika with my parents when I was about four years old. My father also worked for the colonial government and was responsible for most of the irrigation projects etc. in the Mwanza area.

I went to boarding school at Kongwa and later at Iringa before leaving Tanzania in early 1961 after my father was killed.

I have very fond memories of that area in spite of the tragic circumstances that made us return to England.

I do have some photos from that time and would be willing to share them with you at some point in time.

Do you have a list of some of your published work?

Tony

***

Jackie Wigh, Australia, 16 January 2006

Jambo Godfrey!

Thanks for your email regarding TT in the Fifties. I am aware of your book 'Nyerere'.

I was just a toto in the fifties so can't help you there I'm afraid. However, the mother (now deceased) of a friend of mine, wrote a book entitled *My African Affair* by Isabell Florence Lambert. I am sure this book would give you some ideas for your forthcoming book. The ISBN number is 0 86445 117 2 or, you could contact the Lamberts with regard to obtaining a copy.

Actually, I went to school at Mbeya School in the fifties and all I can tell you is I didn't like the headmaster there!!!
Do hope this finds you well.
Mingi salaams!
Jackie

***

From Jackie Wigh, Australia, 17 January 2006

Hello Godfrey

Thanks for your email.

What I could do, if it's any help to you, is to scan some photos I have somewhere. Is anything like Princess Margaret's visit to Arusha any good, or the Aga Khan's visit? (All fifties). I'll get on to that as soon as I can.

I actually have your book (about President Nyerere) and because I have been so busy these last few years never really got around to reading it. I had a look at Amazon and you have 5-stars all round!! Must read it! I'll be in touch.
Kwaheri ndugu.

Jackie

***

From Jackie Wigh, Australia, 23 January 2006

Hello Godfrey ~

Thanks for your email. Will start scanning shortly .....

I've been talking with the bwana and we definitely want *YOU* to have the Princess Margaret program. We want you to have it as a small gift - no return!

We don't have any heirs, as it were, and it would probably land on the tip if anything happens to us. Pity, eh?

Without sounding melodramatic, Tanganyika/Tanzania raised me and educated me and I would love to give a tiny little gift back to one of Tanzania's sons. I *really* want you to have this booklet (112 pages) - really feel you are the right person to 'inherit' it. So ...... if you want it, it's yours, I'll send it you by registered mail - all I need is an address!

All the other stuff we'll scan.

salaams

Jackie (Wigh)

***

From Jackie Wigh, Australia, 27 January 2006

Princess Margaret is on the way to you by registered post. Post Office said it would take up to two weeks to get to you ..... apparently the American side is the slow side :) . In the meantime, Karl is working on the scanning. Unfortunately, all the Aga Khan pictures have no accompanying articles - but they are nice, anyway. They relate to his visit to Arusha in November 1957.

Kwaheri kwa sasa.

Jackie

***

From Godfrey Mwakikagile, 31 January 2006

Hi Jackie,

Please go ahead and send the photos, the postcards, and the letter from Mr. Magambo who worked for PWD! Very historical! It's all going in the book.

It's also interesting to know that you lived in Tanga among other places. My parents were in Tanga in the forties but I have never been there. But I have been to Mwanza and Bukoba.

I never heard of the SS Mariana but I remember the PWD. I even remember the colour of the PWD lorries in the fifties when I was under ten years old. They were painted green on the sides and white on top. And they were Bedford. I remember PWD were initials for Public Works Department. I mention all that in the book.

I also need captions for the photos you sent me. I recognize the Aga Khan but I don't know about the rest. If possible, I would also like to know where and where they were taken.

Asante sana.

Kwaheri.

Godfrey

***

From Jackie Wigh, Australia, 2 February 2006

Hi Godfrey

Thanks for your newsy email.

Yes, it is exciting about your forthcoming book! It will be a real history book indeed.

I'll show Karl your email (when he gets up :)) as he is the fundi on these computer matters.

Re: captions and the AK, Godfrey, I have no idea ..... only that I assume they relate to his visit to Arusha. However, I somehow suspect that maybe the large portrait photo might have been an official photo because on the back is printed 'Studio Moo ....., (copy right reserved) PO Box 562, Dar es Salaam.

I love the photo of the AK disembarking from the East African Airways 'plane - my favourite.

I have sent you are large (unregistered) envelope this week with some photocopies of stuff. If you need any scanning to be done on them, please let us know.

Will get the Tanga shots organised for you, too. Also, one or two other shots. Will organise their captions.

I believe the AK lived in Geneva until his death a few years ago .... The Belerive Foundation or something like that. He was compassionate about animals which I think is wonderful. By the way, your birthday, October 4 ..... is World Animals Day (St Francis of Assisi) - did you know that?

Do hope you're getting lots of input from others on this fabulous project, Godfrey. Well done!
Chat later ....

Jackie

***

From Godfrey Mwakikagile, 4 February 2006

Hi Jackie,

Thank you very much for your very interesting email and for the booklet and other material on Princess Margaret. I received the package yesterday afternoon and I was thrilled!

I'm very grateful to both of you for bestowing this honour on me as the "rightful" heir! I intend to reproduce as much information as I can from the booklet and include it in the book. I'm also going to use the other material you sent me, including some details from the invitation and the old newspapers. It's very historical and I really appreciate that.

I also received this morning some of the photos you sent me. I have not yet looked at all of them but they're very nice. I hope that you also sent me Princess Margaret's picture. If you didn't or don't have it, that's no problem; I'll download one from the internet and add it to the rest of the photos in the book. I saw one in the schedule booklet you sent but I can't scan it.

And I'm going to use in the captions some of the things you

have told me about The Aga Khan's visit to Taganyika in November 1957. It brought back old memories.

As I said before, I went to the former H.H. The Aga Khan High School in Dar es Salaam and completed form VI in 1970. I also lived in H.H. The Aga Khan Hostel in Upanga just a few yards from our school on the United Nations Road in Dar.

Those were some of the best years of my life, and the school was one of the best in the country, probably next to Mkwawa High School (formerly St. Michael's and St. George's) which even during those years when I was a student and thereafter was still considered to be the best high school in Tanzania as much as it was when it was St. Michael's and St. George's.

I have not yet received the other envelope which you sent as unregistered mail but will let you know as soon as it arrives. I'm sure I'm going to use the material and will let you know how much of it I want scanned for the book.

I have been getting lots of inputs from many people and am really excited about this project, one of the most important in my life because of its historical significance; it's also partly biographical. I have already written two chapters about my early life and have more to go. The book is now about 250 pages and I'm not even done yet.

I have learnt something very interesting about my bnirthday. No, I did not know that October 4th was World Animal Day! But I know about St Francis of Assisi, although not much.

Asante sana.

Kwaheri.

Godfrey

***

H.H. The Aga Khan in Arusha, Tanganyika, November 1957. Photo sent by Jackie and Karl Wigh from Australia.

H.H. The Aga Khan in a car in Arusha, Tanganyika, in November 1957. Photo sent by Jackie and Karl Wigh from Australia.

H.H. The Aga Khan in Arusha, Tanganyika, in November 1957. Photo sent by Jackie and Karl Wigh from Australia.

H.H. The Aga Khan, centre and dressed in white, disembarking from an East African Airways (EAA) aeroplane in Arusha, Tanganyika, in November 1957. Photo sent by Jackie and Karl Wigh from Australia.

***

From Alice Shirley, South Africa, 17 January 2006

Dear Godfrey

Jambo Habari yako?

Great receiving your email, especially since we started seeing, corresponding and contacting all our old school friends through this website that was started by a school friend of mine that lives just down the road from me!!

Alice on the left, Alice's mother, and Alice's step-brother Vernon on the right, at Makwaja ranch in Pangani District in the mid-1950s.

    It has brought many friends together from all over the world and in South Africa.
    This all led to a reunion in 2004 and we are having another one in September this year.
    The last one was successful, we had it in Johannesburg.
    The response was excellent and loads of fun.
    Stories abounded and nostalgia took on a whole new meaning.
    Dancing with my chemistry teacher, all of 80+, was great as I had a crush on him at school, as so many other girls had.

Ferry at Pangani in the 1950s.

I am not quite sure what will be of interest to you as I have many stories.

I will however keep it as short as possible and hope that what I write, you may be able to use in your book. If not, it is good to email a fellow East African.

I was born in Eldoret. My ancestors came up from SA on the great trek and settled in Eldoret and Nakuru, where they farmed. I am, I believe, a Kaburu (Swahili for Boer).

My father was an engine driver for EA Railways. When he passed away, my mother remarried and, with new husband, moved to Tanzania to a place called Makwaja where he helped run a cattle ranch for a company called Amboni Sisal Estates. Makwaja is not far from Pangani - it is actually near a place called Mwera.

My memories of my life in Tanzania encompass so much it is difficult to choose which to tell you, but here I go and I will just cover a little bit about my family.

I will start off by sharing some experiences that had an impact on me and were important.

Firstly, with my stepfather and our relationship or lack of it.

He was a racist and was the reason why some of my memories are not as good as others. I will go into that a bit later.

Started school in Arusha School in Arusha. I will always remember Mt Meru and the great Mt Kilimanjaro always in the backround.

Then moved to high school to the great old peanut scheme buildings of Kongwa.

Tumble-down buildings with sack roofs and doors that kept falling off was quite ridiculous but it is from there that I have many fond memories.

If you were not fortunate enough to own a bicycle, you had to lamb shank it and I am talking miles and miles from the mess to the first class room of the day back for lunch to mess then home to your cottage. All this, knowing there are hyenas and lions walking around.

Looking back on it I wonder if it ever crossed our minds that we were in any sort of danger!

Alice's grandmother in front of their "house" in Morogoro. All the pictures from Alice Shirley were taken in the mid- to the late fifties.

In +- 1956 (My dates might not be spot on. Memory does sort of dim at this age) it was off to our brand new smart school at St Michael's and St George's School Iringa. Compared to Kongwa, this was heaven! It is here that things between my father and I came to a head.

In 1961, Iringa became a multi racial school and to quote my father "No child of mine will go to school with non-whites." So I had to give up my final year of schooling and with that my dreams of being an air hostess - as a High School Certificate was one of the necessary qualifications.

Went home for a year that lead up to Independence Day. That was quite a test for us. There was obviously a lot of anger and striking and stones being thrown etc. I have a little story for you here.

One of the strikes we had, no-one was allowed to go out of their compounds and forbidden to work.

We had two house servants. One was called Mbeya and the other Ramsani.

One particular strike my dear friend Mbeya decided to sneak in every morning at 2.30 a.m to do all the ironing, cleaning and all else that had to be done and leave just as the sun rose so that nobody would know what he had done.

That loyalty will live with me forever. When we left he went to Makerere College where I hope he had the success and wonderful life he totally deserves.

No, I have never had really bad times, lived in relative comfort. The experience that I mentioned regarding racism had a large impact on me and when I arrived in this country it was a shock.

SA (South Africa) in the early sixties - what a nightmare. I had at least marched on forward, as the last six months at school we had no problem integrating and our next door neighbours were of a mixed marriage and great friends of ours. So you see, my father was bit weird.

When we had the 2004 reunion, I danced with an Indian class mate. After I had told him the reason for my leaving school early, he proceeded to grab my hands and said "lets dance on your fathers grave" - and with much laughter we did the good old rock 'n roll.

I must have been in Morogoro the same time as you, Godfrey. We used to live there 6 months of the year due to my father's work. I have enclosed a pic of my gran in our house there, a bit shabby but only temporary.

The other pic is of my mum, brother and I in Makwaja Ranch and the other crossing on the ferry at Pangani to get home.

This took forever, especially in the rainy season. No bridges, many rivers. We started off the journey with a long wait for the tide to go out so that we could cross via the sea in a dug out. Then, on to the next river where we crossed over on a raft made up of ten gallon drums strung together by rope and pulled by a tractor on the other side. Then, onto same tractor to next river sans bridge to repeat the whole thing again.

You can imagine my trips home from school: By bus to Dodoma, by train to Morogoro, by bus to Korogwe, by train to Tanga, the Landrover to Pangani across the ferry then the whole dugout tractor drum story then home. By this time I think it was time to go back!! I never complained, though, as I thought this was what life was all about. My kids walked to school - how boring.

I think I have waffled too much but Mbeya used to call me Mama Kangella and not for nothing.

Before I go, my husband's name is Colin. I have a son who lives and works in London and a daughter who is married and is an assistant editor of a gardening magazine, having got a BA degree and diplomas in journalism and photography.

If there is anything else you would like me to go further into, please let me know.
Kwa heri mimi nimekwenda sasa.
Regards,

Alice

***

From Alice Shirley, 23 January 2006

Dear Godfrey

Jambo!
After showing my children the emails (my son is out here from London on holiday)and explaining what they are all about, both exclaimed " what about your other stories Mom, the funny ones."

Since I have been in this country I have had to retell them over and over again to friends, family and co-workers. So I hope you will enjoy. I cannot tell them all as I am not even sure they will be appropriate for your book. Enjoy anyway.

When we lived in Mkwaja we had all sorts of animals: A pet guinea fowl, a women-hating stroppy mongoose, pigs, goats, all of whom by the way were really pets.

The first one was bought to fatten up for Christmas. My brother and I were not having that, so another one was bought and the same thing happened three times. They were so tame they would eat out of our hands follow us everywhere. The pig unfortunately was not so lucky in the end, although I did try.

To get on with my story, as I mentioned earlier, we had chickens that were in a chicken enclosure in our back yard. One night we heard this horrendous noise coming from there. We all jumped up and ran to go and check what was going on. Reaching the back door we found it was locked and not one of us could find the key. We then all aimed for the front door pushing and shoving. You must remember this is all done in the dark, the only light being father's torch that was strapped to his head!!.

My mother and I followed at the rear and as we came around the corner of the house leading to the back yard, my mother started to turn back from where we had just come from shrieking! "Bessie!! (our dog) let go of my chicken, you stupid dog" and all I could see was this four-legged animal with a gasping chicken in its mouth.

It was only when I looked down that I saw Bessie "the stupid dog" standing at my feet, tail wagging and wondering what she had done wrong. Even after shouting to my mother that she nearly had a leopard by its tail, she either did not hear me or she was so caught up in her anger that nothing mattered but to get this wretched beast that was busy pinching one of her beloved chickens.

It did not all end well, my mother survived but the leopard did not. The excitement over, we decided to play a trick on Ramsani, our cook. We lay the leopard in the pathway (that he used every morning to come to work) after propping the animals mouth open with a stick. We then lay in wait for his arrival. Along came Ramsani, paraffin lamp in hand, whistling away.

What happened next was hysterical. The lamp went one way and he the other. It was a long time after that before his walk to work became normal again. The next couple of weeks we would watch as he approached the same spot with much trepidation. I must say he laughed afterwards and he always said he would get us back one day. I must add here that we found our guinea fowl under a bucket after all this commotion. To this day we do not know how that happened. Maybe guineas fowls are so scared of leopards that they can actually pick up a bucket and put it over it over their heads!!!!!!

My other story is again to do with my mother. We had a vegetable patch and grew many fruit trees, and the paw paw tree was a favourite with the monkeys. Every afternoon at about the same time they would come and get their daily ration of paw paws and every time my mother would brandish her broom, which was always strategically placed at the gate. It was such fun to watch, my brother and I would laugh till we cried because they would clutch the paw paw under their armpits and waltz right past her, looking at her as if she was some insane woman, and not taking the slightest bit of interest.

My other quick story involves a lion cub. We had a gardener who used to come once a week to tend our garden. I cannot remember why but he used to have to travel quite far to get to our home.

One day he arrived with a tiny lion cub as a present for me. I was over the moon as I now had a baby. I proceeded to make a bed for it next to mine not thinking of any of the consequences involved and proudly went about loving my new toy. That night, however, did we hear all about it!

The mother lioness prowled around the house all night roaring till the walls of the house shook!! I eventually had to deliver the cub back and only did this the next morning as I did not want a confrontation with this angry Mum!!!!

All ended well, she collected her cub and away they went.

Maybe this will give your readers an idea of how we really lived in the bush. I must say that I miss the bush say and am sorry that I took it all so for granted.
Kwaheri Godfrey
Best regards your newly found rafiki

Alice

***

From Godfrey Mwakikagile, 23 January 2006

Colin & Alice,

Those are wonderful stories! I really enjoyed reading them. Humorous too! Very funny!

I have copied and pasted the entire material in the manuscript and it's going to be published exactly the way you wrote it.

Reading those stories reminded me of a similar experience I had in the late fifties in Rungwe District in the Southern Highlands.

One my uncles shot a leopard in our village. He lived in a village nearby and he was one of only two people who had guns in that area. The other one, in our village, was a much older person and he was not considered to be very good with his gun.

So, some people in my village went to get my uncle. They told him where the leopard was hiding and he went after it. I also followed him, as did a few other people, but he warned us not to get too close.

Within a few minutes he shot the leopard which was hiding up in a tree. He had a reputation as an excellent shooter and fought in World War II. He died in 1998 when I was still in the United States. He was 81.

Thank you very much for the stories and they have helped remind me of some of my own experiences which I'm going to include in the book.

As I said, the book will be out before the end of the year and I will definitely let you know when it's published.

If you have anything else to add, just send it to me.

Kwaheri.

Godfrey

***

From Alice Shirley, South Africa, 24 January 2006

Dear Godfrey

After receiving your email this morning I felt I had to telephone my niece who lives near Cape Town and fill her in on what had been happening.

My niece Jill, to whom I am very close, was always asking me to tell my stories and every couple of months to this very day would say "oh please, one more time". While I was on the phone she said with great excitement "they are going to love the donkey story" - I said, "oh dear! I did not tell him that one." So, apologies Godfrey, and for her sake I will tell you this one. I do not think you are ever going to finish this book with Mama Kangella here carrying on and on.

We lived on a coffee farm near Arusha owned by my grandparents. I was at the tender age of about 5 and my parents thought it would be a good idea if I went to a nursery school run by a local church. My elder brother and I thought this a good idea, but when we were presented with a donkey as a mode of transport we were rather astounded, but were told that we were very fortunate and to stop complaining.

I will tell of the first day we started on our travels and what subsequently happened and continued to happen every day for as long as we attended this funny little school.

We would start early in the morning with our packed lunches. We were both on one donkey, with me behind my brother. About 10 minutes into the journey the donkey would decide to deviate from the path and head straight for a grove of fruit trees. This donkey was kind of stupid and was obviously not aware that it was carrying passengers on its back, and walked under the branches.

The first time we were thrown off, lunch boxes flying and ending up on the ground tangled in blankets. The second day we ducked but to no avail.

Then off for the next part of the journey, very slowly I might say. We had to cross a main road that went from Arusha to Nairobi. Getting that ass to budge across the road was a mammoth task. Then on to the final leg where this animal had no problem budging as it heard the braying of the other donkeys that had arrived at the school from their respective journeys.

Of course with my luck this took place at the top of a hill, with the result that my brother would shout "HANG ON SIS!!!!!" as the beast charged downhill, braying loudly.

I must tell you if you want lessons on how to go down a hill hanging on to a donkey's tail let me know. They should have it as a sport in the Olympics. I would get a gold medal.

Through all that we survived, and to top it all, I always kept an apple for this creature that was responsible for my torn clothes and sore bottom.

Godfrey, I wish you could hear this story directly from my brother. You would be holding your tummy doubled over with laughter the way he tells it..
Regards Mama Kangella
Kwaheri

Alice

***

From Godfrey Mwakikagile, 25 January 2006

Dear Alice,

Habari gani?

I was going to answer you right away after I read the donkey story but got busy trying to work on some photos. I got another free software I think I can use to resize photos and do other things with it after I learn how to use it. It's called Triscape FxFoto and I think it's very easy to use.

I really enjoyed the donkey story! I'm surprised you have not written a book all these years with all the stories you have. You have such a wonderful memory and it's great that you remember them so well. It's a treasure!

You have more stories about living on the farm than I do! And they have helped jog my memory about my childhood enabling me to recall some of the wonderful and scary experiences I had when I was a child.

I remember one vividly.

When I returned to Rungwe District from Manyoni in the Central Province where I tried to enroll in a boarding school in early1960 but was too late for that, my cousins and I had a close encounter with what was probably a python on our farm.

We were eating bananas standing very close to a small river which flows around our farm when I threw a banana peel at a patch of shrubs and told my cousins that our dog, Jack, a German shepherd, was almost killed by a python right in that area.

As soon as the peel hit the patch, we heard some noise as if something big was slithering down the hill towards the river and we were almost sure it was a python. And even today, I believe it was a python because there were pythons in that area.

We were so scared and ran away so fast that we didn't stop until we got to the house which was about 150 yards a way. When we told my parents what happened, they were fully convinced that it was indeed a python.

And I have included that in the book because it's part of my history as a child growing up in the rural areas of the Southern Highlands of Tanganyika.

I have been getting positive responses from a number of ex-Tanganyikans in Britain, Australia, South Africa and other countries and it's very encouraging to hear from them. Your emails and stories are equally encouraging and I hope to finish writing the book before the end of the year.
Send me anything else you want me to include in the book.
Asante sana.
Kwaheri.

Godfrey

***

From Jean Wright, 18, 2006

Dear Godfrey,

Jambo.

I too have lived in Mbeya, as well as Tanga, Mtwara, Dar-es-Salaam, and Bukoba.

I would be happy to contribute some of my childhood memories to your book. What is your deadline?

I am leaving for a family vacation tomorrow and will be back on the 29th Jan so will get down to answering some of your questions upon my return.
Regards,

Jean Wright.

***

From Judi Simonds, South Africa, 19 January 2006

Hi Godfrey
I was very interested in your mail - I would be more than glad to share a
few memories with you - just a bit busy this next few days - but will then
sit down and write a few things down.
 Much looking forward to reading your book!!
 Regards

Judi Simonds

***

From Russ Baker, Florida, USA, 19 January 2006

How was life in Tanganyika in the fifties?

Mainly, the '50s were transition days in Tanganyika. The Africans were pushing towards independence from Great Britain and the British colonial officers were "holdidng on," trying to stem excessive, and what they perceived as radical, "push" but at the same time knowing "self rule" was inevitable.

Relationships, white to African, were changing. An African agricultural officer whom I knew said that the colonial officers were "friends when no other white person was present. We even drank tea and ate together. But, whenever another white person came on the scene, we 'separated' and treated us like his servants"!!

What fond memories do you have? Can you give some examples?

Beyond the satisfaction of the spiritual ministry as a church missionary, fondest memories are of the friendliness of the African; their willingness to accept you "as you were" and overlook faults; their quickness to share what they had even though, as a *mzungu* (white person), it was evident you had a lot more than they did; their joyfulness even in hard times (drought, lack of food, pressures from colonial administrators to do "public work," etc.); the trust of business persons (if you can't pay now, take it on credit and pay later).

Examples of fond memories:

1. "I remember when" - I was unmarried when I went back to Tanganyika in 1956. A year later, the lady who was to be my bride arrived and went to another place to live, to await the wedding day.

The African living in the area where I lived noticed I was away quite a bit. In jest, another missionary told them that I was "out looking for dowry cattle since I had spent all my resources to bring her out from the USA."

Lo, and behold, I was attended on by several of the local church leadership, bringing a fat ram. They said it was to "help me provide the dowry so the wedding could go forward"! That to me revealed much of their real concern and character.

2. As all knew, the day immediately preceding and following independence could be quite tense. Many were convinced that African leadership would lead to repression against both the Asians and the whites. Those fears were unfounded.

With my Land Rover, I was carrying a number of people to the celebrations in Mwanza. Without my knowledge, another passanger tried to climb on when I slowed down at a corner - but he fell and was dragged by the vehicle for several hundred yards before I was made aware of his predicament. Because it was an "accident," I immediately went to the police station to report what happened.

The new African police superintendent took my report and told me to go. He fairly realized that it was an unintentional and unfortunate experience and I was in no way to blame. Fairness, courtesy and efficiency. A great "first experience" with the new independent administration.

3. Relationships were built on honesty and openness. I had been directed to "measure out" a plot of land where a middle school and church compound were to be built.

I drastically calculated the acreage wrongly but the chief and sub-chiefs let me proceed with the measuring. Only later did I recognize my mistake. I made a special trip back to the chief's court, met with the chief and the sub-chiefs, and told them I had made a mistake. We returned to the plot of land and re-measured.

But the fact that a *mzungu* should show up in court and say he "made a mistake" was an astonishment to all and cemented a continuing relationship. I believe that, as a result of that, I was invited by the chief to sit in the court proceedings whenever I could and he always gave me a "seat of honour" among those there.

Do you also remember some of the unpleasant experiences you had?

Unpleasant experiences were, sadly, mainly from the colonial administrators who seemed to enjoy "tying up everything" in administrative bureaucracy and delay and, at the same time, trying to do what they perceived was right for a nation headed into independence.

After independence, the institution of *vijiji vya ujamaa* (ujamaa villages) was very upsetting. Basic supplies became "precious" commodities (with the resultant shortages and payments "under the table" to procure); CCM (*Chama Cha Mapinduzi* - the Party of the Revolution or the Revolutionary Party) became *Chama Cha Mahuni* (the Party of Thugs) or *Chukua Chako Mapema!* (Get Yours Early or Fast!).

Where did you live in Tanganyika?

After "growing up" in Tanganyika from 1937 to 1947 I came

back to the USA for studies and then returned to Tanganyika in December 1956 for work with the Africa Inland Mission/Africa Inland Church, working there until 1982 when I moved to Kenya.

(In Tanganyika, later Tanzania), I lived and worked in the Kwimba, Mwanza and Shinyanga regions but travelled extensively in both Geita and Musoma. All my comments/observations following will be based on living in this area (around or close to Lake Victoria in northern Tanzania).

How would you describe life in Tanganyika in the fifties in general?

Africans are very friendly but, underneath, one could sense a frustration with the slowness of the independence movement.

Travel was safe and roads were regularly (?) maintained though almost all roads out of town were dirt/murram.

Salaries for Africans were quite low though those few shillings had a fair buying power.

There was no electricity outside of major towns; water supplies (outside of towns) were mainly from bore-holes and carried to homes.

Public transport was available though schedules hard to maintain because of the roads - especially during the rains!

Most businesses were owned by either Indians or Arabs and larger businesses were branches of mainly British concerns. Africans did have small shops in rural places but most were engaged in agricultural work. Some worked "for pay" but constancy was hard because many just worked tog et enough to pay the hated "poll tax" after which they would quit and return home.

Skilled workers were mainly from Kenya (Luo or Kikuyu) and often had a difficult time relating to the Tanganyika Africans because of cultural differences.

Since I worked at first in primary education, I was able to interact with what was then termed "educated" school teachers though many in those days had not gone beyond the 8th year of studies before going to Teacher's Training Colleges. They are the ones who mainly provided me with views concerning British rule and the progress towards independence.

The colonial administration supported the construction of primary schools but provided very little for either the actual construction or needed equipment and books. The African chiefs and headmen were interested in the education of their people, and their well-being healthwise, and it was not hard to gain their cooperation and help in the establishment of schools and dispensaries.

What is it that you particularly miss about those days? Can you give a few examples?

I miss the uncomplicated life. There was no fear of robbery or travel danger from persons set to do you harm. I did much *safari* work (work which demanded travelling) for several years using an open-back pickup truck. I slept in the back, under the open sky with only a mosquito net between me and "whatever was out there" (hyenas!). In no way was I fearful of robbery or other personal danger. Now, no sane person would consider sleeping out the same way.

What was your overall impression of Tanganyika as country and in terms of life and its people? Was life good? Or was it hard? Do you remember some of the inconveniences, for example lack of electricity, plumbing, etc., and how they affected your lives?

It was understood that a newly independent Tanganyika/Tanzania would have a hard time economically. Diamonds, sisal, cotton, sugar - those exports could in no way support an infrastructure which included universal health care and education. Continuing grants from the Colonial Office in London and international grants-in-air would be needed for quite some time.

Increased taxation of impoverished people produced strong resentment - even to the extent of some saying that "under the British we would still have been slaves but we would have enough to eat"!

Elections to office under the independent government often were questionable - even to some telling me that the only effective vote they knew of "came out of the end of an AK47!" especially when those being elected supported the *Ujamaa* principle.

Early aspirations and expectations faded, reality finally settled in and as time passed all tried to make the best of their new situations.

How do you remember those days? With fondness, nostalgia or not? And why?

I fondy remember "those days" but, at the same time, recognize that change always comes. I felt that things could get done with the minimum official hassle (after, of course, approvals had been given) and relationships were good and trusting.

What was it that you liked the most about Tanganyika? What vivid memories do you have of the places in which you lived in Tanganyika, and of your interactions with Africans, Asians and Arabs, if any and where - at home or other places? Can you give some examples including stories of such personal experiences or encounters? And some of the exciting or trying moments you had including hardship?

What I liked the most about Tanganyika/Tanzania? It is hard to gauge since, to me, that country was home. Having grown up out there, "using the USA" for education, made it easy for me to return and begin work out there.

From 1956 to about 1972, we lived "in the bush" (but bushes were few - Nera in Kwimba District; Salawe in Shinyanga District; Kola Ndoto in Shinyanga District; Nasa in Mwanza District) and in each place we were content and felt very safe. There was a "laid back" style of living that was very much absent when we moved to Mwanza and later to Nairobi, Kenya.

"Hardship" may mean spending nights stuck in the mud during the rains or running out of sugar or kerosene and having to travel 70 miles to try and purchase some or a bus service that came through only once a week or the inability to help everyone the way you wish you could.

But, all this was a fact of life and you rolled with it making needed adjustments and changes. To this end, I can only say that we having gone to be of service to God and knowing that we were in the place in which He had put us - this mainly made us content and satisfied with what we found and experienced.

Feel free to share any oher experiences you had in those days. I would also like to use some of the old photos you may have from those days if you can scan them and email them to me. They should be no bigger than 6" x 9," the book's size.

Also let me know if I can use your name or if you want the information you give me to be published anonymously.

I'm not sure how helpful any of this information may be. I'm not interested in "mention" but if you feel led to do so, no problem.

I will look through photos/slides that may highlight those days and if I feel there are some that may be useful will let you know.

Sincerely,

Russell H. Baker
Africa Inland Mission/Africa Inland Church, Tanzania

***

From Malcolm Crawford, South Africa, 20 January 2006

Godfrey,

How was life back then?

It was excellent.

What fond memories do you have?

Carefree childhood. Exciting. Stimulating.

Can you give some examples?

Exploring your world in Africa is a better prospect than

exploring the street that you could live in. It is bigger and more unpredictable and in consequence is far more of an adventure. A boy's paradise!

Do you also remember some of the unpleasant experiences you had?

Leaving.

Where did you live in Tanganyika and where did you go to school?

In the bush, literally, my Dad was a driller. So Handeni, Tabora, Serengeti, Olduvai. Then into towns Dodoma, Tanga and Morogoro. School was Mbeya and Iringa.

How would you describe life in Tanganyika in the fifties in general?

Fantastic

What is it that you particularly miss about those days? Can you give a few example?

Freedom, almost total lack of crime, security, space, the smell of the rainy season.

What was your overall impression of Tanganyika as a country and in terms of life and its people? Was life good? Or was it hard?

If you were white then you would have to say good, although life was simple and would lack amenities available in more advanced countries. If you were black then it would be harder (less income). However, I don't remember malnutrition or starvation.

This is a difficult topic as it depends on the perspective you look from. A white person could see a mud hut as hardship. Alternatively, you can say the person had provided an economic house for himself which provided very adequate shelter. There would be whites who felt their simpler lifestyle was a hardship (poor things!)

Do you remember some of the inconveniences, for example lack of electricity, plumbing, etc.?

In the bush we had none of these things. My mother baked in a biscuit tin in a clay oven. My Dad shot for the pot. We had tilly lamps for the evening. God knows what we did for a toilet!

In town we got electricity. Hot water was a horizontal drum on a concrete foundation heated with a wood fire. Ironing was a heavy casting filled with hot charcoal. This would burn everything delicate and was only appropriate for khaki. A source of much annoyance to the "memsahib" who could never understand why there were so many scorch marks. She of course had never tried to use the bloody thing. Fridges were heated with paraffin. Cooking stoves were Aga wood fired. Meat safes stood in tins of paraffin to keep the ants out.

How do you remember those days? With fondness, nostalgia or not? And why?

Nostalgia because it was simple, uncomplicated and honest. It gave a better appreciation of what was produced from this rudimentary equipment.

What was it that you liked the most about Tanganyika?

Space, freedom, variety, great scenery.

What vivid memories do you have of the places in which you lived in Tanganyika, and of your interactions with Africans, Asians and Arabs, if any and where - at home or other places? Can you give some examples including stories of such personal experiences or encounters?

My first friends were watoto and their fathers. Their kindness is remembered. Making toys, how to make a catapult, bows, arrows, traps for birds. The sharing of food. Mahindi roasted over a wood fire. Dried peas and rock salt. Posho with pumba (poor people) white posho without pumba (richer people). Ripe and green mangoes. Sweet tea out of a Kimbo tin off a wood fire (best ever).

Indians to. Free chocolate if you spent enough in their shops! Curry. Chipatis. Samoosas (sambusa).

Iringa became multiracial and we had African team mates in the rugby team.

Sikh engine drivers on EAR&H giving you a tour of the locomotive cab. All the brass highly polished.

Arabs were in dhows in Dar-es-salaam - keep away they might carry you off to Yemen or somewhere!

African dances. Men leaping up and down till they went into a fit and foamed at the mouth and were restrained by others.

African villages where locusts had, or were, eating their entire crop. Very distressing to see.

And of some of the exciting or trying moments you had including hardship?

Exciting moments were avoiding an annoyed elephant whilst changing a flat tyre on an EAR&H bus. Hardship was travelling +- 1000 miles from Mbeya to Tanga over 3 days. First on wooden slats on a bus to Itigi. Leave Mbeya at night to hit Itigi at 12 noon to avoid tsetse fly. Train to Morogoro. Bus from Morogoro to Korogwe. Car from Korogwe to Tanga.

Malcolm

***

From Anna Harrison, 21 January 2006

Hello Godfrey,

It is funny that you should be looking into the 1950's in Tanganyika, as recently I have found some old school chums, through the Iringa website, and have had meetings with two of them which gave us an opportunity to remember the wonderful time we had living in East Africa and going to boarding schools in different parts of the Territory.

Most of my treasured memories are of the time spent at Kongwa which became a school upon the failure of the Groundnut scheme sometime after the second World War (I believe!).

Because the old scheme had built admin buildings and groups of residential 'cottages' the set up was perfect for our school, the admin blocks becoming classrooms and the numerous little houses became our 'dorms'.

This arrangement meant that each cottage slept eight children with the two room unit behind, which may have been servant quarters, used for two prefects, bathrooms or the house matron. This arrangement gave us kids the freedom to get up to all sorts of mischief, particularly on a Sunday afternoon, after Church.

Being at the School for two terms a year meant that we became a close knit family, and learnt to rely on our friends rather than parents, for most of the time.

Also the children came from all over the Territory, of different nationalities, but at that time not integrated with local African children, sadly.

One of my regrets is that I didn't learn proper Ki-Swahili, and only know some vocabulary and how to sing "one man went to mow"!!

I was born in West London in 1943, and was taken to Tanganyika with my family, when my father was demobbed from the Army, travelling by sea on an old P&O ship, arriving in Dar sometime in 1950.

Being only seven then, I can't remember some details, but I do recall the enormous adventure that it was.

We were stationed in Lindi, near the Mozambique border, and I can still see the marvellous sandy beaches and the surf crashing on the reef.

It was good that my Mother had given me some rudimentary lessons in swimming, because my brother and I were soon spending days on the beach and in the shallows, having a great time collecting shells, cowries mainly, and having races with hermit crabs!

We were stationed later, in Tanga and Mwanza, with a sojourn in Ukiriguru (Research Station) and later, 1959/60, in Dar-es-salaam.

I went to school in Arusha, Mbeya, Kongwa and Iringa, the latter for one year to do my overseas school certificate, so I travelled all over the place, by car, Cessna, train and bus!

I remember much of the excitement of these travels, and the wildness of much of the route, the red dust, the mud, the freedom to stay un-scrubbed, and the encountered wildlife. I loved it all!!

Godfrey, I could go on but time is short, so I hope this is useful to you. I do have some small B&W snaps, taken by my Mother, but I am too new to the computer process to send any at this time.

Do ask if you want more, and what sort of photos (subject?) you might be interested in.

I hope the book is filling up and that you have plenty of material to add.

Regards,

Anna Harrison.

***

From Mary Brown, South Africa, 23 January 2006

Jambo Godfrey!!

Good luck with your book!

I have so many vivid memories that I would need to write a book of my own!!

I refer to myself as a "Mwafrica" and feel privileged and blessed to have grown up in an environment of true freedom, no greed, corruption, violence, animosity.

Colour and creed did not come into any equation - all people were one.

Mary Brown and her grandchildren, as she calls them, Sheena and Gabriel, in South Africa. The picture was taken on 21 April 2005. They are the children of her family's domestic helper and she was helping to raise and educate them. As she said in her email in January 2006: "Sheena was with us from a few hours old and is now almost 9. She goes to the same school as my children did. I do not interfere with their culture and feel it is important that they know their roots. Little Gabriel will be a year old next month."

I was free to walk in the bush, in a town or a village without worrying about my safety. Spend the day up a mango tree or eat the fruit of a baobab tree. Pull the stems of long grass then suck the juices when I was thirsty - mix with the different tribes I came across through the years, the Masai, Makondes, Wagogos and others, all happy within their own communities. Christians and Muslims, Arabs and Indians, Ismailis, Italians, Greek, British - black, white, brown and discovering each ones cultures, learning from each and respecting them all.

I shared food and water with all and I received true basic hospitality wherever I happened to be. I went to any church that was close at hand or according to my mood therefore I was brought up with "free" religion. All humans were my friends. All animals were free to roam.

I was truly blessed to have had this experience. I have few photographs but everything is imprinted vividly in my mind.

I weep for my children who have missed out and are subjected to this awful world of today.

What does the future have in store for them? What chance will they have to enjoy the people of this world and what is left of nature?

Slim chance.

I must not carry on otherwise I will be writing for a few months - maybe, I too, should write a book!!!

I would need time anyway to write in detail in reply to your letter and I am rather short of that at this present moment.
Salaama,

Mary Brown

***

From Perry Garlick, Russia, 24 January 2006

Godfrey,

Jambo.

I have no idea how you came across me, I can only presume from the web site iringa.org. Perhaps you were even at school with me ?

I dont know where you live now, are you still in Tanzania ? Anyway with pleasure I will answer your questions, and give you my perspective of Tanaganyika as I remember it.

I lived there as a child from 1948 until 1960 or '61 I can't remember now. I left when I was 14 years old after independence, because unfortunately the farm was nationalised.

My parents were farming in the Southern Highlands, about 15 miles from Mufindi. Our nearest post office was at John's Corner on the great North Road between Mbeya and Iringa.

Our farm was called Tuferu Farm, it was a mixed farm, doing crops, vegetables, flowers, Battery chickens, and cattle. In fact if I recall correctly one of the rivers that ran through the farm was the little Ruaha. Our nearest club was at Soa Hill. Our neighbours were people like the Snapes and the Hales.

In fact some things I remember like yesterday, because for me I had a fabulous childhood growing up in Tanganyika. I loved it, and my heart is still in Africa these days, though I work in Russia, I have a home and family in South Africa, so that's where I will retire.

Where did I go to School? The first one I went to was the Soa Hill mixed (both sexes) primary school. The headmasters name was Geoffrey Holland. I was there from the age of 6 till seven-and-a-half. My father decided that I was not working very hard and enjoying the Girls too much (at 6 and a half!!), and sent me to a Catholic School in Soni called St Michael's in the Usambara mountains. I was at St Michael's School, Soni, until I was 11.

Then I took my 11 + exam, passed and started at St. Michael's and St. George's in Iringa. I was in Oram House. My cousin Sean, and his sister were there as well, plus my very good friend Johnny Ghaui, who lived at Kisolanza Farm closer to Iringa. I was at St. Michael's & St. George's in Iringa till I was 14. My family and I left to return back to England in 1961.

What do I remember? Great times. Wonderful place as a child to grow up. So much freedom as a child to wander round the farm, to go hunting and trapping, with all my African friends who were my age living on the farm.

Riding my bicycle to Mufindi, to Kisolanza farm.- just being able to tell my mother that I was going to visit so and so for a couple of days, putting a bag on the back of a bike, and riding off without a care in the world, and returning 3 days later. Nobody worried, if something went wrong. The bush telegraph worked very well.

Having no electricity, and using Tilley lamps, and Hurricane lanterns, was no hardship. I was taught to be independant at an early age. It has stood me in good stead because I have lived in many other palces in Africa as well, and now live in Russia, and that was rough living in the early 90's. My mother used to take me trout fishing once a year near Mbeya. I can't remember the names of the rivers we used to fish.

I loved camping as a child, and visiting the game parks. We

aslo used to go to Bagamoyo for holidays during the long vac. Fabulous digging in the reefs, swimming and snorkelling. The wonderful Arab doors on the buildings.

Bad times? None really. I remember the friendliness of the people, how they would look after me when I came back from school and the East African Railways and Harbours bus used to drop me at John's Corner, and I would wait there talking and eating until a neighbour or my father came to collect me. Time was not important.

I have always had a great affection for the African people, their wonderful sense of humour, and of course as a child I spoke Swahili fairly fluently, though unfortunately I have forgotten that skill.

I did get malaria a couple of times as well as para typhoid from drinking polluted water. The local Mission Hospital sorted me out from that.

The only really bad experience I had was losing an eye playing cricket at school, when I was 13, which was very sad, as I could not play any sport for a long time afterwards. I spent 3 months in the Ocean Road Hospital in Dar-es-salaam.

I have rambled enough. Thank you for reminding me of a great country, and place to grow up as a child.
Kwaheri

Perry

***

From Charis Radford, Australia, 26 January 2006

Hello Godfrey,

Thank you very much for your reply to my questions. I was most interested in reading it.

Yes, I would enjoy writing about my memories. I may also get my mother to reminisce...she is almost 90 and lived in Tanganyika/Tanzania from 1944 to 1966, living in Rungwe from 1947 to 1958. She always says those days were simply wonderful days....she loved her life there.

You originally said you were from Mbeya region, but were born in Kigoma. Are you an Mnyakusa? We thought your name sounded like it. I'm curious why you were born in Kigoma? I was born in Mbeya, three months before you!

My father, Dick Feuerheerd, became Principal of the Rungwe Teacher Training College. Before that he was working up in the Kigoma region. It's all so very interesting.

I'm wondering if I can have a postal address that I could send copies of photos, I'm not too proficient with computers.

Is it specifically the fifties that you are interested in? I left Tanzania in 1966 as a teenager, having spent one year at Mkwawa High School (formerly St. Michael's and St. George's School).

I have sent a copy of your reply to me to another friend who lives nearby who had had your initial letter...Denton Webster. We have been having a couple of local 'mini reunions' of a few of us who live in this area and were at Iringa School. We all look back with GREAT fondness to that time.

Sincerely,

Charis Radford

***

From Godfrey Mwakikagile, 26 January 2006

Hello Charis,

Thank you very much for your response and for your interest in the project. It's always nice to hear from someone who lived in the same place I did many years ago.

I'm very excited about the project and it will be very nice if your mother also can add something to it. I'm sure she saw a lot and she lived in Tanganyika during a time when life was different from what it is nowadays. Life was simpler, and the people friendlier, in those days. There was hardly any crime even in the fifties when you and I were growing up.

It's also very interesting that you were born and lived in my home region! And that we are the same age, only three months apart! Also one of my sisters was born in Mbeya just like you were.

I remember quite a few things about Mbeya although I was only a child when we lived there. Do you remember a circus they had in Mbeya one day? I was about four or five years old and my parents took me to see the performance. I remember seeing an elephant and many people on that day. I also remember seeing someone with a snake wrapped around his neck.

Were you there on that day or saw other circuses in town? I don't remember if they had other shows after that but they probably did. And I may have seen more than one but I'm not sure. I was too young to remember all that.

And you are right about me. Yes, I am a Nyakyusa, but I was born in Kigoma because my father worked there. He was a medical assistant. He was trained at Muhimbili Hospital in Dar es Salaam in the mid-forties after completing his secondary school education at Malangali, which I'm sure you know of, since you went to Mkwawa High School, formerly St. Michael's and St. George's, in the same district, Iringa, in the beautiful Southern Highlands.

It is really interesting that you and your parents also lived in the same district where I come from. Although I lived in different parts of Tanganyika as a child, and in what became Tanzania when I was a teenager, Rungwe District has always been my home because that is where my parents came from. And that is where they returned. My most memorable years were also in Rungwe District because that is where I grew up. And it is the home district of the Nyakyusa people, of which I am one.

I am interested in the fifties but not exclusively so. Since you lived in Tanganyika, later Tanzania, until 1966, you can write about the sixties as well. I'm going to use it in the book. And if you send me any photos, include the ones you have from the sixties, not just the ones from the fifties. I have received some information from a number of ex-Tanganyikans who also lived in Tanganyika in the sixties and I'm going to use all of it, although most of the material is about the fifties.

I wish I could tell you to go ahead and send me the photos but I can't because I cannot scan them right now. And they could get lost in the mail. I would hate for you to lose such important items. They are a treasure. I'm sure they are of great sentimental value to you and you have kept them for so long. I hope you can find someone who can help you to scan them.

Just take your time and see if you can find someone to help. I would rather wait than see you lose such important photos if I were to ask you to mail them to me. I'm also not very good with computers and am still learning how to use them.

I would love to include your photos in the book and will wait as long as necessary until you get them scanned. But if you can't do it, just send me whatever you write about those days. They were indeed good ol' days and we will never see them again. But we can at least preserve the memories we have of those wonderful years. And that's what I'm trying to do wth this book.

Asante sana.
Kwaheri.

Godfrey

***

From Ben Cooper, Dubai, 29 January 2006

Hi Godfrey,

Sorry about the delay in responding - I was taken aback a little!

To answer your questions-

I was born in Malawi and raised in East Africa up to age 14 - we left during independence years in 1961. As you know, this was during the colonial era and we had little day to day contact with native Africans, but of course the average man in the street was always very polite and the servants we employed were loyal people.

My parents were hard working as they would be anywhere else, earning a living.

I think we miss mostly the weather and the freedom, with so many outdoor activities, sightseeing etc.

Throughout our stay, my two brothers and I went to boarding schools at various places (Kabale, Entebbe, Nakuru, Nairobi Princo, St. Mary's, Iringa St. Michael's) with all the travelling involved. It was a very thriving community and we were very proud of the railways (my Dad worked for EAR&H) and the huge 60 class Garrett locomotives then used - the biggest in the world. At times, we were in western Uganda, then Kisumu, then down at Tabora.

We had horses and pets of all sorts which we took with us when we were transfered to other locations and we used to ride out into the bundu which was quite exciting - we had a privileged life you might say, but it's all relative, isn't it - those were post-war days and my Dad did serve in the King's African Rifles and spoke well of his African troops.

At Iringa school, we welcomed the first African and Indian students at independence and I remember them being very clever and with sporting ability - this was just before we finally and sadly left Africa as my Dad's job was Africanised.

We do as old pupils visit the school in Iringa and are welcomed very well by the African students and it's nice to be able to contribute with small donations now and again which is very small repayment for all the wonderful times Africa gave to us so long ago.

We are proud to call ourselves African as you can imagine we have reunions across the world still to remember old times and many of us still speak a few words of Swahili.

Inconveniences? In Uganda we lived in the bundu building the railway extension to Fort Portal - we had oil lamps not even a generator and collected rain water for drinking, but this was normal after a few years.

Our schooling was by correspondence but as kids these were exciting times. The railway film unit used to come and show movies time to time on outside screen and the tribesmen would come with their spears, lined-up at the back row. I don't remember trying or difficult moments but leaving our parents for long periods seemed hard - does boarding school make you a better man? - I have mixed feelings about this.

Godfrey, I wish you well and a Happy New Year and hope to chat to you some more. I am a mzee now, working in Dubai and retiring in a few years to Cyprus - people say I have got Africa in my blood and will not go back to UK!!!

Take care, and if you have news on Susan Lockhart from

1950's please let me know.

Ben Cooper

***

From Tony Stylianou, South Africa, 29 January 2006

Dear Godfrey,

Your address was passed on to me by Rudene Gerber who had it passed on by Valerie Robinson.

I was born in Moshi in 1940 and grew up in Arusha. I went to Arusha School and later to the Prince of Wales School in Nairobi.

My father was in business in Arusha where he had a factory manufacturing macaroni and other pastas. He also had a coffee plantation at Usa River.

Our family home (in Arusha) was on Haile Selassie Road, formerly known as Churchill Road. The house next door is now State House and belonged to my mother's sister and brother in law, Christopher Kikkides MBE, who incidentally was a member of Legislative Council and later an MP.

I married a teacher who came from the UK to teach at Arusha school, and three of my children were born in Arusha.

We immigrated to South Africa at the end of 1965. We farm near Kidd's Beach some 30 kms from East London and we spend every week end in Port Alfred where we have a home.

Since 1993 I have been visiting Tanzania at least once a year. Last year I was there during May, July and August.

I have many photographs and records of our life from the 40's to the 60's, maybe we can share some of them.

Get in touch and let's see what we can do.

Regards,

Tony Stylianou.

***

From Vanessa Beeman, UK, 9 February 2006

Dear Godfrey,

I haven't got a scanner, so have been waiting for my husband to have time to scan a few photos which may be of interest, but as time is passing, I thought I would send this and do the photos separately!

My parents, Kaspar and Eileen went out to Shinyanga to the Tsetse Department in 1937, and stayed for forty years! They loved East Africa, and my father always worked in pest control, especially disease vectors such as mosquitoes and tsetse. It is great that they apparently still have a photo of him at the Tropical Pesticide research labs in Arusha.

My sister was born on a Mission at Kolodoto (?) near Shinyanga in 1940, and I was born in Nairobi in 1945.

We lived in Entebbe for a while, but at Arusha 1950 - 1967. I went to Arusha Primary School and St. Michael's and St. George's in Iringa.

It was a very happy childhood - great freedom, wide open spaces, no polllution, and the Tanzanians are great with children. In addition of course there was the wildlife.

The electricity went off sometimes, but we had paraffin lamps, and our water was a Tanganyika boiler: an oil drum with a wood fire beneath. We cooked with *kuni* (firewood) in the early days.

Vanessa's father Kasper Hocking, second from front, in the canoe with his colleagues on a tse-tse-fly patrol near Mwanza in the late 1950s.

Arusha had plentiful water: we were blessed with the mountain streams. The climate was excellent.

I think of it all with great fondness and went back recently to find it more populous, but the folks friendly, and the wildlife parks excellent.

'Mungu ibariki Tanzania'

Vanessa Beeman

***

From Vanessa Beeman, Constantine, Kernow, 28 February 2006

Hi Godfrey,

H/W (I hope !) three pics. The one in the canoe is my father (second from front) and colleagues on tsetse patrol near Mwanza somewhere, my mother sits on the verandah of our PWD house in Arusha, and myself, sister Shelagh and mother are watching game at Ngurdoto crater near Arusha. My parents are Kaspar & Eileen Hocking, now 93 & 92 respectively!

Kwaheri kwa sasa

Vanessa

***

David Leonard, 10 February 2006

Dear Godfrey,

    My apologies for taking nearly a month to get back to you, but I've been doing alot of flying which has been my profession for the last 40 years. From Super Cubs to four engine Boeings.

    You certainly wont remember him but I am to be blessed next week with a visit from an old teacher from St Michael's and St George's specifically Allan Klube, who now, for his sins, lives in England.

    This in some haste as our machine is down and I'm using a cyber cafe.

    I know Kigoma well, as from Geita we used to spend our Christmas on the Liembe between Kigoma and Mpulungu in Northern Zambia towing barges of freight while we sat around playing 78s and trying to avoid my father, who could be relied on to turn up anytime I lit a cigarette (I was 15 but I gave that up quite quickly). Visited Ujiji to see where Livingstone met Stanley on several of our trips. Ditto Morogoro, Mbeya and Kilosa at all of which three latter places, we played rugby.

    You may remember Mzungu who was the last DC at Handeni. He was from memory a Mr Milner who's son was at school with me.

    Strange that you refer to the colonial government, there are very few of us left who remember those days.

I was in Tanga when the Brit Marines put down the mutiny in Dar in '64 and subsequently Julius Nyerere formed the United Republic of Tanganyika and Zanzibar. Known, as I'm sure you know, as Tanzania.

I remember Julius Kambarage quite well as he was the Tanu Rep. who negotiated with my father about working conditions at the gold mine where I was raised near Mwanza.

Delighted that you are writing a book about Tanganyika - if you need any help with specific parts, you have only to call.

Tanganyika was a wonderful country and still is. Though it went trhough that bad period of Ujamaa.

Look forward to hearing from you again when mayhap. I can be more informative and not under the same time constraints.
Kwaheri Ndugu.

David

Appendix I:

Sykes of Tanzania Remembers the Fifties

Peter Colmore:
The Man With the Midas Touch

A personal memoir of East Africa's first and most succesful impresario by his longtime friend and business associate, the equally illustrious ALLY SYKES of Tanzania.

In 1958 I formed my first company, Sykes Sales Promotion Consultancy, and an old friend, Peter Colmore, who had by then built up a very successful sales promotion business in Nairobi, appointed me his agent in Tanganyika.

I first met Peter in Nairobi in 1942, during the Second World War. I was at Kabete waiting to be transported overseas for active service. We met at a record shop - East African Music Store. Both of us were in the uniform of the King's African Rifles (KAR), so we exchanged greetings and a few words. Our meeting in this record shop was an omen, because later our relationship would evolve around music and the business enterprise we would build.

Colmore was at that time a lieutenant and aide de camp to General Sir William Platt, Commander in Chief of the East African Forces. I was a lance corporal.

After the war, I disembarked at Mombasa and came to Nairobi looking for a job. Peace had created new opportunities to those who wanted to settle in Kenya. I went to look for Colmore. He had started his own real estate business, Colban Ltd, in partnership with an English lady. Colmore now put me in charge of the office. My job was to take prospective buyers to properties offered for sale and to negotiate the price, leaving Colmore to seal the deal after I had completed the groundwork. I also acted as a public relations officer for the agency.

At that time, under colonial rule, it was a prestigious job indeed for an African. I got on well with Colmore and we decided to add a sideline to the real estate agency to boost our earnings. We decided to start a band. Since I was in the Entertainment Unit during the war, it was not difficult for me to organise one.

Colmore brought in an African band from Southern Rhodesia (now Zimbabwe); at that time Kenyan musicians had not yet taken up playing modern instruments. This band from Rhodesia had African musicians who played the piano, saxophone and trumpets. Colmore put me in charge and I was responsible for the general management of the band and for fixing their engagements. The band became very popular in Nairobi as it had talented musicians. We played mainly for white audiences, because that was where the money was. At first the band was known as the Ally Sykes Band, but later it came to be known as the Peter Colmore African Band.

Colmore is reputed to have owned the first tape recorder in Kenya. He bought the machine from an army officer. In those days, a tape recorder did not use emulsion tape but paper tape and was called the "sound mirror". It was a dramatic breakthrough after the tedious chore of recording on disc. Colmore used to record the American Top Ten from the Voice of America with this tape recorder and the band would practice these songs and play them to their audiences. In this way, American pop songs found their way into the dance halls of Nairobi soon after they were released in New York, Los Angeles and London.

The quality of our music was excellent. At that time, we played more for the love of art than for commercial gain. Colmore used to come to Dar es Salaam to record local bands like Ulanga Jazz Band, Morogoro Jazz Band, Home Boys and others. He was responsible for recording for His Master's Voice (HMV) Blue Label and for Jambo Records, which was owned by his friend, Dr Guy Johnson.

Colmore was the pioneer of disc cutting in East Africa. I was involved in all these ventures. We promoted many bands from Tanganyika and Kenya. Colmore later founded his own recording company - High Fidelity Productions Ltd. There was never a day when High Fidelity Productions was not on the airwaves either in Tanganyika, Kenya or Uganda. Our advertisements were all over East Africa. Colmore also composed his own tunes to go with the programmes. These signature tunes soon became synonymous with the products.

Colmore also promoted entertainers and comedians such as Omari Sulemani, known as Mzee Pembe, Halima bint Said, and others. He also promoted musicians such as Franck Humplick, Mathias Mulamba, Esther John and John Mwale, and got the Kenya Broadcasting Corporation to take on famous radio announcers like Stephen Kikumu, Julius Kilua and Said Omari.

I also broadcast radio shows for Philips Company of Holland in Dar es Salaam. I used my band for sales promotion. When we began promoting the Shell Company of East Africa Ltd, I changed the band's name to the Shell Merry Makers.

Colmore himself was a gifted stage artist. His talent for mimicry invariably had his audiences rolling about with laughter. He was a regular performer at the Nairobi Royal Theatre. Our band also played at the Royal Theatre, adding flavour to the shows. These shows were later linked with publicity of products manufactured by multinational companies.

We represented, promoted, and were consultants to Coca Cola (East Africa) Ltd, Cooper Motor Corporation Ltd, Allsopp (EA) Ltd, Shell Company of East Africa Ltd, Aspro Nicholas Ltd, Gailey and Roberts Ltd, Bata Shoe Company Ltd, Kenya Broadcasting Service, Cotton Lint and Seed Marketing Board and Raleigh Industries of East Africa Ltd.

We were also commercial representatives in Kenya for the Tanganyika Broadcasting Corporation (TBC), now Radio Tanzania Dar es Salaam. The head office of this massive sales promotion venture was in Nairobi's Delamere Avenue, now Kenyatta Avenue.

Peter Colmore built some products into household names around East Africa. The best musicians East Africa had ever known were used to promote these products.

Colmore signed on Edward Masengo, the gifted guitarist from Elizabethville, Belgian Congo, to promote Coca-Cola. Masengo had come to Nairobi with a group called Je-Co-Ke meaning Jeunes Comediens Katanga. Colmore, who was already in broadcasting, was informed that there was a young man in town who played terrific guitar.

Colmore went looking for Masengo and found him in a filthy lodging on River Road. He was sitting on the floor playing his guitar with people gathered around him listening to his music. This was the beginning of the association between Colmore and Masengo.

There was the famous poster of Masengo with his guitar, holding a bottle of Coca-Cola. There was also the famous photograph of Msafiri Morimori the trombone player. These pictures were regularly printed in newspapers around East Africa.

The sales of the product rose as the market responded to the artist, and the music of the artist was promoted through his being associated with the product.Colmore entrusted me with the management of this nascent sales promotion venture in Tanganyika.

Through Masengo, Colmore signed the talented singer and guitarist Jean Mwenda Bosco, also from Elizabethville. Masengo and Bosco were cousins. In January 1959, Peter Colmore and Edward Masengo flew to Elizabethville to fetch Bosco for a short contract to promote Aspro. The Belgian government made Colmore pay 30,000 francs as deposit to make sure that he would return Bosco back to Congo.

Bosco was already a household name in East Africa, but no one had seen even his photograph or knew what he looked like because he had never travelled outside Congo. At that time, he was recording with a South African recording company, Gallatone.

Bosco stayed in Nairobi for six months. Colmore took Bosco on a countrywide tour of Kenya promoting Aspro as relief for headaches, fever and flu. The effect he had on the sales of Aspro was phenomenal. At that time, Bosco was 29 years old and at the prime of his career. Before he left for home, Bosco composed a song, Shangwe Mkubwa (Let's Praise the Boss), in praise of Peter Colmore, in which he sang of his flight from Elizabethville to Nairobi. Music critics of those times were of the opinion that of all his compositions, this was the best.

Colmore also arranged for Masengo and Bosco to perform together at dance halls in Nairobi. By the time Masengo left Kenya for home, he was already a rich young man. Masengo married a beautiful Maasai girl, Lucie Akukuu Mainge and had a daughter, whom they named Jojo. This marriage took place in April 1959.

In December 1960, we brought Masengo over to Dar es Salaam for a series of shows. The late Julius Nyerere, my friend and colleague, was the guest of honour at the show at Arnautoglo Hall. Colmore had come over from Nairobi for the show and I took the opportunity to introduce him to Nyerere. I took Colmore to Nyerere's house at Magomeni Majumba Sita. We found Nyerere in a state of distress - he had just heard reports from Congo that Lumumba had been killed.

As members of Tanu and citizens of a country on the brink of achieving independence, we followed the news from Congo with great interest. And the events now unfolding were extremely distressing for most of us. I had a special interest, as at that time I believe I was the only person in Tanu who had been to Congo and had first-hand experience of the ruthlessness of Belgian colonialism.

Masengo was also very sad to hear of the news that Katanga, his home province, had under Moise Tshombe seceded from the Congo Republic. So the only thing I can remember of that day when I took Colmore to Nyerere is how sad we all were about what had happened.

However, we took the opportunity while in Dar to have Masengo record his old songs with Tanganyika Broadcasting Corporation. Back in Nairobi, both Colmore and Masengo wrote to me, Colmore thanking me for introducing him to Nyerere and Masengo for successfully managing his tour and shows. Colmore told me how grateful he was to Nyerere for showing a firm stand on the Congo problem.

At that time, Masengo was incorporated into High Fidelity

Productions as one of the directors. Colmore was a man of foresight; he realised that we would need the support of Nyerere if we were to expand our business in free Tanganyika. Our business interests there were already growing rapidly. Colmore built a house in Moshi and used to drive over from Nairobi every weekend.

After independence and following the Arusha Declaration of 1967, the government passed the Leadership Code. The code prohibited civil servants from engaging in business, drawing more than one salary, owning property or holding shares in a private company. The code even prevented any civil servant from renting out property.

In 1971, the government passed the Acquisition of Buildings Act. By the stroke of a pen, all buildings with a value of more than a hundred thousand shillings became government property. We too lost some property through nationalisation, including the office, which was owned by Colmore.

Colmore could not stand the political climate and so he sold the company to me and returned to Nairobi. But we remained friends. The last time I saw him was few months ago. He was on his deathbed and when he spoke to me he was barely audible.

Yes, Peter Colmore had a Midas touch. Whatever he touched turned into gold. We had a friendship that lasted 62 years. And over that period I was a witness to that magic.

From *The East African*, Nairobi, Kenya, 16 February 2004.

Appendix II:

Paramount Chief Thomas Marealle Reflects on the Fifties: An Interview

A Man with A Mission

By Heckton Chuwa, Moshi

The 10th of November used to be the Chagga Day, something which not many of the current generation know about. In the past, the Chagga were seen as one of the wealthiest, most highly organised and modern tribes.

On the 9th of November *The Express* interviewed the last ruler of the Chagga, Chief Thomas Marealle II OBE, at his home in Shanty Town Moshi, Kilimanjaro Region.

During his time as Chief, Marealle worked hard to create strong chieftainships in the country, with councils working for development. Thanks to his education and later awards, Marealle, after being stripped of his title, continued to work for development under the auspices of the United Nations.

The Express:
When did you become chief of the Chagga?

Chief Marealle:

Officially, this was on the 17th January, 1952, the day I was inaugurated after winning the chieftainship elections.

The Express:

Winning the elections? But do not chiefs and kings inherit their thrones?

Chief Marealle:

Definitely. But in my case it was a little bit different. After my grandfather Chief Marealle I died, my father was to inherit the throne but it passed him because of the war between the Germans and the British. The war made the colonial powers and the local people unable to concentrate on local administration matters.

The Express:

So what happened?

Chief Marealle:

After the war had ended the British who were then ruling Tanganyika imposed Divisional Chiefs in 1946 that were known locally as Mitoris, but this did not please the local people who wanted to have there own local leadership.

The Express:

Did the people stage an uprising?

Chief Marealle:

No, although there was one indirectly. The Chagga led by the leader of all the Chagga clans, Petro Njau in 1949 formed the Kilimanjaro Chagga Citizens Union, KCCU, with the main objective to establish local self government.

The Express:

Was it successful?

Chief Marealle:

Yes. The Provincial Commissioner (PC) of that time convened a big meeting which comprised of different leaders from religious organisations and the Divisional Chiefs among them. They discussed the contents of the proposed KCCU constitution which called for a Paramount Chief of the Chagga. The motion was passed and the Chagga got their constitution in 1951, making the Chagga the first local community to have our own constitution in the then Tanganyika.

The Express:

Who were your main opponents in the contest for the

chieftainship?

Chief Marealle:

There were three of them, all of them Divisional Chiefs: Abdi Shangali of Hai; Petro Marealle of Vunjo and John Maruma of Rombo.

The Express:

What did you do before you became a chief?

Chief Marealle:

I was the Manager and founder of the Tanganyika Broadcasting Corporation.

The Express:

During the colonial era, it must have been very unusual for a local person to get such a big post. How did you get it?

Chief Marealle:

It is unquestionable because of my education. I had come back from England where I went for my higher education. I studied economics and political economics at the London School of Economics, and Public Administration at the Trinity College.

The Express:

Tell us briefly about the Chiefdom.

Chief Marealle:

There was a supreme council known as the Chagga Council, which had complete autonomy. The Council was divided into committees which ran the daily administration services of the chiefdom. The paramount chief was the chairman of all the committees.

The Express:

Can you tell us about the Chagga Day and how it all started?

Chief Marealle:

This was the Chagga chiefdom's version of an Independence Day, because it was the day when the Chagga people got what they wanted most: self local administration. Its origination dates back to the day when I was nominated as the Chief of the Chagga, the 10th November, 1951.

The Express:

How did the celebrations of the Chagga Day look like?

Chief Marealle:

Very colourful! We started the day by attending prayers in our respective areas of worship; at the churches for Christians and mosques for Muslims. After the prayers we used to march to a place known as Kiboriloni to perform traditional Chagga rituals to mark the day, after which I delivered my traditional Chagga Day speech. It included the past year's performance of the monarch and the future plans.

The Express:
Did the celebrations end there?
Chief Marealle:
No. After my speech we settled for lunch together with other invited guests and after the afternoon rest, all council members used to watch football matches in the evening. Later in the evening, all leaders of the Chagga Council together with invited guests exchanged views as far as development were concerned. Those who performed well in development of the chiefdom were rewarded.

The Express:
Did you have any relations with other chiefdoms?
Chief Marealle:
Yes. I suggested to the then governor of Tanganyika to convey a conference of the local chiefs in the country with the intention of creating unity among us and also to discuss our problems so that we could help each other to solve them.

The Express:
Did this work?
Chief Marealle:
Yes, the Governor agreed and the first conference was conveyed at Mzumbe, Morogoro. Mwani Ntare, ruler of the Waha from Kasulu Kigoma was elected the Chairperson. That was in 1957. I was elected the Chairperson the next year and Chief Adam Sapi Mkwawa was elected my deputy. We agreed to select an official with the then British leadership, C.I.Meek, for the post of Secretary General. He acted as a coordinator between the Conference of the Chiefs and the Governor.

The Express:
How did your people benefit from your chieftainship?
Chief Marealle:
Many got education, the primary education was free and the parents of those who went for higher studies were asked to pay what they could and the remaining was then subsidised by the

Chagga Council treasury. Some went to the Makerere University. We also build our own State House and Parliament and our people were provided with clean water.

The Express:

Did you ever get any subsidies or any other type of help from the government?

Chief Marealle:

I remember getting two voluntary government contributions. The first was 50 per cent towards the expansion of educational services and 75 per cent towards water supplies.

The Express:

What are your fondest memories from the time of your chieftainship?

Chief Marealle:

First I was very glad that I was able to serve my people and share with them my achievements as far as my education was concerned. My achievements and good relations with the British leadership made the Governor choose me to represent Tanganyika at the coronation of Her Majesty the Queen of England Queen Elizabeth II. I was also chosen to represent Tanganyika at the Independence Day of Ghana of which the late Richard Nixon then the US President attended. I addressed the United Nations Assembly and I was awarded with the British Empire's OBE on the 12th June 1958.

The Express:

How did the chiefdom come to an end?

Chief Marealle:

This was after the declaration of the abolition of the Chieftains by the government in 1961.

The Express:

How did you feel when the chiefdom ended?

Chief Marealle:

I didn't feel anything because I had left the chieftain in 1960.

The Express:

Why?

Chief Marealle:

Plans were then underway to join the traditional chiefdoms with the new political administration systems that I didn't see as fair. I had sworn that I couldn't involve my God-given chieftainship with modern politics.

The Express:
Do people still recognise you as their Chief?
Chief Marealle:
Yes, especially those who remember my achievements. Even those who benefited during our administration do visit me here, others come for advice.

The Express:
What did you do after you were stripped off your title?
Chief Marealle:
Because of my achievements, I was called to join the United Nation's FAO/WFP programme. I was in charge of all aid directed to Third World countries. I was based in Rome, Italy for the entire 13 years of my service.

The Express:
What are you now doing for a living?
Chief Marealle:
I am a retired diplomat.

The Express:
I do thank you, Your Majesty. Long live the King.
Chief Marealle:
Thank you. And May God bless you.

From *The Express*, Dar es Salaam, Tanzania.

Appendix III:

The Fifties in Tanganyika: A Tanzanian Journalist Remembers

One of the first Tanzanian pioneer journalists

By Peter Msungu

John Innocent Hungu

On October, 1957, John Innocent Hungu, was appointed Editor of *Baragumu*, on secondment from the public relations department, which later changed to Tanzania Information Services. The then youthful public relations assistant had joined the department in 1956.

"There were no formal local courses for journalists then. It was assumed that Cambridge Certificate holders, me being one of them, could undergo what the colonial officers termed as 'on the job training' and we did that successfully," John Innocent Hungu, recalls vividly.

Narrating the brief history of newspapers in this country during colonial days, Mr.Hungu explained that on January 22, 1958, the colonial government transferred the ownership of its three Kiswahili newspapers, namely, *Mambo Leo*, *Baragumu* and *Mwangaza*, to an independent company, called Tanganyika National Newspaper Ltd.

As his second name(Innocent), would suggest, Mr.Hungu, now 67, looks very innocent and many of his close confidants have many a time asked him why he never chose to become a priest.

"John takes things seriously, especially when it comes to discussing human issues, or even an ordinary issue concerning work. He would leave no stone unturned, and it is here you would discover he is a serious gentleman," narrates a former workmate from the colonial era, adding that once Hungu believes in a certain discipline, you cannot convince him to abandon his belief.

It is for this reason that he was dismissed from service when it was discovered that he was working for a political newspaper, *Mwafrika*, during his spare time. He firmly believed politics was the number one saviour of Tanganyikans."Why should someone want to transfer me to Tanga where I would lose touch with my *Mwafrika* newspaper?" he once asked.

"Come 25 April, 1959, I am dismissed from government service after I refused to be be transferred to Tanga, and secondly for being discovered working in my spare time for a political newspaper, *Mwafrika*, during the struggle for independence," John Hungu recalls.

Born in January 1937 in Tukuyu, Mbeya Region, Hungu first attended a Native Authority primary school in Tukuyu before joining Mchikichini Primary School in Dar es Salaam where he finished his primary education in 1949. Between 1950 and 1952, he studied at Kichwele Secondary School before proceeding to Mzumbe secondary school where he completed his secondary education.

After his dismissal from government service, he joined the Tanganyika African Newspaper Company Ltd as an assistant editor on the *Mwafrika* newspaper where he stayed for three years from 1959-1961.

"Immediately after independence, the paper was sold to the Nation Group of Newspapers, Nairobi, which to me was a big blunder for a political newspaper to be sold to a tycoon who was not a Tanzanian," he lamented.

"As is usual, I had to start looking for a new job in order to sustain my life and that of my younger brothers who had not started schooling. And in the course of my endeavors I got a job with the United States Information Services(USIS) where I stayed for two years before joining the Tanganyika Broadcasting Corporation as Assistant News Editor for both the English and Kiswahili news programmes," Hungu said.

Indeed, Mr.Hungu has had a varied working life, for between 1964 and 1969, he was editor of the *Ushirika* newspaper, the mass communication organ of the Tanzania Cooperative Movement(CUT).

And between 1971 and 1972, he was appointed editor of the most famous religious newspaper in the country, *Kiongozi*, published by the Catholic Secretariat, Dar es Salaam.

He told this reporter during the interview that he had always dreamt that one day he would travel to a foreign country where he would live and work seriously to earn a living.

"So from *Kiongozi* newspaper, I started a long journey to India where I served the government of India at All India Radio, New Delhi, as journalist/cum broadcaster for 28 years," Mr.Hungu explained happily, adding that he went to that great country of Mahatma Gandhi to learn first-hand her philosophies and to study, practise, and integrate them into hi daily life, he said.

Asked to give his personal opion on present-day India, he had the following to say: "When I left India in 2001, things had politically changed. The present regime under Prime Minister A.B. Vajpayee seems to tilt more towards Western Europe, rather than Africa. The government does not seem to realise that India has a lot to gain by cooperating with Africa, as was the case in the past during Indira Gandhi's rule. Indira was a true daughter of Africa," Mr.Hungu remarked.

Talking of his other extra-curricula activities, the still going-strong journalist said in 1971 that he published a book titled *Uhuru na Taifa Tanzania*, a history of Tanzania and TANU before and after independence.

A reviewer of that book, the late Kusai Kamisa, then a journalist of high repute with the *Daily News/Sunday News*, said the book was uniquely concise, and perhaps the first Swahili book by a Tanzanian to cover Tanzania's history before and after independence up to 1967 when the Arusha Declaration was adopted.

In his foreword to that book, the former Minister of State for Regional Administration and Rural Development, Peter Kisumo, commended John Hungu for his efforts in writing the vital book which, although small, contains virtually everything one wants to know about Tanzania historically.

Asked to mention a few names of people he believes pioneered the journalism industry in Tanzania, he said it was not difficult as some are still alive. He mentioned Joseph Yinza, the first Tanzanian Director of Information Services; the late Aidan Cheche, Hubert Cheche, Lawrence Munubi, Felix Ishengoma, John Hungu, Athumani Zayumba, Peter Maravi, Joseph Patila, and Mr.C.Lupindu.

He said most of these veteran journalists first worked with *Mambo Leo*, *Mwangaza* and *Baragumu* newspapers before later joining the Tanzania Information Services in the years after independence.

Mr.Hungu also worked as a stringer for the BBC Swahili programmes during his stay in India from 1973 - 2001.

The veteran journalist/broadcaster is happily married and blessed with five children, two girls and three boys, three of whom have been to universities in India.

"As of now, both of my children are still outside the country working and or pursuing further studies in various disciplines," he proudly said, adding, "they look forward to joining us here in Tanzania in the not-too-distant future."

"I am now enjoying a happy retirement after serving the government of India for 28 years," he concluded.

From the *Sunday Observer*, Dar es Salaam, 3 March 2004.

Appendix IV:

Remembering Tanganyika That Was: Recollections of a Greek Settler

Grandfather Gregory Emmanuel "Nisiotis" (1875 - 1977)

This is the story of Grandfather Gregory's life from information contributed by his sons, Constantine (Costas) and Dimitri G. Emmanuel, and his daughter, Eleni P. Lekanidou (nee Emmanuel).

By Gregory C. Emmanuel, December 2000

On their trip to Tenedos in July 1998, Dimitri G. Emmanuel and his family, and his sister Eleni P. Lekanidou, located the ancestral family house where their father grew up. The house, which was built by their grandfather Constantine N. Emmanuel "Nisiotis" around 1853, is still in excellent shape and now is a hotel.
The Turkish lady that owned it kindly let them in to look around. Eleni and Dimitri also located the white marble headstone from their grandfather's Constantine's grave.

It was found some distance away from the desecrated Greek Orthodox cemetery and lay beneath some bushes along the sides of the town's main square. The lettering on the headstone was made by pouring molten lead into the lettering incised in the marble.

The lead letters that were originally there have all been removed, but one can still see the small holes that were used to fasten them to the marble.

As a boy, Grandfather Gregory attended the best Greek school in Asia Minor, the Grand National Academy in Constantinople, graduating in 1894.

In 1895 he signed his French-Greek dictionary using the family nickname, Nisiotis. You can read all about the origins and evolution of the family surname here.

Soon after his father passed away, Grandfather Gregory left Tenedos on one of the family's sailing ships (probably the 200-ton bratsera Agia Trias) with a cargo of the family's wine and sailed up the Black Sea coast to Romania.

He arrived there only to find that another captain from Tenedos, also with a cargo of wine, had come ahead of him and flooded the market, so Grandfather couldn't sell his wine.

Instead, he opened a taverna and over the next few months disposed of all his cargo, selling it as the taverna's house wine. Following his trip to Romania Grandfather returned to Tenedos and, after some time, left for Egypt, which had a large and thriving Greek community, to seek his fortune.

There he worked as an engineer for the Suez Canal. In Alexandria he met Constantine Meimaridis, a good friend of his from Tenedos, who persuaded him that there were good prospects in East Africa.

At that time there was a great deal of railway-related construction going on in the Kilimanjaro area of Deutsch-Ostafrika (present-day Tanzania), and a lot of cargo was being landed in Mombasa, British East Africa (present-day Kenya), and transported by train to Voi. From Voi cargo was hauled by ox-wagon over a rough track through thick bush to Moshi (present-day Old Moshi), Deutsch-Ostafrika, as there was no road or railway line connecting the two towns.

But the ox-wagons couldn't haul very bulky or heavy loads.

Meimaridis had purchased a steam traction engine, or road locomotive, and intended to take over the heavy transport business between Voi and Moshi, a distance of about 90 miles. He offered a partnership to Grandfather, who accepted.

Sometime in the early 1900s the two friends sailed from Alexandria to Mombasa, where the dismantled and crated steam engine waited. (They became two of the first Greeks in East Africa, and many of the Greeks who later settled in Tanganyika were their relatives and friends from Tenedos).

The two men loaded everything on the train and went up the line to Voi, where they established themselves and assembled the large machine with the help of an Indian mechanic.

The machine was named Tinga-Tinga, a phonetic Swahili nickname derived from the pinging noises the large flywheel made as it turned.

But Tinga-Tinga was just too heavy and cumbersome to negotiate the primitive track. It often sank through the soft sand and got stuck, or it would smash through the crude wooden bridges at stream crossings, and in the rainy season it would get thoroughly bogged down in the viscous African mud.

The number of successful trips made are unknown and we have no descriptions of these trips.

Around 1908 The plan to revolutionize the cargo hauling business in East Africa was given up and the partnership dissolved. As compensation, Meimaridis gave Tinga-Tinga to Grandfather, who put it to good use. For the next two years he hauled building materials and other heavy freight around the Moshi area, and sometimes used it as a tractor, contracting with farmers to plough their fields.

Tinga-Tinga was eventually sold to a German settler in the Moshi area, who dismantled it and mounted the boiler and engine on a permanent base to power a saw-mill, where it operated until the end of its useful life. In West Kilimanjaro, Tanganyika, a short distance north of Engare Nairobi, there is a place marked on the maps as Tinga Tinga. The origin of the name is unknown, but perhaps some other steam traction engine met its end at that location.

After the Tinga-Tinga venture, Grandfather became a contractor for the Dar-es-Salaam to Kigoma (on Lake

Tanganyika) railway construction project, where he made good money. In early 1920 he returned to the Moshi area and, after borrowing money from another Greek from Tenedos, Nicholaos Christofis, he bought two farms from the original German owners and so became one of the first Greeks to settle permanently in Tanganyika.

Christofis became Grandfather's silent partner. Also, he was my father's (Costas) godfather. He was bought out by Costas, Dimitri, and Nikos Emmanuel in 1946. Both farms were located in the foothills of Mt. Kilimanjaro, just north of Moshi. Chombo was a fairly well developed coffee estate at Uru, while Lambo had been abandoned for some years and had just a few scraggly coffee trees in it, at Machame.

Grandfather lived at Chombo, where his first house had mud walls, an earthen floor, and a grass thatched roof. The house at Lambo, which was built of large river stones with a corrugated metal roof, was much smaller then than it is now. There was no verandah at the Lambo house; instead, a huge bougainvillea covered the whole front of the building and part of the roof.

When Grandfather went to take possession he found a large male lion snoozing under the bougainvillea. Fortunately it ran off into the bush when it realized there were people about.

In 1920, when he was 45 years old, Grandfather returned to Tenedos to find a bride and get married. On that trip he wrote a postcard to a friend in East Africa, telling him how hard it was to find a bride. However, on September 9, he married Irini D. Perrou, my grandmother, who was 24 years old at the time. She was a refined, cultured woman, who spoke French and played the piano. She was also very high-strung, a contrast to Grandfather, who was calm and quiet to an extreme.

Sometime after their return to East Africa, probably in 1921, Grandfather tore down the mud house at Chombo and built a new one, of cement blocks with a metal roof.

For the next four years Grandfather and Grandmother were busy having children; in 1922 they had a daughter, my aunt Eleni Lekanidou, in '23 my father, Constantine (Costas), was born , and in '24 and '25 they had two more sons, Dimitrios (Dimitris) and Nicholas (Nikos), my uncles.

In 1922 Greece's initially successful campaign to recapture

Constantinople and the formerly Greek lands of Asia Minor ended in disastrous defeat. With the 1923 Treaty of Lausane, Tenedos and the Moskhonisia, the Emmanuels' ancestral homelands, were formally ceded to the newly formed, ultra-nationalistic and militant Turkish state which had replaced the moribund Ottoman Empire.

During the pogroms and the exchange of populations between Greece and Turkey that followed, about 1.3 million Greeks left their homes in Asia Minor and sought refuge in mainland Greece and other countries. As a result, during the 1920s the Greek population of East Africa grew dramatically. A large number of Greeks, many from Tenedos, came to Tanganyika, where Greeks became the second largest expatriate European community (Germans being the largest group).

In both Moshi and Arusha there were thriving Greek communities and the need arose for a Greek school. As the house at Lambo was vacant, Grandfather leased it to the Greek community and it became the first Greek school in East Africa. It was a boarding school and was the first school attended by my father, Costas. (He told me that a student who sleepwalked was taken during the night by a leopard.)

Sometime in the 1920s Grandfather acquired his first car. Being a thrifty person, he economized on fuel by shifting into neutral and freewheeling all the way from his farm down to Moshi, a distance of about 10 miles. Of course, this played hell with the brakes. Also, it is said that the grevillia trees that lined the narrow, potholed dirt road on both sides bore scrape marks as evidence of his passage.

My father, Costas, told me this story from the early 1930s:

> One night all of us were piled in Father's car, a Ford Model A, returning to Chombo in a heavy rain sometime in the masika (rainy season). There were Nikos, Eleni, Dimitris, your grandmother Irini, myself, and your grandfather Gregory, who was driving.
>
> There was also another Greek in there with us. Well, at some point we got stuck in the mud and we all got out while the old man, my father, tried to jack the car up. But there was too much mud and the jack wouldn't work.
>
> So your grandfather asked the Greek fellow to go find a block of wood to put under the jack, and off the fellow went into the coffee trees to look for a suitable piece of wood, in total darkness, in the rain. He didn't have matches or a torch (flashlight) with him.

After a while he came back holding something big and shiny, and it looked heavy. When he got close to us the thing he was carrying started to move and he dropped it and ran yelling back to the car. It turns out that in the dark he had picked up a large coiled python, mistaking it for a block of wood.

Grandfather and Grandmother wanted their children to have a Greek education, but as the school at Lambo offered only a primary education, they decided to send the children to Greece.

In 1933, Grandmother Irini and her four children left for Greece on the Deutsch-Ostafrika Linie ship S.S.Usukuma.

In Athens the boys were enrolled in the Athens College, considered to be Greece's best school at the time. They leased a house at 163 Kifisias Avenue in Ambelokipi, a suburb of Athens. Grandfather came to see them for short visit in 1937 and then returned to Tanganyika.

Three years later, on October 28, 1940, war came to Greece when the Italian Army invaded through Albania. Grandmother wanted to return to Tanganyika and, after a lot of searching, she found tickets on a ship leaving for Egypt.

On their way to the harbor to board it, the ship was bombed and sank, so Grandmother Irini and her children were trapped in Greece for the duration of the war and for part of the Greek civil war which followed, enduring incredible hardships.

Irini and her three sons were finally able to leave and rejoin Grandfather in Tanganyika in 1945, after a separation of 8 years. Their daughter Eleni and her family arrived in Tanganyika the following year.

At that time Grandfather worked the coffee farm at Chombo. His partnership with his nephew, Stelios, to develop the property at Lambo had just ended with the completion of agreed-upon work. So his eldest son, Constantine (Costas, my father), took over as manager at Lambo.

After the war the price of coffee was very high and Grandfather was able to pay off all the debts incurred by Grandmother during the occupation fairly quickly. (Paying off these wartime debts was an accomplishment; many people refused to do so, instead accusing their lenders of taking unfair advantage of them during the war).

Since Grandfather was now financially solvent, his sons persuaded him to end the one-sided partnership with Christofis.

Grandfather agreed and his son Dimitri went to see Christofis at his residence in Cairo. Christofis agreed to the dissolution, so the four brothers bought him out and in partnership with their father became the outright owners of Lambo and developed it as a sisal estate.

My mother told me that when I was born in 1953 Grandfather was very excited because I would be the first grandson who would bear his name. During the few weeks after I was born, he would visit every day to make sure that my eyes stayed blue, like his.

Grandfather continued working the coffee estate at Chombo until 1960. That same year Grandmother Irini passed on at the age of 64. Chombo was then sold and Grandfather retired; he was then 85. He left East Africa and returned to Greece for good in 1964, the same year as his son Dimitri. In Athens he lived in an apartment at Spartis 7 Street, in the same building as his daughter Eleni, who lived on the 7th floor.

Grandfather's life in Athens was radically different from his way of life in Tanganyika. He usually wore a dark suit and a tie, and sometimes a hat. Every day his routine was exactly the same. He got up, shaved, had a healthy breakfast, and would go for a walk which ended at Platia Amerikis.

He always patronized the same kafenio, where he sat with his friends discussing the news of the day, reading the paper, and watching people go by. Then lunch with some wine, a nap, and in the afternoon another walk and another kafenio session. Back to his house for dinner and some more wine, and then he would read and go to sleep.

He ate a lot of yogurt, vegetables, and fruit, loved fish, and always drank wine with his meals. His habits were so regular you could set your watch by him. His children paid a housekeeper to clean and cook for him.

In Athens, Grandfather had a tan Peugeot 403 car and a hired driver, Anestis, who was a Greek refuge from Asia Minor. In the 1960s, when I was in boarding school at the Athens College, Grandfather would sometimes come to school to pick me up for the weekend and deliver me to my aunt Eleni, my guardian (as my parents were in in Africa). One time he took me to see the war movie "The Sands of Iwo Jima" just to please me.

When my family moved to Athens and lived in the apartment

at Spartis 3, Grandfather would often come to visit. He would sit quietly, not saying much at all, and not hearing much either because he was losing his hearing, while we would try and make shouted, uneasy conversation. But Grandfather was quite content to sit quietly, just enjoying the companionship. A few hours later he would slowly get up and wander on home.

When TV first came to Greece in the late 1960s Grandfather bought one and spent most evenings watching terrible, black and white Greek movies or the news. Sometimes my sister, Elli, and I would go over and watch the Lucy Show or Lassie. We would leave with our ear drums ringing as the volume was always too loud.

Grandfather spoke Greek, Turkish, English, Swahili, and some French. He was a tall, good looking man. One summer in the 1970s he came to visit us on his way to his afternoon kafenio session. He had just returned from a week-long holiday at Loutraki, a popular seaside vacation spot, and he looked great; he was deeply tanned and his blue eyes sparkled, and he was full of humor.

As he left for the kafenio he chuckled and said, "Well, I guess I'll go to the kafenio to see which one of my friends died while I was gone, and which one is left." He was in his late 90s then and had just started to use a walking stick.

Once, my uncle Dimitri and I were talking to Grandfather about his days on Tenedos and about the sailing ship that his family owned. To our great surprise, he easily drew a remarkably accurate outline of it on a piece of paper.

In 1977 Grandfather Gregory fell in his bathtub and broke his hip. He was taken to the KAT hospital in Athens and to everyone's amazement the broken bones healed. Unfortunately, the prolonged period of immobility and lying on his back required to heal his hip led to pneumonia.

On May 24 he passed away from complications due to pneumonia, at the age of 102. My Uncle Dimitri says that he was "blessed to the end of his long life with an amazing clarity of mind and remarkable memory."

Lambo Sisal Estate (1921 – 2000)

The information in this story is from my father, Constantine G. Emmanuel, who shared it with me in Athens, Greece, during autumn 2000.

By Gregory C. Emmanuel, December 2000

In 1921 Grandfather Gregory Emmanuel bought Lambo and a coffee estate called Chombo from the original German owners.

To do so he borrowed money from Nicholaos Christofis, a wealthy Greek also from Tenedos, who became Grandfather's silent partner. (Christofis never worked the farm, only shared in the profits.)

Later he became Constantine (Costas) G. Emmanuel's godfather. Costas has the original survey map of Lambo, drawn with white lines on dark blue, which was drafted at the time of purchase and registered at the Moschi (Moshi) land office.

Lambo lies on the foothills of Mt. Kilimanjaro, at 3,000 feet, about 10 miles west of Moshi, at Machame.

When Grandfather bought it, Lambo had only a few coffee trees and the house, which had been abandoned for some time. The house had thick walls built of river rock and a corrugated sheet metal roof. There was no verandah at the front, just a flat area of packed earth covered by a huge bougainvillia which also covered a substantial part of the house.

When Grandfather went to take possession, he discovered a male lion sleeping at the front of the house under the bougainvillia. Fortunately the lion took off when it realized there were humans about.

Since Grandfather lived at Chombo, the Greek Community leased the Lambo house from him and operated it as the first Greek school in Tanganyika. It was a boarding school until the 1930's, with about 20 boarders, and it was the first school that Costas attended.

He told me that one time a boy who walked in his sleep was taken by a leopard in the night.

Grandfather planted the first sisal at Lambo. He had an agreement to share the costs of installing and operating a sisal decorticator with his neighbor, an Italian farmer named Mongardi (Dado's father), who also intended to plant sisal. But World War II came and Mongardi, fearing internment by the British, left Tanganyika for Italy.

When he returned to Africa after the war he was too old to start in sisal, so Grandfather developed the plantation and built the sisal factory with his sons. Dado, old man Mongardi's son, was one of Costa's best friends and hunting companions.

Dado's children, Georgio, Massimo (who was the same age as I and was one of my best friends), and Roberto were our constant playmates and good friends. Massimo passed away when we were in our twenties and I was devastated.

Grandmother Irini, Costas, and his siblings (Eleni, Dimitris and Nicos) left Africa in 1933 and returned in 1945 after surviving the horrors of the German occupation and the first battles of the civil war in Athens. Eleni and her family returned to Tanganyika a year later.

For the first few months after he returned Costas stayed on at Chombo with his parents, then he moved to Lambo and lived with Stelios, his uncle (Aunt Marika, Grandfather Gregory's sister, was Stelio's mother).

At that time a partnership between Grandfather and Stelios was dissolved as the agreed upon work was completed (plant a small area with corn, install a small 50HP Robey decorticator and some raspadoria). When Stelios left, Costas became Lambo's general manager.

The salary of a manamba (contract farm laborer in the days before trade unions) in 1945 was 50 Tanganyika cents per day, plus 1 lb. of maize flour, 6 oz. of beans, salt, and a small amount of karanga (peanuts or groundnuts) or cottonseed oil, and some fruit.

The manamba signed contracts for a year. They were conscripted by the colonial government, usually from the Wagogo tribe, which was going through a period of severe famine and drought at the time.

When trade unions came to Tanganyika, they demanded that a higher percentage of a worker's wages should be paid in cash instead of food. Unfortunately this resulted in a noticeable increase in drinking and malnutrition.

After the war the price of coffee was so high that Grandfather was able to pay off all the debts incurred by Grandmother during the occupation fairly quickly. Paying off these wartime debts was rare; many Greeks refused to do so, instead accusing their lenders of taking unfair advantage of them during the war.

Since Grandfather was now financially solvent his sons persuaded him to end the one-sided partnership with Christofis. Grandfather agreed, so Dimitris went to see Christofis in Cairo, where he lived. Christofis agreed to the dissolution, so the three brothers bought him out and in partnership with their father became the outright owners of Lambo and developed it as a sisal estate.

During the Korean War (1951-52) the price of sisal skyrocketed (£250/- per ton FOB New York) because it was a strategic material, and the Emmanuels made good profits. With this money they bought Silverdale Estate and planted more sisal, thus enlarging Lambo.

They also built the foreman's house (Christos Yarinakis and his sister, Fofo, lived there) near the main Moshi-Arusha road. In addition, they installed a large Robey decorticator (corona) and a hydraulic baling press.

The Robey was a huge, beautiful machine, with revolving drums of shiny brass, flapping canvas drive-belts, and a feeder chain that looked like a gigantic bicycle chain. It was eventually replaced by a more business-like German Krupp decorticator, which was installed on concrete foundations and under a steel I-beam roof specially designed by Costa's best friend, Costas Kalliambetsos.

During this time they also bought the Tongoni Sisal Estate in Tanga in partnership with Pygmalis Karageorgelis and another Greek named Stavropoulos. It was a terribly humid place and everything was coated with a gritty film of red dust that never washed away.

Grandmother Irini passed away in 1961. That same year Chombo was sold so that Grandfather, who was 85, could retire. In December of that year Tanganyika gained its independence from Britain (and later changed its name to Tanzania).

In 1964 Grandfather finally left Africa and returned to Greece, retiring to a small flat on the 1st floor of the apartment building at Spartis 7 Street where he lived until 1978, when he passed on at the age of 103. His daughter, Eleni P. Lekanidou, lived on the 6th floor of the same building.

Talk of possible nationalization of white-owned farms and a general slump in the price of sisal made profits dwindle, and in 1964 the Tongoni farm was sold. In its place the Emmanuels bought Lewa Sisal Estate (a larger farm, also in Tanga) in partnership with Nicos Zannetos, George Issaias, and Pygmali Karageorgelis. Also in 1964, Dimitri Emmanuel left Tanzania for Greece, where for many years he worked in a shipping office in Piraeus.

The Lewa shareholders also became involved in a shipping company of their own, but the ships were not profitable because they were World War II vintage Liberty ships that needed either a lot of maintenance or outright replacement.

At the same time the shipping market slumped and they lost a lot of money before liquidating the company. Dimitri took me aboard the company's S.S. Eland when it was in the roads off Piraeus and I remember a large steel cutout of an eland's head on the ship's funnel and in the ship's mess eating watermelon with feta cheese for the first time.

In 1967 the Arusha Declaration was signed and soon after the first white-owned farms were nationalized. As Lewa was considered to be owned by resident rather than expatriate whites, it was nationalized only by 60% instead of 100%.

Eventually some compensation money was paid to the shareholders and with his share Costas bought an apartment at Spartis 3 Street in Athens.

Lambo and many other white-owned farms in the Machame and West Kilimanjaro areas were nationalized 100% in 1972, the year I entered the Metsovion Technical University in Athens. The house, Land Rovers, tractors--everything was lost.

As for our personal things, Costas sold almost everything (all our books, clothes, toys, furniture, camping equipment, etc.) to a Catholic convent; whatever wasn't sold was given away. He left the house an empty shell, without even light bulbs.

The only things he took with him were his personal car (a

Ford Cortina with plates MSA 10) and his clothes. Behind his office he buried a cigar tin with a $20 banknote inside it, as the possession of foreign currency was a crime; this tin is probably still buried there. He had to borrow cash to cover his daily expenses as his personal bank account was frozen.

After nationalization Costas rented a house at Arusha Chini, next to Thanos Papadopoulos. The house had a swimming pool, and I remember swimming there as a child when the Wells' lived there. Now the pool was empty, with scummy water full of insect larvae and tadpoles at the bottom.

During this time Costas worked with his brother, Nicos, farming seed beans in the Sanya Plains, next to Kilimanjaro International Airport.

They were the first to farm that area.

Sometimes we lived in tents at Sanya, constantly choking in clouds of powdery gray dust, with never enough water. I roughly surveyed this farm and drafted a map, which my father, Costas, kept and gave me in November 2000.

When Costas left Tanzania in 1974 he went to Greece, where he worked in a shipping office as an accountant. In 1977 he returned to Tanzania and with Uncle Nikos traveled to Dar-Es-Salaam where they negotiated a compensation price for their nationalized farms with the government of Tanzania.

This was wasted time and effort, as to this day compensation for the loss of the farms has not been paid out.

Costas returned to Greece. In 1978 Costas left Greece and went to Kenya to manage the Dwa Estate at Kibwezi. He bought a small farm at Hosti, on Crete, in 1981, and adjoining property in 1987. Costas worked at Dwa until 1990, when he returned to Greece, dividing his time between Athens and Crete. He never went back to Tanzania.

I last saw Lambo in 1974. The fields were neglected, with abandoned farm equipment in them and deep erosion gullies.

In the mid-1990's my uncle Dimitri B. Georgiadis visited Tanzania and Lambo. He sent us some photos that show no trace of the garden or the trees around the house. The house itself looked abandoned.

In November 2000, my parents (Ketty and Costas), my aunt (Eleni Lekanidou), my wife (Lacen Horter), and I went to the village of Mili on the island of Naxos to celebrate my Uncle Niko's 75th birthday.

He told us that after nationalization in 1972 the co-op running the farm so grossly mismanaged the estate that all production was stopped; the house was abandoned and was in a state of partial ruin.

Appendix V:

Other European Immigrants Remember Those Days in Tanganyika

Well...I arrived in Tanganyika about 74 years ago. By that I mean that I was born here of Greek parents.

My father came to Tanganyika in 1906 and he came specifically to work in a coffee estate, which belonged to a relative of his. That coffee estate exists even today and it is on the Kibosho road, as you go towards the Wildlife College on Kilimanjaro.

Yep, well father initially came to help this relative of his to start his coffee factory, to build his coffee factory and help him with the plantation in general.

I may add that this plantation was the first commercial plantation of coffee on Kilimanjaro. The first coffee there, was planted there around 1900, around the turn of the century.

After setting up the coffee factory, my father was given the job of going to the port of Mombasa to unload a big steam engine, which had been ordered by the owner of this coffee estate, in order to do some transport business.

That machine was offloaded from the ship, of course it was all in pieces and father had to assemble it, and together with three waggons and they were all... they were all transported to Voi by train. From Voi the engine was started up and it was driven all the way to Moshi, because there was no railway line in those days between Voi and Moshi.

So that was father's job, it was very tough task, but eventually they managed to get to Moshi, and in fact they started having a transport... a transport business between Moshi and Voi, in the railway line.

But, after two or three trips, they found out that this engine was a very heavy one, and if there was any slight rain, it was impossible to move.

And it was becoming more and more difficult because sometimes they ran out of water. Of course, fuel was plentiful because they had, they could use firewood.

So, after their final trip, the engine was brought back to Moshi and it was used as a stationary engine, providing power to a sawmill on Kilimanjaro; and the remnants of this engine to this day exist on Kilimanjaro.

And... father was involved, as I said, in coffee from his first day in Tanganyika, but he acquired his first coffee estate in 1921. That was an ex-German property, which the British administration was selling as custodian, custodians of enemy property.

So, that was the first estate in 1921. That estate again exists, it is called Chambo, and there is also another estate which he purchased in 1922, called Lambo. That estate was a large-scale plantation, which initially had caoutchouc trees planted, but after the failure of the price of caoutchouc, complete collapse of the price; and the caoutchouc was uprooted and they started planting sizzle and eventually it became a large sizle estate.

Hum ... Coming back to me, after schooling in Greece, we came back in 1945 to Tanganyika, and I had a short spell as a teacher in a Greek school... the first Greek school in Tanganyika.

Fortunately that lasted only a year and a half, and I found out soon that I was not made to be a teacher.

So I started trying to become a farmer, under my father's guidance, I was involved in coffee growing, and... I think it went off quite well because, after a few years, we started up another estate here in Lambo, and also we purchased this Makuru estate, where we are now taking this film.

That estate again was an ex German estate, but it had been run down completely by its previous owner, and we purchased that estate in 1957, and started planting new coffee, and improved everything : the irrigation system, the factory and eventually, by the time the Tanzania government decided to nationalize large-scale coffee estate on Kilimanjaro.

This estate was producing about a hundred tons of coffee a year, and I can say it was a good-quality coffee.

So, in 1973, we were nationalized, it was a very tough experience; we were told, we were asked to, to attend a meeting called by the authorities, and we were told that as of the next day, our farms would be nationalized and that we had to give them up to government and we were promised full and fair compensation, which took some years to materialize, but anyway that was 1973.

So, after... this enforced abandonment of coffee growing, I started farming on leased land about 150 kilometres away from here... from home. It was very tough, but we managed somehow.

I was growing seeds for export, mainly seed beans and some flower seeds, and that lasted for about 12 years until conditions became very difficult and I had to stop.

In the meantime, policies changed in Tanzania and due to the fact that coffee estates which had been nationalized were very badly neglected and run down, and the result was that the government decided that they should be rehabilitated, and that farmers were prepared to take'em up on a lease basis could come in back again and work in those estates.

And I am happy to say I was the first one who got in to my ex-coffee estate in 1995.

So... I'm back again after all these years in coffee growing, and I'm very happy about it !

Source: www.canalu.com/vo/2101277029/0/transcription.htm

***

Yes, as I was saying, that estate before nationalization was producing about one hundred tons of coffee per annum.

The year I got in the estate in 1995, it had produced nothing : zero kilos, so I started from a very low basis, and slowly by 1998, production reached 50 tons, and if all goes well, in 2 or 3 years' time, it should be a hundred tons.

The Greek community on Kilimanjaro had a big impact on coffee production, in fact I should say about 90% of the Greeks living in all Kilimanjaro were coffee growers and... they were producing very good coffee.

The community itself was very progressive. As I said they built the first Greek school, the first church and they were an example to the rest of the Greek communities in Tanganyika.

Where do we go from here? The Greeks came to Kilimanjaro, I think, following those who came first. By that I mean that a few very adventurous people.

Greek people, arrived on Kilimanjaro during the German times, and they settled here, they liked the area of course it was one of the nicest and still is one of the nicest in Tanzania, and then the relatives came, and friends and so on so you find mainly that people who came from one part of Greece settled, say, on Kilimanjaro... and then in Arusha you have people from another part, mainly from Cyprus.

And so on... And of course all that came to an end after nationalization, all the Greeks left, with my own exception, except for me, because there were more than 300 souls, Greeks, on Kilimanjaro and right now I am the only one... no, no! with the exception of Gikos... Gikos, he settled there very recently.
That's all.

Q : And how the Greeks got the skills on coffee production?

A lot of them were peasant farmers, they were not highly educated sort of class of people with a few exceptions of course. But, they didn't know about coffee, it was a question of trial and error at the beginning. Eventually, I must say that they became very very good at it.

We have the same example in sisal.

Greeks owned the largest number of sisal estates and I think probably one thing that helped a lot is that they had a very good understanding with the people, with the local people, with labour, and they got on very well.

So, these are some of the reasons I should say.

Q : The other communities...

Yes, the Asians were not involved in farming initially. They were mainly in trade, they were traders. Even on the mountain there were small-scale traders.

This is a place which now... the place has been taken by indigenous Africans. But there was a time when every village had its own Indian shop and... of course later on they were excluded from having shops in the mountain and they concentrated in the town. So they were involved in trade, but other nationalities who were involved in coffee were British, Italian, Swiss and German of course.

Some of the Germans were allowed to come back and continue farming after the war.

But the Greek community was probably the largest settlement of coffee growers on Kilimanjaro...plantation growers.

As I said I came back into the estate in 1995 under a lease agreement with the Inshara rural cooperative society, primary cooperative society which owns the farm.

The lease is for a limited number of years, renewable, subject to renewal. But there is an annual payment of lease, which is a considerable amount and the local people benefit a lot from this.

So far, from the money they have collected from the lease they have built a bridge over a river, they have built classrooms in schools in the villages they built a dispensary, they built a mill for grinding maize and... in general I think they are benefiting far more than what they were when they were running the estate.

In fact, it was a loss at the time, it was a big loss to them and to the country itself. Because we are paying the workers regularly, we pay our taxes regularly and the traders around the village are very happy because there is some money for the people to buy things with and I think it's a mutually satisfactory arrangement.

Source: www.canalu.com/vo/2101277029/1/transcription.htm

***

Childhood Memories of Tanganyika

By Mike K-H

Going to school in East Africa was always an adventure for an eight-to-ten-year-old. But sometimes an adult would have described it that way, too.

We lived in Tanga, a coral harbor in Tanganyika Territory, as it was then called. During the school vacation periods, this was as close to paradise as any child could imagine.

At home, I could read and make models.

On foot, I could brave robber crabs and buy tasty parrot fish as they were landed from dugout canoes.

After sunset, I could kick the water into phosphorescence.

By bicycle, I could visit friends' houses, or go right through town to the Swimming Club or the Sailing Club.

At the age of eight, I learned to swim. Doing my breast-stroke, touching down between strokes, I followed the front of the low cliff between the two clubs on a rising tide. I had put my foot down twice before I realised that it wasn't touching anything any more.

The climate was considered unhealthy during the really hot and humid periods. In any case, at a hundred and ten in the shade and around eighty percent humidity, most kids would have had a hard time forgetting that the beach was five minutes away.

We all went up-country to boarding schools, some of us starting at the age of six-and-a-half. One or two kids used to get homesick occasionally, but their peers always comforted them. The rest of us enjoyed every minute of it, and would have found day school very boring.

From Tanga, I went to Lushoto, in the Usambara highlands. This was a short trip, accomplished in a single day. Some kids had steamer trips, overnight train trips, or even stopovers in hotels, as part of their journey to school. If an adult went with them it was purely by chance. One or two teenage students making even longer journeys were all we usually had in the way of a guide or supervisor.

The normal procedure for me was to board a train soon after daylight, and get off around mid-day at Mombo. From there I would catch a school bus (an ex-army truck, really) for the long haul up the escarpment to Lushoto.

The train was fun. Drawn by a wood-fired steam loco, it had open verandahs at the ends of the carriages, just like the ones in the Westerns. I didn't really like the bus journey very much. It usually made me feel sick.

This time, I had been ill and was returning to school late. The rains had started and several sections of rail had been washed away. The road (not metaled in those days) wasn't in too good a state either.

No problem. I was going to fly for the first time in my life.

I'm not sure if many US citizens would recognise it, but my plane was known and loved by all British aircraft buffs - a de Haviland Dragon Rapide, called a Dominie in its military form. This was a twin-engined biplane with beautiful slim, elliptical-plan wings and (if I remember correctly) Gypsy Queen engines. The fuselage was slab-sided, like a refined version of the much larger planes used in the early days of Imperial Airways.

I don't remember how many passengers the Rapide carried - I think it was about nine, and I was sitting in one of the pair of seats behind the pilot.

We flew low. I could see herds of antelope and other wildlife on the plains below us. I could also feel my stomach churning as we bumped around in the powerful thermals, and it was very hot and stuffy.

One of the passengers asked the pilot if he could do anything to increase the ventilation. He opened a window. HE OPENED A WINDOW. It didn't make much difference.

Mombo airfield's only building was a corrugated iron shed. Outside, the plane had faded into the shimmering haze. Inside, we wilted. Someone served Pepsis at blood temperature.

I was met by a woman I did not know, who said she was giving me a lift up to Lushoto. She was driving one of the most popular vehicles of the time - a Ford V8 Pilot 'Box Body' esate car. Real wood, they used in those days.

She gave me a huge, red apple.

She was a chatty woman, who looked at you while she spoke. This was our undoing, because we were driving the hairpins up the scarp of the Usambara Mountains when she looked up and realised she was heading over the precipice.

She swerved back violently, and hit the cliff on the inside of the bend.

Clouds of steam issued from under the hood, and she stopped talking. Luckily, it was only a few minutes before a bus appeared, and the driver soon mended the split radiator hose with a strip of inner tube.

We set off again, with eyes more carefully on the road, after no more than fifteen minutes.

Nothing else happened.

By the time we reached school, I was getting bored

Source: Mike K-H: Off to School I Go - Childhood Memories of Africa:
www.franceforfreebooters.com/different/school.htm

***

A White Tanganyikan Remembers Life in the Fifties

Fetching the Mail:
A Rite of Passage in the life of Steve Van Nattan

It was turning out to be a rather typical vacation at home (from Rift Valley Academy where I went to boarding school) and my Dad decided I was old enough to go for the mail.

Now, most of you would not have to be very old to think that was a big event, right? Well, we lived in Kibara on the shore of Lake Victoria, and the post office was 60 miles away over terrible road.

In those days, many mission stations, schools, and businesses in Tanganyika got their mail in a bag. The postmaster could fill your "private bag" and seal it, and he would send it to you by bus if you requested it, but along the way various bus drivers and "tani boys" might open it to see what could be procured.

So most people sent someone to escort the mail bag back to their station.

A word about "tani boys." A "tani boy" is a very special hired hand who rides your truck. He helps load it and dig it out of the mud, and in the old days, he would crank the engine while the Bwana would try to start it. Thus, his title, "tani boy," is a corruption of what the Bwana yelled when he wanted it cranked-- "Turn, boy!"

As progress came, and as electric starters became standard equipment, the "tani boy" became the guy who collected the tickets on busses and shoved the last poor victim through the back door. To increase profits, the "tani boy" would stuff the coach of the bus so full of passangers that he would end up hanging onto the back steps of the bus, or he would climb up on top of the bus and lay on top of the baggage.

Well, the day of my rite of passage had arrived. I was to take the empty mail bag from Kibara to Nansio and exchange it for a full one and bring it home, and I would be on my own. Kibara, our local town, was a dusty small town like a thousand other dusty little towns in Africa. Business was carried on by several concerns.

There were the Indians from India in the biggest shops who offered every conceivable gong and trinket an African could want. From the walls and ceiling cascaded down an inventory that, in the USA or the UK, would fill a rather large store, but in Kibara these shops looked very small from the street.

Africans also owned small shops, like the bicycle shop and a tea shop. Luo tribal fishermen, who lived on the papyrus shelf along the lake shore, would be hanging around the main street trying to sell dried fish. The arrival of a bus was a pretty major event in Kibara.

Folks went to the doorways to see who would get on and off of the bus. Mail and supply orders from far away would be dragged off of the top of the bus. The "tani boy" might have a few chickens he wanted to sell to anyone willing to pay the price. Negotiations were fast and doubtful. Then off the bus tore in a towering cloud of dust.

African busses in the 1950s were not like anything you ever saw. A company in the capital city of Tanganyika, Dar es Salaam, would order a chassis and drive train complete to be shipped from the UK. Bedfords and Leylands were the companies of choice.

Once the bus chassis was in Africa, the local company who ordered it would then build a body or coachworks on it. The body, in the 1950s would be built of wood, and it would be bulky and heavy. Some companies did pretty good work, but after 50,000 miles of washboard roads, the wooden framed coachworks would be real loose in the joints, dear reader.

Now, the bus that pulled into Kibara that morning very early was well used. The back was for general class travelers. It would seat perhaps 35 people on wooden benches and maybe 20 more sitting on oil tins down the aisle and on one another's laps.

There were laws about overloading, but the rule of thumb was, "If your thumb could fit inside, shove on in." My Dad made sure I got to ride First Class, which meant I rode in the front seat with the driver. It cost two shillings more, but it was worth it.

There was no cab as such for the driver. You see, the whole coachworks had to be supplied after arrival in Africa. The wooden framework came all the way forward, and the windshield was mounted in the wooden works.

So, as we wound through the countryside of Tanganyika at breakneck speed, I watched the whole coachworks shift at each turn. There would be a distinct creaking groan from all sides as the coach lurched to the right and then back to the left. In the upper right corner above my head I could see right into the sky at times as the coachworks opened to add ventilation.

As we progressed down the road, people would run out into the road to flag down the bus. Each time the driver stopped, he would rush the people faster and faster until they could hardly get in the back door before he was under way again. I could not understand why this mad rush.

We finally reached some hill country where there were long hills down to bridges and back up-- over and over. The bus driver would press the accelerator flat to the floor going down hill until we were careening along in terror, then BANG, hit the bridge deck with a crash, then up the far hill in an effort to stay in at least third gear.

I could not keep quiet any longer. I casually asked the driver why the hurry. The driver told me that there was another bus coming along behind us. Well, I wondered out loud what difference that made. He told me he wanted to be the first bus to the Rugezi ferry crossing from the mainland to Ukerewe island.

Thanks to Mike Patterson from the UK, whose father served under the colonial office on Ukerewe Island, for the photo of the Rugezi ferry. - Steve Van Nattan.

You see, we lived on a peninsula which terminated in an island named Ukerewe. Only one road went to the island, and a ferry crossing was mandatory to get onto the island and to the big town of Nansio where the Post Office and government offices were. I thought about this for a while.

Then reality sunk in. When an ordinary automobile crossed over on the ferry, it could be loaded, and all the passengers could stay aboard. But these ferries were small pontoon arrangements. The hired helpers would drag the chain or cable up from the lake floor over the ferry and drag the ferry along that way.

Since this was a lake, and there was no current as at a river crossing, the system worked just fine. But, when a bus came along, the thing was almost too much for the ferry WITHOUT the passengers.

So, the passengers ALL had to cross in dugout canoes. This meant that a complex and lengthy process was followed since the whole top of the bus would also have perhaps two tons of chickens, bags of corn, hoes, plows, and just about anything your could imagine. Much of it might have to be offloaded and, with the passengers, ferried across in the dugout canoes.

The second bus to the ferry crossing would have a very long wait while the first bus was processed across. I forgot the terror of the moment and turned to the driver and yelled, "Haraka, haraka, rafiki." Roughly, that means in Swahili, "Get going!" The driver lost all inhibitions. A representative of the White race had just given him permission to put the pedal to the metal, and HE DID!

He still needed to stop and pick up more passengers though since the "tani boy" in the back assured him he could cram in a few more. Hey, that's profit, right? Speed and capitalism must be balanced in order to pay the bills. So, stops were perilous, and everyone watched to the rear for the other bus. As we topped the hill going down to the landing of the ferry, Layland Motor Works of England would have been proud. The brakes worked splendidly.

Coachworks of Africa, and chassis of the UK, were still in reasonably good fellowship. Best of all, there was not one car or bus at the ferry landing ahead of us. Cheers went up for the driver, and, on my part, a prayer of thanks for deliverance went up to the Lord.

The process of crossing the ferry was nerve wracking for the passengers. One of the luxuries of "going First Class" was to ride the ferry across since there were only two of us in First Class with the driver. So, I escaped crossing in a dugout canoe.

The prospect of this is not the canoe ride itself-- the terror is that they always overload them due to the fact that another bus is coming soon.

And sure enough, the second bus rolled over the hill just as we were grinding onto the ferry in low gear. Various groans could be heard from the second bus, "Bahati mbaya" (bad luck) and "Min Allah" (Allah's will). In the rodeo of African transportation though, our driver went up a couple of notches in fame.

The crossing was as uneventful as it can be in Africa. One

canoe had to be bailed constantly to keep it afloat, but the passengers were always willing, what with the alternatives. On the other side, we loaded up, and the ride to Nansio was leisurly since there was no more pressure to arrive first.

Nansio is a combination of port, government center, commercial chaos, and gossip city. The four principle merchants in those days were Walji, Virji, Damji Mamji, and JP Patel. Walji was the most friendly and the most crooked, but he had the best inventory. JP Patel was the most honest and helpful but lacked the funds to build a large inventory. Damji Mamji was probably a great guy, but we never shopped there-- I don't know why.

I went around to Walji's and bought some candy or something to munch on. Walji insisted on hearing how all of my family were doing, and he made me promise to take greetings to my father. Walji was crooked in pricing and quite able to gouge if he could get away with it, but he seemed genuinely sincere in his care of my parents.

A Hindu merchant is an obscure and perplexing person all of the time. If honesty pays off best, he is as honest as anyone you ever knew. If lying and tricks turn the best profit, count your fingers. Once the Hindu cleans up on you, he reverts to sincere concern and friendliness, and he will demand that you stay for a cup of tea. A Muslim merchant is just as friendly, but he is not a crook in business.

There was a soda pop bottling concern nearby, so I went over there for a cold soda. That was a real luxury in Africa in the 1950s. There was no electricity in the city during daylight hours, so the refrigerators, Servels from Sweden, were run on kerosene. Several merchants kept cold soda in an aging Servel in the back room.

Whiskey was on hand for the Catholic priests. The flavors of soda pop were only limited by the imagination of the merchant and had nothing to do with the flavor of the beverage. My favorite was ice cream soda, which tasted more like rose water.

I wanted to catch the first bus back home, so I went on to the Post Office to get the mail. Switching bags was no trick, and off I went to the bus park. Now, in all of Africa, except possibly where civilization has intruded in South Africa, the bus leaves when it is full, and no sooner. So, to get out of town quickly, I had to walk the line of busses and read their destinations.

The ones headed for far away destinations would leave first since they had the prospect of picking up added passengers along the way to fill the bus. I made my choice and was delighted to find it was about to leave. Again, I managed to acquire a First Class ticket and a place in the front seat with the driver.

By now it was very hot, perhaps 1 o'clock in the afternoon. Nansio had taken on the mid-day odors of frying onions for the evening meal, mixed with various varieties of manure, dried fish, and elderly cuts of beef hanging in the meat market in the center of town.

The dogs were in slow motion, as were many of the inhabitants. The driver was in a subdued mood due to the mid-day heat, but he was happy to see the bus full.

Mama would have enough cash to buy more beans and cassava for the babies when he got home tomorrow. With some luck they could buy a goat for the coming celebration of their son's return from the government school in Mwanza.

Life was good, and I was heading home. Speed would not be so high a priority since the next bus was not nearly full and would not be trying to pass us on the way back to the ferry.

The driver's section of the bus was comfortable enough, but the back of the bus was an oven. It would have been better if the poor passengers had not been crammed in like sardines. In any case, we made the ferry and crossed without a hitch, and we were on the mainland cruising along fine when someone in the back lost their lunch.

The bumps on the road, along with the sweltering heat, had taken their toll. The groans were audible as people got sick one by one by proxy. Each sick passenger inspired one behind him, and on those bus lines there were no little brown bags provided, like on your favorite airline.

Well, it was getting tense and depressing. What was needed was a distraction. In Africa, in Tanganyika, circa 1956, on any given day along the roads and pathways, distractions are pretty easy to come by. Thus, a dear old man riding a bicycle was our distraction.

In all of Africa, there is a special kind of bicycle sold in nearly every Indian shop. It is made in England or Hong Kong, and it is more like a truck than a bicycle. I believe China still makes these vehicles by the hundreds of millions and ships them around the world.

Three Pigeons was the most famous brand in East Africa. This bicycle can be loaded until you would be in awe and expect it to break in half. A whole family can climb aboard.

A special carrier is attached on the rear which is massive and holds a great load. The bicycle is then peddled slowly since it is so heavy. It can be loaded even heavier, but the owner must walk it down the road since it would fall over if he tried to ride it.

As we cruised along in the bus, we came to an area where the road made slow graceful curves back and forth as huge clumps of wait-a-bit thorn bushes were negotiated. Roads in Africa don't go through such obstacles-- they simply go around them. The "right of way" is whichever way provides the least resistance. Each of these "bushes" was really huge, averaging maybe fifteen feet high and 40 feet across.

As we rumbled along this way in the heat, we came around a particularly large bush of wait-a-bit thorns-- perhaps 200 feet in diameter. Half way around the curve, we met an old gentleman on a bicycle, fully loaded with some unknown cargo, and just creeping along.

The bus driver blasted the horn, and I thought we would run right over the old man. Well, the fellow did the only thing he could do-- he turned and parked the bike in the thorn bush. The bus zipped past his rear wheel missing it by inches.

The wait-a-bit thorn bush was so thick that after he crunched into the bush, and after we tore on down the road, he was left there perfectly upright, sitting motionless on his bicycle, and totally supported by the thorn bush. The wait-a-bit thorns were supporting him as they clung to his clothing.

Now, African wait-a-bit thorns are like millions of fish hooks and grow on canes similar to roses. If you even brush up against them, you are caught solidly. To pull away would mean the end of your clothes and probably some nasty cuts. They can be escaped from only by stopping and peeling the branches off slowly, thorn by thorn.

Now, imagine yourself on a bicycle, completely encased in, and propped up by, a million wait-a-bit thorns and no way to back out.

Well, Africans don't deal with disaster like Westerners. The whole bus load of passengers saw every detail of the scene and action as we tore by, and they all broke up in hilarious laughter. Africans laugh at disaster, even if they are the one suffering.

I don't know about the old man. It just might have been too much for him to be merry at that point. But, the driver broke into such fits of laughter that he nearly drove into a tree.

The roaring of laughter went on for miles, but finally it settled down. After a period of quiet, an old gentleman in the back began to tell a story. "Once upon a time there was an old man named Tembo. He needed to get some corn to market to sell, and he wanted to buy some things. So he set off early one morning from his village and on his bicycle to go to the market in Nansio." On and on the story went.

Finally I realized that this fellow was telling the story of the old man on the bicycle in the thorn bush. When the story teller finally got to the part where the old man met the bus, all of the passengers were on pins and needles. As the story teller described the crunch of the bicycle into the thorn bush, the whole bus broke up all over again, including the driver.

This went on all the way home to Kibara. Over and over the story teller would tell the story, every time the same plot, and the passengers loved it. It also helped all of us forget the heat and stench of lost lunches.

I suppose life is very different today. The busses are much nicer. They build them with steel coachworks now, and there are nicer seats and better ventilation.

But, somewhere on the Kibara planes, late at night around a low fire, I dare say you can still hear a story about the old man on the bicycle and the wait-a-bit thorns. Some things are just too good to change.

Source: "Fetching the Mail" - Steve Van Nattan Tells About Life in Africa: www.blessedquietness.com/yarn/mail.htm

***

Teaching in East Africa: Destination Unknown

By Mrs. B. Lakin

Fed up with shortages and rationing still in force after the war, and more than fed up with cycling through all weathers to my teaching post in Essex, I decided to seek employment in a sunnier corner of the earth. My choice fell on Tanganyika (as it was called then).

Knowing nothing of the place, except its position on the map, (and that I had had to look up), I was allocated a berth on a cargo-passenger ship in September 1951. I did not know how to prepare myself for this voyage - and there was no such thing as counselling in those days - so I bought a camera and a pair of sunglasses and set sail.

For some obscure reason it was the policy of the Colonial Office not to divulge the final destination until arrival at Mombasa so I, and others also on their way out to the unknown just relaxed and enjoyed the voyage. Being a cargo vessel it took six weeks and called at Marseilles, Genoa, Port Said, Aden and finally Mombasa.

On opening the letter which was waiting for me there, I was informed that I was to be stationed at Arusha. I didn't know it then but there were only two European schools in the country, so there wasn't really a wide choice. However, the school at Arusha was being extended and while this building was going on, an annexe was used to cope with the overflow of pupils, and it was to this annex I was to be sent.

Life on a slow train through Africa was certainly an eye-opener and going through the Tsavo, where stories of man-eating lions abounded, was really exciting.

My train destination was Moshi, the railhead for Arusha. Moshi is near Kilimanjaro, the "Little Hill of the White Spirit", so named to denigrate its feeling of self importance and persuade it that it was not all-powerful.

I arrived at Moshi station to find no one to meet me. However, ever friendly folk soon contacted the right people and I was duly collected. I was not able to visit the main school during the two days I was in Arusha because there was a case of polio and the place was in quarantine.

All of this I accepted quite philosophically but was a little put out to discover that the annex was 100 miles away. It was at a place out in the wilds called Oldeani and was not too far from the Ngorongoro crater.

The school there housed about 40 children with a matron, first teacher, his wife who was the housekeeper, and me, the second teacher. I had my own room, which included a chemical toilet.

Whoever had fitted this was not much of a handyman as the flue pipe went out through the roof leaving a gap, so using the loo on rainy days necessitated the use of an umbrella.

Soon after I arrived we congregated one evening in the master's flat enjoying a sundowner when the door was flung open and the night watchman burst in. He was a local gentleman dressed in a piece of cloth, knotted over one shoulder, carrying a lamp and a spear and at that moment he was rather paler than most Africans.

"Chui! Chui!," he shouted and it was quickly explained to me that that meant leopard.

The next day, local farmers set up a trap in the form of a tent and with an inverted V-shaped opening. The trap contained bait and a rifle fixed upside-down with a piece of string attached from the trigger to the ground.

The leopard fell for this and a shot was heard, but when the trap was inspected it was discovered that the opening had been too wide and the leopard must have been shot in the shoulder and not the head. So now we had a wounded leopard wandering around! However, he was so weak that he was soon tracked and shot.

After a few weeks at the annexe it was decided that my talents were more suited to the main school so at the end of term I made the journey back to Arusha. This was by bus with the children, and I was given a snake-bite outfit for use in the possible event of someone meeting a snake.

The outfit consisted of a razor blade and some potassium permanganate crystals and I was supposed to cut the bitten area and rub in the pot.

Well, I can tell you that when we did stop for nature's calls modesty was not observed and no one was allowed further than 10 yards from the bus.

This was the beginning of my life in Africa and I have loved every minute of it since, but for a new, raw girl from the UK it certainly was an exciting start.

Source: Expat World, *The Weekly Telegraph*, London, 29 September 2003.

Appendix VI:
Princess Margaret in Tanganyika

Princess Margaret at a state banquet in Tanganyika in October 1956.

I wish to express my profound gratitude to Jackie and Karl Wigh, ex-Tanganyikans living in Australia, for sending me some newspaper articles from the 1950s published in the Tanganyika *Sunday News*, a sister paper of the *Tanganyika Standard*, whose editorial staff I joined in June 1969 as a news reporter when I was still a high school student in Dar es Salaam.

They sent me some other material including a 112-page booklet on Princess Margaret's visit to Tanganyika in October 1956. The booklet is entitled, *Tanganyika: The Royal Visit of Her Royal Highness The Princess Margaret October 1956.*

I was seven years old, attending Kyimbila Primary School near Tukuyu in Rungwe District in the Southern Highlands. She was 26 and first arrived in Tanganyika on October 8th four days after my birthday.

She visited a number of places in Tanganyika: Dar es Salaam, her first stop; Tanga; Mbeya and Sao Hill, both in the Southern Highlands; Tabora, Mwanza, Mwadui, Arusha and Moshi.

This is the summary of events from the booklet the Wighs sent me on her visit to Tanganyika which may be of some interest to some people for different reasons including nostalgia of a bygone era when life was simpler and the people friendlier, as they reminisce on how life was in those days in the 1950s in this East African country:

Monday, 8th October: Dar es Salaam - Arrival and opening of deep water quay; Processional drive through town; Luncheon at port; State Dinner.

Tuesday, 9th October: Dar es Salaam - Baraza; Luncheon with Legislative Council; Dinner with Governor-General of Belgian Congo.

Wednesday, 10th October: Tanga - Hospital; Baraza; Luncheon with Sisal Growers.

Wednesaday, 10th October: Dar es Salaam - Dinner on S.S. *Kenya*.

Thursday, 11th October: Dar es Salaam - Opening of General Hospital; Arnautoglu Hall; Garden Party; Dinner and Masque at Government House.

Friday, 12th October: Mbeya - Baraza where children from all schools in the Southern Highlands Province will sing "Tanganyika, also attended by the Provincial Commissioner Griffiths"; Luncheon at Mbeya School.

Friday, 12th October: Sao Hill - Tea at Southern Highlands Club.

Saturday, 13th October: Tabora - Baraza; Luncheon at Tabora Hotel; Government Secondary Boys' School.

Sunday, 14th October: Mwanza - Church.

Monday, 15th October: Mwanza - Reception; Aga Khan School; Baraza.

Monday, 15th October: Mwadui - Luncheon with Dr. Williamson; visit to diamond mine.

Tuesday, 16th October: Arusha - Baraza; Lake Duluti; Ngurdoto Crater.

Wednesday, 17th October: Arusha - European School; Reception; Dinner with Town Council.

Tuesday, 18th October: Moshi - Trade and Agricultural Show; Chagga Council; Luncheon with Coffee Producers; Departure.

Princess Margaret's visit got extensive coverage in Tanganyika's leading English newspaper, the *Standard* and its sister paper the *Sunday News*, as much it did in British newspapers.

They all had many eye-catching headlines including one in the British *Daily Mail* which said, "Angry Settlers Boycott Visit by Princess." This was in reference to the white settlers in the Southern Highlands Province where I come from; although what was called a boycott by some, not all, of the settlers was given different interpretations by different people for different reasons - if it was indeed a boycott at all, or simply dissatisfaction with the way things were handled during Princess Margaret's visit to the province, excluding some of the white settlers from the some of the official events, or simply failing to invite them for whatever reason, as seemed to be the case according to some people.

One of the items Jackie and Karl Wigh sent me from Australia when I was writing this book was a four-page coverage from the Tanganyika *Sunday News*, October 21, 1956, full of pictures on the royal visit to different parts of the country; including a clipping with an article entitled "Ambassadress Princess Gave

E.A. (East Africa) 'Shot in Arm'" by a *Sunday News* reporter. The article also provides some insights into the kind of mentality that was prevalent in those days among some people associated with the British empire:

The influence towards stabilising the East African territories exerted by the 'travelling Princess ambassadress' will be invaluable. 'It will give the local government a little more time to get on with their plans for developing multi-racial states before Nasser and Nehru get their toe in the door.'

That is the half-way summing up of Princess Margaret's East African tour made in the London *Daily Mail* a few days ago by their special correspondent Kenneth Ames. 'East Africa, politically speaking, needs a severe shot in the arm,' Ames cabled. 'Along came Princess Margaret three weeks ago to begin to administer it with unconscious dexterity.'

Red-tape curtain

After describing Egyptian propaganda from Cairo Radio and Indian propaganda from 'a secret, high-powered transmitter across the Indian Ocean near Bombay,' beamed at East Africa, he added: 'In some places I was told that pro-Egyptian sentiments were growing rapidly and had only been stopped short by the arrival of Princess Margaret.'

Ames's comment later in the cable, that not enough of the people have had the opportunity of getting more than a fleeting glimpse of the Princess has been echoed by many other writers travelling with the Royal tour. Leader of the attack against the red-tape curtain was Douglas Williams, doyen of the Royal tour press corps, who constantly hammered home, in the columns of the London *Daily Telegraph*, the complaint that too many of the Princess's activities were restricted to rigid official functions.

No human touch

Of the Princess's arrival in Tanganyika to open the deep water berths at Dar es Salaam, Williams wrote: 'It was unfortunate that the Britannia had to berth in an enclosed dock, unseen by the general public. The only spectators were privileged guests by special invitation.'

And the *Daily Telegraph* columnist, 'Peterborough,' commented, 'The human touch, conspicuously absent so far, looks like remaining so unless her Tanganyika and Kenya programme is modified. In Mombasa, Mauritius and Zanzibar she was not given a single chance to talk to the natives. Only a couple of hundred people specially invited by the East African Railways or the government were able to watch the Princess's arrival at Dar es Salaam on Monday. All that the crowds on the waterfront could see was a distant view of Britannia docking. No stands were put up for the general public.'

The Princess's informal meeting with the dancers at the Dar es Salaam baraza, however, was welcomed by most correspondents as a happy break through the hedge of officialdom surrounding her. 'It has reacted like champagne on all sections of the community,' David Wynne-Morgan cabled his newspaper, the London *Daily Express*. 'Yes,' shouted the *Express* sub-editors in a six-column headline, 'the princess may mix now - official all-clear - but 'it might have been nasty."

The Rhodesia Herald took it more seriously. Under a front-page headline - 'Princess Nearly Lost in Tanganyika Crowd of 60,000' - its correspondent reported 'Another hectic mob scene nearly marred Princess Margaret's inspection of a baraza of 60,000 African tribesmen in Dar es Salaam today.' And in a leading article, *The Rhodesia Herald* said: 'Twice during her present tour Princess Margaret has been in danger from runaway public fervour, first in Mauritius and now in Tanganyika.

Hypnotic tom-toms

'Africans, Asians and Creoles, in a frenzy of excitement, made nonsense of police precautions and might well have caused physical harm to Her Royal Highness.....

'....with the hypnotic beat of the tom-toms drumming up primitive emotions, the East African authorities should have been reminded of the explosive human material with which they might have to deal. If the normal police force was small, special constables should have been enrolled. From now on Royalty intends increasingly to visit the Dominions and Colonies. So let other governments take heed; however willing members of the Royal Family may be to meet the people, they must be firmly protected from such scenes as those which have attended the tour of Princess Margaret.'

Anne Lloyd, of the *Daily Mirror*, spoke of the Princess's smile 'that charmed away all the anxiety - that everything must be 'just so' - that her visit caused.'

No clowning

She mentioned the case of diver Peter Williams who was presented when the Princess opened the deep water berths. 'Railways and Harbour Authority wanted to present him in a diving kit minus its heavy lead weights,' said Miss Lloyd. 'But when they suggested it to Clarence House, back came the reply: 'Certainly not. It would be clowning before Royalty."

Railway officials wanted to lay on kingfish in aspic for the Princess at the luncheon at the docks, but the local medical authorities stepped in and banned it. 'It was the local medical authorities again who caused the typhoid scare,' Miss Lloyd added. 'Every steward who was to serve the Princess had to go through tests lasting seven days - tests twice as stringent as many of the same men passed before serving the Queen when she was here as Princess Elizabeth. Princess Margaret took normal precautions against the disease before coming here.'

Settler boycott

Correspondents found some exciting descriptive scenes to cable and many of them did full justice to the colourful up-country barazas. But in the Southern Highlands, the *Daily Mail* man reported further evidence of the red-tape curtain.

On the front page of this leading British daily, under the heading, 'Angry Settlers Boycott Visit by Princess,' Ames reported, 'Planters and settlers in the Tanganyika Southern Highlands farming region today boycotted Princess Margaret's one-day visit after they had been excluded from receptions to meet her.' He quoted one settler as saying, 'The settlers feel they have been slighted. They feel they have played their part in building up the country and this should be their day. Even minor government officials who have only been six weeks in Tanganyika have been invited to meet the Princess, but not the settlers or their wives who are very disgruntled.'

Bitter feud

The *Daily Express* carried no mention of the bycott. Instead, they followed in their next issue with a cable that 'Princess Margaret, wthout knowing it, placed herself in the middle of a bitter political feud when she stayed yesterday with the Dowager Lady Chesham at Rungemba in the Southern Highlands.

'The question of white mastery or multi-racialism is still a tense one in this mandated territory and Lady Chesham is one of the most fervent multi-racialists in Tanganyika. She is one of the leaders of the United Tanganyika Party, which believes in the closest co-operation between all communities. So firm are her beliefs that she is converting the house in which she entertained the Princess into a multi-racial school. Ironically, her husband, Lord Chesham, wo died three years ago, conceived the idea of turning the Sao Hill area f the Southern Highlands into a white settlers' area like the White Highlands in Kenya. The plan fell through because of lack of interest.'

Too soon

Asked about the Tanganyika Government's reaction to overseas press coverage of the Tanganyika visit, the Director of Public Relations, Mr. Kenneth Dobson, said it was a little too early to make a considered comment. He thought that, on the whole, the correspondents had done well, but he was not in a position yet to comment on specific points raised by them, such as the allegations that the Princess was unable to meet the ordinary people because she was hedged in by officialdom.

On the Princess's visit to Zanzibar, the *Daily Telegraph* reported, 'As representative of the British Crown she will leave behind her a memory of grace, charm and simplicity which will do much to buttress British prestige and British sympathies in this predominantly Arab Kingdom.'

Divorce probe

The *Daily Mirror* carried a report that the Royal Tour Executive Officer there, Mrs. Cecily Evans, had to conduct a private probe into the past lives of the 220 people in 'the British colony' there - because of an official 'hint' on divorce.

Authorities in Dar es Salaam had told her, said the *Mirror*, 'It would be most improper if persons who have been divorced were at a garden party to meet the Princess.' But, after screening all the names, Mrs. Evans discovered no one had been divorced.

***

The Tanganyika *Sunday News* of October 21st also had many other stories which had nothing to do with Princess Margaret's 11-day visit to Tanganyika but which may remind many ex-Tanganyikans who read this book of their lives there in the 1950s and of the country they left behind when they moved to other parts of the world.

The clippings from the paper Jackie and Karl Wigh sent me from Australia, which had to do with the royal tour of this East African country, had headlines such as "'New Passenger Train Services': To meet increasing local demands on the Southern Province Railway, the third-class passenger train services between Mtwara and Nachingwea....".

Other reports in the paper included, "'53 Times Round the World': Dar es Salaam Motor Transport company's 37 buses travelled a total of 1,308,511 miles last year - the equivalent of nearly 53 complete journeys round the world. The territory's latest development report states that nearly 10,000,000 passengers were carried compared with 7,080,000 in 1952 - when the year's mileage with 24 buses totalled just over 800,000."

There was also one sad story headlined "'Man Dies After Bee Attack':

A European died from shock after being attacked by a swarm of bees in Dodoma. He was Mr. P. Evelegh, aged 65, who arrived in Dodoma from Dar es Salaam a week earlier to take up an appointment with the Department of Geological Survey as a works foreman. Mr. Evelegh was arranging stores for a safari when the accident occurred.

The Medical Officer at Dodoma Hospital, Dr. Tiagi, said that the deceased had been stung about 50 times. The dead man, who was employed for many years at the Geita Gold Mining Company, leaves a widow in Dar es Salaam. A number of passers-by were stung severely, including an Italian petrol lorry driver and Mr. J.R. Dolphin-Rowland, of the Water Development and Irrigation Department, who received 26 stings, mostly on head and neck."

There was also a photo in the same newspaper, unfortunately only a very small part of the newspaper clipping showing some men dressed in suits, with the caption: "Demonstrators on Tanganyika Tour." And another one, a complete photo, with the following description: "'The End of Princess Margaret's Elevenday Visit to the Land of the Twiga': Princess Margaret feeds the giraffe at Mr. A. Kuenzier's zoo farm, eight miles from Arusha. It was at the farm that the Princess was presented with a pair of zebra which are being shipped to England for her. She also saw a baby elephant, ostritches and wildebeeste."

Those were just some of the stories from Tanganyika in the 1950s, years and a country many people, including many ex-Tanganyikans who moved to different parts of the world, remember with nostalgia. And they provided an inspiration for this book which I would not have been able to write without those memories. They are indeed times to remember.

***